MADOFF

MADOFF

Corruption, Deceit, and the Making of the
World's Most Notorious Ponzi Scheme

PETER SANDER

THE LYONS PRESS
Guilford, Connecticut
An imprint of The Globe Pequot Press

The Lyons Press is an imprint of The Globe Pequot Press.

Text designed by Sheryl P. Kober

Library of Congress Cataloging-in-Publication Data is available on file.

ISBN 978-1-59921-811-3

Printed in the United States of America

10 9 8 7 6 5 4 3 2 1

The will to believe something that is convenient to believe is strong in all realms.

—*Kurt Andersen, novelist and host of Public Radio's* Studio 360

CONTENTS

ACKNOWLEDGMENTS

The Bernard Madoff story is a rapidly moving one, generating new news almost every day; it was a challenge to keep pace with these developments and what they mean to all of us. So first and foremost I must acknowledge my family, my wife, Jennifer, and young sons, Julian and Jonathan, for putting up with my commitment to the task and taking care of those other tasks that would normally be on my plate. And, boys, thank you for serving as a steady reminder that financial scams don't just happen on Wall Street.

To bring this story public as soon as possible, this book was developed on an aggressive schedule. As such I must also recognize the Globe Pequot Press team, including Jennifer Taber, Gene Brissie, and Gary Krebs, for putting up with my occasional battle fatigue and making it all happen. Beyond that, I also offer my special thanks to my exercise buddies (you know who you are) for keeping me in the physical and mental form necessary to accomplish such a task. And I must also thank the numbers of journalists, investigators, and researchers who have put together pieces of this complex story from which I've drawn, and of those I must single out Harry Markopolos for his unique genius and foresight in the Madoff matter.

Finally, I have great sympathy for the many, many victims of the Madoff debacle. I dedicate this book to those victims and sincerely hope, as a result, we rise to an environment where such a thing could never happen again.

INTRODUCTION

On December 15, 2008, the Honorable Louis L. Stanton, a Federal Judge in the United States District Court for the Southern District of New York, appointed Irving Picard as Trustee for the liquidation of Bernard L. Madoff Investments Securities LLC ("BMIS") pursuant to the Securities Investor Protection Act ("SIPA") as set forth in the attached order.

So reads the epitaph on the tombstone-like webpage at www .madoff.com marking the remains of Bernard L. Madoff Investment Securities, LLC, a matter of days after that fateful December 11, 2008, morning when the scandal broke. That and some other protocol about how to fill out a claim for SIPC insurance under the Securities Investor Protection Act of 1970.

Nothing about the company. Nothing about your investments, should you be among the unlucky. Nothing about the firm's history, what it did, what it owned, where it went wrong. Nothing about Mr. Madoff. No "About Us" or "Contact Us" page. No pictures of beautiful Florida sunsets or Wall Street skyscrapers or the oval, red-granite Lipstick Building on Third Avenue in New York City, where he apparently conducted most of his business.

Just an epitaph in white letters on a solid black background.

What happened? What happened to the $50 billion (yes, that's *billion* with a "b") entrusted to this firm by thousands of investors, as many as 4,000 of whom may have lost everything they had, in the greatest investment scandal of all time? Fifty billion? How does one guy lose $50 billion—of other people's money?

- Fifty billion is about $163 for each of the 305 million people estimated to be living in the U.S. in December 2008.
- Fifty billion is more net worth than Warren Buffett accumulated in sixty years of investing.
- Fifty billion is more than all but six U.S. states spend each year.
- Fifty billion is more than the annual budgets of the U.S. Departments of Labor, Interior, Transportation, Treasury, and NASA—*combined.*

It's big enough to prompt the following from the Securities and Exchange Commission (SEC), who arguably committed a gross oversight in their oversight of the Madoff firm. "Our complaint alleges a stunning fraud that appears to be of epic proportions," stated Andrew Calamari, the SEC's associate director of enforcement in New York.

Got that right.

And who's the "perp" that pulled this one off? Bernie Madoff. That's "made-off." Like, made off with all your dough. But what was really going on?

Was it all about greed? On Madoff's part, perhaps yes, perhaps no. Perhaps it was about a genuine instinct to serve his investors well—consistently well—that simply got out of hand. He may have made some promises that were too big to keep. He may have made those promises figuring that someday he'd hit an investment home run and be able to recover, or catch up, to pay investors legitimately—which, of course, fell out of reach when the markets turned south in 2008.

Or, Madoff's scheme may have been deliberate and maliciously calculated from the beginning. It may have been cleverly crafted and hidden in such a way that he and only he could have known about it—and be held responsible for it. He may be smiling today, knowing that for years, he was able to hide the scheme from faithful clients, regulators, firm employees, and even his own family. The devil is in the details—and those details surface daily in the new information and confessions coming forth from Mr. Madoff himself and those who surrounded him.

Greed may or may not have been Madoff's motive, but it was almost certainly *not* the motive for his clients. That's one factor that makes this scandal different from the many hedge-fund blowups and other scandals of recent years. For the most part, Madoff's clients appear simply to have been seeking steady returns. Yes, better-than-market returns, in the 10 to 15 percent range, but not huge returns, the more than 20 percent often promised by his more-aggressive hedge-fund brethren. Indeed, Madoff's clients were probably looking for two things: steady returns *modestly* ahead of the market; and the ability to entrust their investing and wealth-management business to someone else.

Even more than client trust, perhaps the more puzzling issue is the persistent hands-off treatment by the SEC and other regulators. Were they duped, just like the clients? Or was there some other reason why they simply chose not to peek behind the curtain for the most part? Even to the point of avoiding financial analyst and skeptic Harry Markopolos, who started blowing his whistle to the SEC in 1999 and did it more loudly and formally in 2005, leading to a brief 2006 investigation that was later closed without consequence. Why did they cast such a blind eye, and how will the scandal affect SEC regulations from here on out?

There are many more questions, and readers and writers alike are wondering: What's the rest of the story? Who is, and who *was*, Bernie Madoff? How did he get his start and rise to become a big Wall Street player? How did he create the blind trust that convinced so many investors to part with their fortunes without asking questions? How did he avoid regulators for so long? Who are his victims, and what went through their minds when they trusted him—and later, when the scandal went public? Why did he do what he did in the first place? And how can we as prudent investors and citizens avoid such a debacle in the future?

These and many more topics are the business of *Madoff: Corruption, Deceit, and the Making of the World's Most Notorious Ponzi Scheme.* Here's how the story (as known during the winter of 2009) will be told.

Chapter 1, "Mr. Ponzi's Scheme—and Other Famous Ponzi Swindlers," describes Ponzi schemes in general, along with their creator and his imitators. Examples of other Ponzi schemes are given, with chilling parallels to what Madoff himself pulled off.

Chapter 2, "Queens Kid Makes Good," details the early days of Bernard Madoff—his childhood and family, vignettes of the Queens neighborhoods he grew up in, and his education and early career, including how he got started in the securities business and the trappings of his wealth at the end.

Chapter 3, "Building the Madoff Brand," covers his growth from market maker to money manager, and the evolution of Bernard Madoff Investment Securities. This chapter outlines how Madoff made money in the trading business, how he became recognized as a Wall Street pioneer through his broker-dealer business and electronic trading, and how his more-aggressive tactics made him into an industry leader.

Chapter 4, "Blind Trust: Recruiting the Best and the Brightest," explores how he infiltrated wealthy Jewish and international circles, his sales pitch and tactics, and the feeder funds and recruiters that were part of his scheme. A brief explanation of hedge funds is included, along with how Madoff became a money manager and hedge-fund operator.

Chapter 5, "One Step Ahead of the Regulators," discusses the SEC—what it is and what it does—along with important securities laws in the Madoff case. This chapter will also cover the important investigations, especially the chillingly foretelling exposé of investment analyst Harry Markopolos, who blew the whistle loudly three years before the scandal was uncovered. And finally, the chapter will cover what the SEC did—and didn't do—once the Madoff scandal broke.

Chapter 6, "'It's All Just One Big Lie,'" details the events leading up to the arrest, along with the SEC complaint, the arrest itself, and the early proceedings of the investigation and the pursuit of justice. This chapter also examines whether the reported Madoff investment returns were even possible, or were they a lie, too?

Chapter 7, "Collateral Damage," explores the profound impacts on investment funds, individuals, charities, and other parties. Who lost money, how much, and what victims had to say at the "Ground Zero" locales of Palm Beach and New York will also be described, along with the early effects on the financial industry as a whole.

Chapter 8, "Chosen Again: The Profound Effects on the Jewish World," offers a deeper examination of the impact on the Jewish community, including foundations, charities, and other nonprofit organizations. Also covered is the evidence of a rise of a new wave of anti-Semitism and the more abstract impacts on the Jewish psyche and sense of place in the world.

Chapter 9, "The Psychology of Trust," takes a look at thoughts and theories on what makes an investment crook tick, why they do what they do, and why it works. It also looks at the other side of the table: the psychology of trust and reasons why some otherwise-savvy investors may follow blindly.

Chapter 10, "The Madoff Legacy," investigates how the Madoff scandal will impact regulations and regulatory enforcement, the Wall Street image and business practices, what it means for individual investors, and what investors should do in the future to guard against such schemes and manage their money wisely.

It should be recognized that this book reflects the current facts of the investigations as of the end of January 2009, fewer than two months after the scandal broke. The investigation and its consequences are likely to go on for years, and more facts will inevitably surface about the scandal and about Madoff himself. It isn't likely, however, that those facts will reveal anything more than additional details about the main story: The Madoff scandal is one of the biggest and most brash crimes of all time, causing all to wonder how it ever could have happened in the first place. With that in mind, read on . . .

CHAPTER 1

Mr. Ponzi's Scheme—and Other Famed Ponzi Swindlers

How did he get away with it for so long?
—Almost everyone close to the case

Headline: MADOFF SCANDAL IS LARGEST BIANCHI SCHEME.

Bet you haven't seen that one yet, in your newspaper or anywhere else. Although they share similar Italian origins, the name *Bianchi* doesn't quite roll off the tongue the way *Ponzi* does. But it could easily have been the term we use today for a pyramid scam. Why? Because it was one of a variety of names that Charles Ponzi himself used throughout his career.

Unlike Mr. Madoff, who kept his ruse going for many decades, Ponzi and his investors went on a swift and wild ride that started and stopped in less than a year. He began in the late winter of 1920, and it all came crashing down by July of that same year. He wasn't the first to invent the swindler's method of paying early investors with money from later investors, but it was his name—the Ponzi name he was using at the time—that stuck.

A Ponzi Definition

The term *Ponzi scheme* is really an American colloquialism for what is known around the world as a *pyramid scheme*. Although Charles Ponzi put a brand name on the classic method, he was hardly the only one to create, profit, and get in trouble from such a crime.

So what is a pyramid scheme, anyway? Perhaps fittingly, we should look to the Securities and Exchange Commission—the SEC—for a definition:

> *In the classic "pyramid" scheme, participants attempt to make money solely by recruiting new participants into the program. The hallmark of these schemes is the promise of sky-high returns in a short period of time for doing nothing other than handing over your money and getting others to do the same.*
>
> *The fraudsters behind a pyramid scheme may go to great lengths to make the program look like a legitimate multi-level marketing program. But despite their claims to have legitimate products or services to sell, these fraudsters simply use money coming in from new recruits to pay off early-stage investors. But eventually the pyramid will collapse. At some point the schemes get too big, the promoter cannot raise enough money from new investors to pay earlier investors, and many people lose their money.*

So there is little doubt, by Madoff's own account and the investigation that has followed, that Madoff is guilty of such a scheme. When he started it, and why, still isn't clear, but it follows the SEC definition pretty closely. As will be described in chapter 5, it's too bad the SEC didn't take a fresh look at this definition when they examined his business several times before the scandal broke.

Before getting into the main course of the Madoff story, as an hors d'oeuvre, the story of Ponzi schemes as they have been carried out by others, including Mr. Ponzi himself, is served.

Ivar Kreuger—The Swedish Match King

Most headlines these days are giving Bernard Madoff credit for developing the "largest Ponzi scheme of all time." Just how to determine which has been the biggest financial scam of all time is a matter of some dispute. Until the final figures are in on Mr. Madoff, some financial historians insist that this title should remain with a man named Ivar Kreuger.

In 1961 renowned economist John Kenneth Galbraith called Kreuger "the Leonardo" of financial scammers. He advised that "Boiler-room operators, peddlers of stocks in the imaginary Canadian mines, mutual-fund managers whose genius and imagination are unconstrained by integrity, as well as less exotic larcenists, should read about Kreuger."

What had this man done so masterfully? He'd managed to corner the world market on matches. Yes, matches. The kind you light a cigar with. Swedish safety matches. Ever heard that old warning that lighting three cigarettes on one match is unlucky? (The third guy will be shot, as the enemy will have spotted your position and pulled the trigger by the time you light the third cigarette.) Kreuger himself created and spread this admonition in an effort to sell more matches.

But it wasn't his ability to sell matches that led history to remember him. It was the way he built up his empire. He acquired match factories around Europe in the early 1920s and then began approaching cash-strapped governments with a sweetheart deal: If the government gave him the match monopoly in their country, he would loan them money. Some countries, still reeling from the devastation that followed World War I, borrowed enormous sums, including France, which borrowed $75 million in 1927. Even small countries like Bolivia got involved, borrowing $2 million from Kreuger in 1930.

According to the *Economist,* Kreuger had a plan designed to bring him prosperity: "His monopoly and skilled marketing would increase sales. Governments taxed matches, so the higher sales would raise tax revenues used to repay the loans. It was, boasted Kreuger, an almost foolproof business plan: the loans were secured against revenues that he controlled; the monopolies, meanwhile, ensured generous returns."

Turns out that he couldn't make enough money from selling matches to keep up, and soon, he was paying dividends to investors out of capital instead of actual earnings. He loaned money to governments and bought companies using that company's own cash, or cash from a company previously acquired. With some financial engineering and bogus reporting, he was able to report profits where there were none, and pay dividends to boot. By 1931 he controlled some 200 companies, and his reported net worth in 1929 was thought to be the equivalent of $100 billion today.

But true to Ponzi-scheme fashion, the 1929 stock market crash led to the exposure of his accounting, which ultimately proved fatal to Kreuger and his empire. It was a giant pyramid scheme. Just before a meeting with one of the bankers he relied upon, Kreuger shot himself in Paris in March of 1932.

As it turns out, tightlipped Bernie Madoff may have learned a thing or two from the Swedish Match King. When interviewed by the *Saturday Evening Post* in the 1920s about the reason for his success, Kreuger told the reporter: "Silence, more silence, and even more silence."

Reed Slatkin and the Scientologists

Not content to rest on his dot.com laurels, Reed Slatkin, a cofounder of Internet service provider Earthlink, became a money manager and built his own pyramid empire involving the Church of Scientology. It was a complicated scheme involving payment of false returns to investors, some of whom in turn donated them to the Church.

Slatkin was a former Scientology minister, and many of his victims were members of the Church of Scientology. His fraudulent financial empire lasted for fifteen years before dissolving into bankruptcy proceedings in 2001. He took some $593 million from investors, $240 million of which was lost. Taken into custody in April 2002, Slatkin pleaded guilty to fifteen counts of fraud, conspiracy, and money laundering. He did cooperate with authorities, but, as the judge pointed out when sentencing him, "The cooperation has been, shall we say, somewhat checkered."

During the sentencing phase Slatkin did try to argue that much of what he did was done out of fear of fellow Scientologists who allegedly urged him to continue his scam so they could profit. The judge was not impressed, and proceeded to sentence him to fourteen years in prison. Among the investors in Reed Slatkin's Ponzi scheme were Greta Van Susteren of Fox News and her husband, John Coale. When interviewed about his investment by the *National Post,* Coale admitted: "For a couple of years I looked like an investment genius. Now I'm just a dope."

The Associated Press reported in November of 2008 that The Church of Scientology would pay back $3.5 million of the money they'd received from investing with Slatkin.

As will be seen, this scheme resembled Madoff's in that it worked inside a group of people with common interests, common bonds, and common trust—a church. Such an approach is now referred to as *affinity fraud.*

Lou Pearlman and the Backstreet Boys

In November 2008, publisher HarperCollins released the book *The Hit Charade: Lou Pearlman, Boy Bands, and the Biggest Ponzi Scheme in U.S. History.* Oops. Pearlman bilked investors out of $300 million, so that must have seemed like an easy claim to make at the time. At what editorial meeting could anyone ever have imagined that just weeks after the book's release, that amount would seem like lunch money compared to Madoff's scheme?

Lou Pearlman, the founder of the Backstreet Boys, pled guilty in March 2008 to charges of conspiracy, money laundering, and making false statements during a bankruptcy proceeding. The boy-band mogul had been running two shell companies for years, enticing mainly retired Floridians to invest in companies that existed only on paper. The statements he sent investors showed profits that also existed only on paper.

NOWADAYS THERE'S A WEBSITE FOR EVERYTHING

Been defrauded? Start a website. That seems to be the natural way to respond these days, particularly when there are large numbers of victims who want information, and who need to be in touch with each other for legal updates. The victims of Lou Pearlman can head to www.scammedbypearlman.com, and download form letters urging tax relief for victims of financial fraud. Investors taken by Reed Slatkin can stay abreast of developments on www.slatkinfraud.com.

Some might think it odd that such a site has not yet been created for Madoff and his victims, outside of the bankruptcy trustee's update, posted on www.madoff.com.

And we'll see how Bernard Madoff, too, employed this latter tactic.

Lou Pearlman is currently serving twenty-five years in prison, although the judge suggested he could knock off one year of his sentence for every million dollars he recovered for his victims. When requesting leniency during the sentencing hearing, Pearlman's attorney explained to the judge, "Mr. Pearlman *did* live large, if you will, but Judge, he was in the entertainment business."

Born on the Bayou—The Bayou Hedge Fund Group

Samuel Israel III came from a long line of distinguished moneymen. His grandfather created a successful commodities firm in New Orleans, which his family ran for a hundred years before selling it for tens of millions to the brokerage firm of Donaldson, Lufkin & Jenrette. The Israel connection inspired great confidence in investors throughout the South.

Investors in the Stamford, Connecticut–based Bayou Hedge Fund Group, founded in 1996, were reassured by the frequent updates they received from Israel. Weekly e-mail updates arrived and client statements were mailed on time. But alas, in the company's history, it never actually posted a year-end profit, and its client statements were entirely fictitious—as were the forged audited statements it used to hide its losses.

Israel lost $450 million of his investors' money. The fraud was discovered when a client first attempted to call the firm and got no answer. He then visited the firm's offices and found them empty, but the back door open. He went inside and found a six-page confession and suicide note from CPA Dan Marino, Israel's business partner.

The 2005 SEC complaint alleged that, among other things:

- Israel, Marino (the CPA), and Bayou Management overstated the Funds' 2003 performance by claiming a $43 million profit in the four hedge funds, while trading records show that the Funds actually lost $49 million.
- In 1999, Marino created a sham accounting firm named "Richmond-Fairfield Associates" that he used to fabricate annual "independent" audits of the Funds, attesting to the fake results that he and Israel had assigned to the Funds.
- Israel and Marino stole investor funds by annually withdrawing from the Funds' "incentive fees" that they were not entitled to, because the Funds never returned a year-end profit.
- By mid-2004, Israel and Marino had largely suspended trading securities on behalf of the Funds. They had transferred all remaining Fund assets, consisting of approximately $150 million, to Israel and other non-Bayou-related entities, for investment in fraudulent prime bank note trading programs and venture capital investments in non-public start-up companies.
- Despite having abandoned their hedge-fund strategy in 2004, Bayou Management continued to send periodic financial statements to investors describing purportedly profitable hedge-fund trading activities through mid-2005.

Bernard Madoff apparently used some of these tactics, too: the not-so-independent audits, the suspension of real trading activities, and likely the collection of fees for "profits" not earned. And once again we see the manufacturing of fictitious statements.

Madoff hasn't done anything like what Israel did after his conviction—at least, not yet. Israel pled guilty quickly, but then

> ## SUICIDE IS PAINLESS
>
> *Suicide is painless.*
>
> Indeed it is . . . especially if it doesn't happen. Israel wrote that message in the dust on the hood of the 2006 GMC Envoy he abandoned on a bridge over the Hudson River in an effort to dupe authorities into believing he'd jumped. After being allowed to drive himself to prison, he instead tried to flee with a phony suicide scheme. Federal investigators didn't spend much time looking in the water for a body, but instead expected that he would eventually wash up at an airport or a border crossing.
>
> He didn't. Instead he ended up in a parked RV with his girlfriend, and then turned himself in to authorities about three weeks later.

faked his suicide in an effort to escape imprisonment. After a month on the run, he surrendered in Southwick, Massachusetts, and is currently serving a twenty-year sentence in prison. Marino did not commit suicide, but instead is serving a similar sentence. Israel still has a modest presence in the news, however—most recently because his girlfriend tried to send him $300 in the pages of a magazine in mid-January 2009.

One Dinner Party You Don't Want to Attend

It isn't just high-level investors who are duped by pyramid schemes; they flourish at all levels of the socioeconomic scale. The early 2000s saw a women's movement known as "The Dinner Party" sweep through the United States, the UK, and Canada. Suburban housewives, business owners, and mid-level employees were all swept up by its central message—that by participating, you are actually helping others.

You're smart enough to know you didn't really win the Irish National Lottery. You're smart enough to know that a Nigerian prince doesn't really need your help to get his millions out of the country, despite all of those enticing e-mails you've received.

But what if someone tells you:

You are helping other women . . .

The church members are counting on you . . .

No, this isn't illegal—it's all about giving back and being helped in return . . .

Ask yourself this question: What does your heart say?

This powerful set of closing lines is part of the standard pitch for a "charitable gifting concept" that appears under names like Women Empowering Women or The Dinner Party. Whatever it's called, it is illegal. With this "gifting" pyramid, attendees at a recruitment meeting look at a chart that shows how they will move around the "table" as other women join in and pay up after them, until their name is at the "dessert" spot and they receive the money—as much as $40,000.

This is worth repeating: The pyramid scheme was literally laid out before participants in black and white. Like a child's board game, you could reach out and trace with your finger the path that you'd have to take in order to hit the jackpot. Yet women around the world still succumbed, handing over their money and their hopes and dreams. Why? Because everyone else was so enthusiastic about it. Because everyone else assured them that it was a wonderful thing for women, for entrepreneurs, for stay-at-home moms—giving them the chance to suddenly receive a windfall that would help them pursue their dreams. They could have it, too, if they'd just "gift" the reasonable sum of $5,000 . . .

Now this one bears little resemblance to Madoff's scam in its basic tactics. Madoff wouldn't have been caught dead drawing a picture of his scheme for anyone. And he didn't use the "hard-sell" lines. But as for capturing and capitalizing on the enthusiasm of other clients—that was a big part of the Madoff plot.

Low Tides Reveal Everything

Warren Buffett has famously observed that when the tide goes out, you find out who has been swimming naked. Newspaper accounts are rolling in from all parts of the country about more financially naked swimmers splashing to shore, tossed up by the sinking and stinking market that no longer supports their methods.

A Snake River Snake?

The *Wall Street Journal* reported on January 17, 2009, that Idaho securities regulators were looking into hedge-fund manager Daren Palmer of Idaho Falls, investigating claims that he'd operated a long-running Ponzi scheme involving as much as $100 million.

Missing in Florida

At the same time newspapers also carried reports of Arthur G. Nadel, an aging Florida hedge-fund manager who had recently disappeared from his home in Sarasota with millions of his investors' money. His seventy-five-year-old wife said that he had been distraught over the situation. Sources say Nadel's hedge fund may have lost as much as $350 million, but a business partner believes that figure might have been overstated because performance results were exaggerated.

Pennsylvania Ponzi

Another investment fraud case is unfolding in Pennsylvania. The U.S. Commodity Futures Trading Commission and the SEC brought civil charges in early January 2009 against Joseph S. Forte of Broomall, Pennsylvania, who is accused of running a $50 million Ponzi scheme. Authorities say Forte had recently confessed to federal officials after his alleged Ponzi scheme fell apart. According to the SEC, Forte obtained the $50 million from as many as eighty different investors through the sale of securities in the form of limited partnership interests in his firm, Joseph Forte, L.P. They claim he told the investors he would invest their money into an account that trades in securities futures contracts, including S&P 500 stock index futures.

The Confession Line Forms on the Right

Walter Lukken, the acting chairman during January 2009 of the Commodity Futures Trading Commission, the SEC's counterpart in the futures markets, said in an interview that since news of Mr. Madoff's alleged fraud emerged a month ago, his agency had seen a jump in the number of similar cases. "A lot of it is confessions. They are throwing themselves at the mercy of the 'CFTC court,' " he said. In 2008 the CFTC prosecuted fifteen cases alleging the running of Ponzi schemes. The number will certainly be higher in 2009, Mr. Lukken noted, "if it keeps going at this rate."

Well, it sure seems that the Ponzi scheme is alive and well in America, at least in the hedge-fund world. Madoff certainly turned out to be the biggest and the best—but not the only—adherent to the idea. He probably didn't think he had so many imitators.

Finally, Mr. Ponzi and His Scheme

So what did Mr. Ponzi actually do? Just what was his scam? His rapid rise and fall came quickly, as the original Ponzi scheme lasted less than a year. Charles (or Carlo, his given name) Ponzi began in late winter of 1920, and it all came crashing down by July of that same year.

The scam was done with international postal-reply coupons. Those are the flimsy little slips of paper that you send through the mail overseas so that your recipient can easily write you back without paying postage. Ponzi came up with a clever idea: He claimed it was possible to make a profit because of currency fluctuations (buy one in Italian lira, for example, then cash it out in U.S. dollars). Clever enough, but after several months it became clear that there weren't enough of the reply coupons in existence to account for the enormous profits he was promising to his eventual 17,000 investors, mostly in the Boston area.

Interestingly, the SEC website describes what Ponzi did:

> *Ponzi told investors that he could provide a 40% return in just 90 days compared with 5% for bank savings accounts. Ponzi was deluged with funds from investors, taking in $1 million during one three-hour period—and this was 1921! Though a few early investors were paid off to make the scheme look legitimate, an investigation found that Ponzi had only purchased about $30 worth of the international mail coupons. Decades later, the Ponzi scheme continues to work on the "rob-Peter-to-pay-Paul" principle, as money from new investors is used to pay off earlier investors until the whole scheme collapses.*

A PUBLIC RELATIONS DILEMMA

It hasn't appeared yet, and it's a toss-up whether the SEC website (www.sec.gov) will have a section devoted to Madoff once the investigation is over and the case is resolved. On the one hand, it would serve to educate investors, much as the website's Ponzi entry is meant to do; on the other hand, it doesn't make the SEC look too good, does it?

Charles Ponzi pled guilty to one charge and was sentenced to five years. The State of Massachusetts also filed charges against him, and he eventually served another seven years.

A Con Man, Through and Through

Charles Ponzi will also be remembered for his involvement in yet another scam. In the mid-1920s, Florida swampland became rather popular among con men of all walks of life, and Ponzi was no exception. In between jail terms (after a requested pardon was denied), he made his way to Florida and joined in on the "boom."

Deported to Italy after his second prison release, Ponzi eventually made it down to Brazil to work for the Italian airline that later became Alitalia. Some sources say he got the job directly from Italian dictator Benito Mussolini. He tried to get in on a scam involving currency smuggling by some airline employees; when they refused, he became one of the "good guys" and tipped off Brazilian authorities. Three top airline officials were arrested, and the airline went bust during World War II. Ponzi found himself jobless and teaching English while collecting unemployment in Brazil. He died penniless in the charity ward of a hospital in Rio de Janeiro on January 17, 1949.

Not the Only, and Not the Last

As far as pyramid schemes go—and investing schemes in general, for that matter—Bernie Madoff may be the biggest thus far, but he'll hardly be the last. Financial manipulations have gone on for years. We've been through Michael Milken and Kenneth Lay, and all of the scams mentioned above. These types of schemes have no borders, as we found out in January 2009 when Ramalinga Raju of India's Satyam Computer Services admitted to a billion-dollar corporate financial reporting fraud.

While investing and corporate financial fraud have been in the limelight for years, one gets the feeling, especially in the unregulated, greed-fueled hedge-fund circles, that many, many more Madoff-like schemes could be out there. The Madoff revelations, painful as they are, will likely help to expose them and possibly correct some of the faults in the system that allow them to happen. We can only hope so.

At this point, the best we can do is learn what happened, and why, and use those lessons to fix the system and become more prudent investors. The rest of this book examines Madoff, his scheme, and his legacy.

CHAPTER 2

Queens Kid Makes Good

If you had said to me that Bernie was going to be chairman of the NASDAQ and make all this money, I never would have believed it possible.

—Fletcher Eberle,
Far Rockaway High School swim team co-captain

Who is Bernard Madoff?

Good question. And it's being asked by lots of people in lots of places these days. By investors, regulators, financial industry leaders, charity and foundation professionals, and prominent members of the Jewish community, just to name a few. And it's being asked in dozens of languages around the world, for the impact of Madoff spreads well beyond U.S. borders.

And it's a question that's likely to be asked for years to come.

For, truth be told, it's hard to get a clear picture of where this guy really came from. Just as with his investments and business matters in general, one who tries to draw a clear picture of Madoff's background quickly discovers a virtual vacuum of facts, or even stories, about his life.

It's pretty clear from the record that *does* exist that Madoff was—at best—a pretty ordinary, unremarkable kid growing up. Beyond that, few specifics point to a stellar or noteworthy career in the securities business—or any other business, for that matter. Likewise, there isn't much, save for a few morsels

16

here and there, to point to shady dealings or any of his current notoriety.

As one tries to research Madoff's background, one gets the feeling, whether true or not, that many of the more revealing facts were simply wiped from the record. For instance, a close check of the facts and media investigations, at least to date, fails to reveal much about who his parents were, what they did for a living, specific addresses where he grew up, or any of the family's history or ancestry. There is little reference or record of his school days, his marriage to Ruth Madoff, or his early family life.

And some of his early dealings don't add up completely; just how *did* he accumulate the $5,000 he supposedly started his securities ventures with in 1960? How did he get into and pay for Hofstra University? Did he really graduate from that institution, and what did he do while he was there? What did he intend to do with his degree? Ordinarily, one might not be so concerned about such gaps in one's résumé, but given what Mr. Madoff pulled off later in life, should these mysteries have tipped us off? And how much of the Bernie Madoff story is real, and how much is based on myth, anyway?

One can only wonder.

Perhaps an exploration of the early Bernard Madoff, from birth and early life to his early career as a securities industry player, will provide some answers.

Birth and Early Life

It is generally accepted that Bernard Lawrence Madoff was born on April 29, 1938, in the Laurelton area of Queens, New York, to a fairly average Jewish family. His birth and early years were spent in Laurelton and in Rockaway Beach on the Rockaway Peninsula, a short spit of barrier land in extreme southern Queens on western Long Island, about sixteen miles southeast of midtown Manhattan. Laurelton and Rockaway Beach are separated by the grounds of what is now the JFK International Airport.

The name "Rockaway Beach," the beachfront geography, and the proximity to New York City suggest a pretty glamorous place, yet the Rockaway Peninsula is a predominantly working-class place of little glamour, particularly as it has evolved over the years. The Laurelton and Rockaway Beach areas of Bernard Madoff's youth afforded plenty of opportunities to play street and sandlot baseball and to swim in the Atlantic Ocean in the summer. And that's likely what Madoff spent most of his time doing, while probably idolizing the Brooklyn Dodgers and dreaming of becoming a baseball star like most kids did in the area, at the time, in the 1940s and '50s. Not much is known or has been said about his personality, but CNN reporter Allan Chernoff, after interviewing some local contemporaries, noted that Madoff "was said to be shy, but had an intense competitive streak." Carol Marston, co-webmaster of the Far Rockaway High School Online Alumni Association website, was quoted as saying: "He never stood out."

Special treats might have involved trips to the local Rockaway Playland; more ambitious journeys may have taken him to Coney Island, or even into Manhattan. But there's little evidence to suggest there was anything remarkable or unusual about young Bernie's childhood.

Parents and Family Background

Not much has come forth about Bernard Madoff's parents or family ancestry. It seems that they were a low key and typically Jewish middle class family, likely of Russian origins. Russian and Ukrainian immigrants were common in this area; in fact some beach signs in nearby Brighton Beach are bilingual—Russian and English.

In a series of *New York Times* interviews with elementary school classmates, none could recall much about Madoff's parents. Their names were Ralph and Sylvia. From SEC documents it was discovered that there was a brokerage firm registered in Sylvia's name called Gibraltar Securities, but not much is known about that business. It apparently was a small operation, for in the early 1960s the SEC investigated whether small firms such as hers had filed proper financial reports. Shortly thereafter, Ms. Madoff withdrew her registration.

There may be more reasons for the withdrawal. Reports say that Ralph Madoff was really the securities broker and had tax problems, owing the IRS some $13,000. Did he put Sylvia's name on the brokerage business to keep the authorities away? That's not known, and both parents died in the 1970s.

It's a good guess, however, that Bernard Madoff got his first exposure to the securities business through his parents.

Rockaway, Near and Far

If we can't find out enough about the man, perhaps we can learn more by learning about the community he came from. With that thought in mind, here is a short vignette of Bernard Madoff's Rockaway Peninsula hometown.

Take a quick glance at the Rockaway Peninsula on a map and you might expect it to be a rich and historic beachfront enclave—like Miami Beach to Miami or even, well—a Palm Beach in Florida. Beaches adorn this narrow peninsula, separated from the mainland by Jamaica Bay but connected by two different highway bridges and served by the Far Rockaway branch of the Long Island Rail Road.

But the Rockaways—Rockaway Beach and the larger Far Rockaway—exhibit few of the traits of more-desirable beachfront areas, at least today. Earlier photos from the mid-1930s show a beachfront boardwalk typical of many Long Island and New Jersey shore communities. But inland from the boardwalk were very ordinary homes one might expect to find in TV's *All in the Family*. Sprinkled among them were rows of cookie-cutter "bungalows," obviously catering to shorebirds of more modest means. The skies over the Rockaway Peninsula were filled with airplanes, as a new airfield—first known as Idlewild Airport, and later, New York International—came onto the scene in 1943. That facility, now JFK International, is just three miles to the northwest across the eastern portion of Jamaica Bay. Laurelton is just north of JFK, and the famed Aqueduct Racetrack, which must have drawn well from the working-class Laurelton and Rockaway ranks, is just west of that.

Today, Far Rockaway and the Rockaway Beach areas are dotted with older homes, nondescript mid-rise apartments, a few newer high-rises, and a fairly unremarkable downtown strip slated for renewal, like many others in the region. There are vacant lots and traces of a more-prosperous past, an area of recreation and fun close to nearby New York City. But it's obvious that improved transportation and greater wealth among most New Yorkers have driven most of the more-amenable beach communities farther east, along Long Island and elsewhere.

By the Numbers

The Rockaway area's blue-collar character is confirmed by the demographics. According to 2008 U.S. Census estimates, the median household income in Rockaway Beach and Far Rockaway (zip codes 11691 and 11693) is $30,667, compared to a U.S. average of $44,684. Almost 85 percent of households have an income of less than $75,000. Only 9.4 percent of residents have a four-year college degree, compared to about 15.2 percent nationwide. The average home is forty-three years old compared to a U.S. average of twenty-seven years, and some 71.5 percent of homes are rented, compared to a U.S. average of 21.4 percent. And the population is 10.7 percent Jewish, compared to a U.S. average of about 2.2 percent.

So, aside from the Jewish concentration, Rockaway Beach is no Palm Beach. Not even close.

My Hometown Rockaway

While Rockaway wouldn't be featured on an episode of *Lifestyles of the Rich and Famous,* it does have a strong sense of community and community pride. One needs to look no further than the aforementioned Far Rockaway High School (FRHS) Online Alumni Association (www.farrockaway.com) to find evidence. Here can be found a treasure trove of stories about past Rockaway citizens, where they are now, and what they're doing. And there are hundreds of pictures of the current and former Rockaway communities and beaches. There are two books available, unimaginatively titled *My Home Town Far Rockaway, Book One* and *My Home Town Far Rockaway, Book Two,* leather-bound and written by an anonymous Rockaway resident, fan, and evangelist.

So would, by chance, www.farrockaway.com be an excellent source for Bernie Madoff background trivia? One would think, but as is happening elsewhere, his memory has been pretty much scrubbed if it was ever there in the first place. The only mention of Madoff in this extensive, thirty-two-page site comes from one of the webmasters, obviously annoyed at the attention and requests for more background. The article entry is titled "Yes, Bernie Madoff Was a Graduate of FRHS, Class of 1956," and then, grudgingly: "Since the story broke last week, I have been inundated with e-mails from alumni, as well as print and TV reporters, wanting to know more about Bernie. According to the story that appeared in the *New York Daily News*, it seems that Bernie, Class of 1956, may turn out to be the world's biggest swindler. The story has been reprinted below," followed by Douglas Feiden's widely distributed story of December 21, 2008, with the headline BERNARD MADOFF HAD A JOB SAVING LIVES; NOW HE'S KILLED DREAMS.

One gets the feeling that Far Rockaway is still a proud community despite the existence of Bernard Madoff.

High School Days

Research also yields little about Madoff's high school days or teen years. As pointed out by the alumni association site and easily confirmed, Madoff graduated from Far Rockaway High School in 1956. FRHS is one of the larger high schools in the area, located in a fairly typical East Coast, nondescript, three-story building in the center of Far Rockaway. Although serving a fairly average population, Far Rockaway High School is the alma mater of financier Carl Icahn, psychologist and personality Dr. Joyce Brothers, and three Nobel Prize winners.

Madoff's time at Far Rockaway High School days was, like most else, apparently quiet and uneventful, and not terribly given to academics. Dozens of scholastic awards were given out at the 1956 commencement ceremony; Madoff received none of them. In the article mentioned above, Doug Feiden quoted former swim team co-captain Fletcher Eberle as saying: "The Bernie I knew was a good-natured, happy-go-lucky guy, always smiling and kidding, who swam the butterfly very well and never got overly serious," and then: "If you had said to me that Bernie was going to be chairman of the NASDAQ Stock Exchange and make all this money, I never would have believed it possible." Not too surprisingly, Madoff spent a lot of time at the beach, eventually getting a job as a lifeguard at the Silver Point Beach Club in nearby Atlantic Beach. That lifeguard job inspired the headline of Feiden's article, and also, by many accounts, contributed to the $5,000 he supposedly earned and put into play as seed money for his first venture into the securities industry.

FRHS is also where he met his sweetheart and eventual wife, Ruth Madoff, class of 1958.

College Days

There's little doubt that Bernard Madoff attended college, although like much of his other earlier records, there are gaps and questions about his college record, the purpose for which he attended college, and even whether or not he graduated. This much seems clear: He stayed close to home, and did not major in or concentrate on anything that would take him close to the Wall Street world he would eventually enter. He dabbled with law school, but did not major in business or study any of the enabling technologies that would have foreshadowed his career as a Wall Street trader or pioneer in the world of electronic trading. And there's nothing to indicate that he was a stellar or even particularly ambitious student.

That's not to say that he didn't have dreams (or delusions) of a greater academic background. He has been quoted as saying he wished he had attended Harvard or the University of Pennsylvania's Wharton School of Business. Some said he was concerned about his "lack of a pedigree," and his failure to become an alumnus of a major school. But others, including one Wall Street executive who worked with him, depicted Madoff as a street-smart entity "too cool for school."

Alabama and Hofstra

It isn't exactly clear why, but upon graduating from Far Rockaway High School in 1956, Bernard Madoff decided to enroll at the University of Alabama. From most accounts of his time there, given by contemporary classmates, he was unremarkable as a student or athlete, but became a fraternity brother in the Jewish fraternity Sigma Alpha Mu (known as the "Sammy house"). From one picture published in the *New York Times,* he was a handsome guy with sort of a Tony Randall look. One classmate remembers him importing a "looker" from New York for a dance, another remembers him as not being "outstanding with girls." So we really don't know, and some classmates didn't remember him at all.

It also isn't clear why he stayed for only one year. The next year, he came back to Queens and transferred to what was then known as Hofstra College, located in the quintessentially middle-class Long Island suburb of Hempstead in the late 1950s. We're left to wonder where he lived or how he got to and from college. He might have accessed Long Island Rail Road connections from the Far Rockaway branch, either through Jamaica (the long way around) or to West Hempstead, still a couple miles short of campus; or possibly he traveled by car (or bus) east up Peninsula Boulevard to the Sunrise Highway, then north on Uniondale Avenue.

For some investigators, it's not even clear that he finished. Most accounts say Madoff began Hofstra College in 1957 and graduated with a political science degree in 1960, although there's no clear notion of what he intended to do with a political science degree in 1960.

Hofstra College became Hofstra University in 1963. The largest private school in Long Island, Hofstra features a broad range of academic disciplines in liberal arts, applied sciences, and business. It also has a well-known law school, which by some accounts Madoff attended but did not graduate from, and has recently announced plans to create a medical school. There are some 12,600 students today, and Hofstra is a well-regarded institution especially in the New York area.

From 2004 until his December 2008 arrest, Madoff served as a trustee of Hofstra University.

The Controversy

A look at the 1960 Hofstra University yearbook should bring some information to light about Mr. Madoff, yet it does not. Apparently he wasn't mentioned, nor did he appear in any photos, in that yearbook. Classmates interviewed did not remember him, either. But a Hofstra official did confirm his 1960 graduation, and the fact that he majored in political science. The official suggested that he may have graduated early, thus negating his appearance in the yearbook. But one wonders, in light of more recent news, just what to believe.

Law School

Not much is known about this, either, but Bernard Madoff did attend Brooklyn Law School for one year, starting in 1960 in the fall after graduating from Hofstra. Reports say he attended school in the morning and ran his side business, installing and maintaining irrigation sprinkler systems, in the afternoon. As we'll see, this business gave him the initial funds to start his securities business, and the few kernels of legal knowledge probably didn't hurt that effort.

Ruth Madoff

Bernard Madoff apparently met his future bride, Ruth Madoff, then known as Ruth Alpern, sometime during high school.

An attractive, petite, and spunky blonde almost three years Bernie's junior, she also grew up in Queens, graduating from Far Rockaway High School in 1958. Her father Saul Alpern was an accountant, which probably gave rise to her eventual role as bookkeeper and administrator for Bernie Madoff's firm. After graduation, she attended Queens College, a well-established four-year and graduate college in the City University of New York (CUNY) system. Queens College is primarily set up for commuters, and Ruth likely commuted up the Van Wyck Expressway to the neighborhood of Flushing in the northern part of Queens.

She graduated from Queens in 1961 on an apparently accelerated schedule; it isn't clear what she majored in. They married in the early 1960s. She and Bernie made substantial contributions to Queens College in recent years, and beginning in 1993, she served on the Queens College Foundation board before resigning in the wake of the scandal.

Somewhere along the way, Ruth decided to go to graduate school at New York University to get a Master of Science degree in nutrition. She became a noted cook and authority on Jewish cooking, eventually becoming the co-editor of *Great Chefs of America Cook Kosher: Over 175 Recipes from America's Greatest Restaurants,* a work of 185 pages published in 1996.

Aside from this publishing venture, Ruth apparently ran the household (eventually to become many households) and attended various social events with Bernie, mainly in New York and Palm Beach. Of course, she also raised the couple's two boys, Mark and Andrew, born in the mid-1960s, and she has been involved in some of the couple's philanthropic work, covered in chapter 3 and elsewhere. She has been under investigation by the SEC for possibly helping to maintain secret records, including some fund payments. Her name reportedly appears on certain transactions in the business, and many are wondering how she could have not had a big role in the scandal, with her work in the "back office" administrative operations of the Madoff firm.

A Scrapbook Gets Scrapped

Michael Skakun is a well-known independent writer and author in Jewish circles, frequently published in a prominent Jewish publication known as the *Jewish Daily Forward,* or simply "*The Forward.*" A popular speaker on an assortment of topics of Jewish interest, he also has another specialty—creating memoirs.

Kenneth Libo is an adjunct professor of history at New York's Hunter College, and has authored or coauthored several prominent Jewish histories, including *World of Our Fathers, How We Lived,* and *We Lived There Too: Pioneer Jews in the American West.* Libo also has numerous articles to his credit in the *New York Times* and other top publications.

So what does this have to do with the Madoff saga?

It's obvious that Skakun and Libo would be a perfect team to put together a family memoir, especially for a Jewish family. And they were called on to do so, in 2003, by Ruth Madoff. The assignment was to put together a scrapbook as a special gift in honor of Bernie Madoff's sixty-fifth birthday. The story goes something like this, based on Skakun and Libo's account, later published in *The Forward* and elsewhere. On a wet gray day, scribes-for-hire Skakun and Libo showed up under the awning of the posh but low-key, Upper East Side co-op building where the Madoffs lived. Sheltered from the downpour, they folded their umbrellas, went inside, and took the elevator to the Madoff abode. There is no way to describe their impressions better than they do in *The Forward:*

The ample Madoff foyer and living room burst with what appeared to us as classical knockoffs, the regal effect spoiled by overexertion. Gold sconces lined the stenciled wallpaper, a Napoleonic-style desk stood to the side, and the Greek and Egyptian statues vied with each other to set a mood of antique decorum. Arabesque-styled Central Asian rugs beguiled our vision with looping patterns and impressive symmetries, further softening our footfalls.

They sat down at a table with a copy of Ruth's kosher cookbook in front of them. The assignment, she said, was to "give [her husband] a birthday present he won't forget." As reported, she added this comment: "Bernie is turning 65. Other men slow down; take it easy, not him. He's got the whole world on his head."

The birthday present was to be a scrapbook with "pictures, photos, invitations . . . the works." But as she explained the assignment, she also cautioned that Bernie is "cautious," a man who "wanted things in their proper place," a "man who never wanted to be caught off guard." The goal was "to charm him without startling him."

Out came the photos: Bernie playing baseball as a youth, Bernie as a lifeguard, Bernie as a young family man. As they all looked at the pictures, Ruth became wistful and withdrawn, eventually gathering the pictures and announcing "let me mull this over," at which time she "whisked [Skakun and Libo] out the door."

The inevitable phone call came the next day. The project was over before it had begun. Ruth had changed her mind, noting that sixty-five was an age "betwixt and between"; the project would be better done at age seventy, a "fuller measure of life."

The rest is history. And we all get a firsthand glimpse of the Madoff reluctance to illuminate pieces of the past—the way they play their cards close to the vest, reluctant to reveal anything about their life, even to themselves. Realizing this is a private, not a public matter, could we, should we, have taken this as an omen of the future? One can only wonder.

Also interesting is the revelation (and irony) that Madoff was a man who wanted to be charmed without being startled. If only he had had the same consideration for his many clients.

Firm Beginnings

Most accounts have Bernard Madoff starting his own investment firm in 1960, without much fanfare. For seed money he used the $5,000 he'd supposedly earned during his high school and college days working as a lifeguard and installing irrigation

---

THE $5,000 QUESTION

John Carney, managing editor of the Wall Street online journal *Clusterstock*, poses a really interesting question: How could Bernie Madoff have earned his seed money of $5,000 in the late 1950s, while attending college, in the lifeguarding and sprinkler installation business? Sure, it's plausible today—but back then, $5,000 was a huge amount (the equivalent of about $35,000 in today's dollars), especially when you consider that the median wage earner income was $5,600 at the time.

Good question. As Carney puts it: "The idea that Madoff made this much working part-time jobs while going to college doesn't pass the sniff test."

Hard to disagree with that.

---

sprinklers. If he did indeed start the firm in 1960, right after he graduated from Hofstra, he certainly didn't waste any time.

From the beginning, the firm was known as Bernard L. Madoff Investment Securities (today known as Bernard L. Madoff Investment Securities, LLC.) And from the beginning, the firm was a family business, initially run by Bernie and Ruth, who handled the bookkeeping. The early beginnings of Bernard L. Madoff Investment Securities (now known infamously as "BMIS") and how it evolved are examined more thoroughly in the next chapter.

Andrew and Mark

Perhaps it would have made sense to discuss Bernard Madoff's two sons, Mark and Andrew, immediately after introducing Ruth. But, in sequence, BMIS came first. Later on, both sons would join the business as entry-level trading assistants, and would eventually become well known in the securities industry themselves.

Like the other Madoffs in question, little is known about the boys' childhood, except that much of it was spent in a newer but unremarkable ranch-style home in Roslyn, New York, a small, predominantly Jewish suburb of 2,500 residents on the northern edge of Long Island. Located along the Oyster Bay branch of the Long Island Rail Road, Roslyn is not far from the wealthy enclave of Great Neck and about twenty-five miles from Manhattan.

Mark Madoff came first, born in 1964. He attended the University of Michigan, graduating in 1986 and then joining the family business. Eventually, he became co-director of trading, specializing in "listed" securities—that is, securities that are also traded on the New York Stock Exchange (NYSE). He currently lives in a large home in the tony suburban town of Greenwich, Connecticut.

Andrew "Andy" Madoff was born in 1966. He graduated from the University of Pennsylvania's Wharton School of Business in 1988 and also joined the firm at that time. He has also managed trading operations for BMIS, focusing primarily on companies in the NASDAQ market, and has served as a member of NASDAQ's Technology Advisory Council. Andrew reportedly contracted lymphoma in 2003, now in remission, and from then on played an active role in the Lymphoma Research Foundation, joining the board of directors and eventually becoming chairman. The family has contributed substantially to this foundation.

As involved as the two sons were in BMIS, it appears that their roles were primarily confined to trading operations—not the money management or investment advisory operations that ultimately collapsed in the Ponzi scheme. As will be shown in chapter 6, they were instrumental in revealing the scandal to authorities after their father revealed it to them. While they will be part of the legal investigation, they are currently not under indictment or suspected of any crimes. It is also reported that Andrew had some money invested with his father at the time the scandal was revealed. Mark had invested in the Madoff fund, too, but withdrew the investment several years ago. Investigators are wondering what he knew at the time of that withdrawal, but the funds may have been used to buy the Greenwich home.

All in the Family

Ruth, Mark, and Andrew all became part of the family business, but the family connection hardly stops there. Bernard Madoff's younger brother Peter also became part of BMIS. Like Ruth Madoff, Peter graduated from Queens College. Some accounts have him joining Bernie's firm in 1965, before he got his law degree from Fordham University; at least one account has him joining the firm in 1970. Either way, Peter brought a legal- and technology-oriented mind to the firm, and eventually became the senior managing director and head of trading operations.

In 1967, the same year he graduated from law school, Peter had a daughter named Shana. She eventually graduated from Fordham and joined BMIS in 1995 as a compliance attorney. Shana raised some eyebrows through her marriage to former securities regulator Eric Swanson in 2007.

Bernie and Peter also had a sister named Sondra, and her son Charles Weiner joined the firm in 1978 in an administrative role, eventually becoming director of administration. A second son of Peter's joined the firm briefly before leaving for a journalism career; he later died of lymphoma at the age of thirty-two.

BMIS apparently had all the camaraderie and positive energy one would hope to find in a successful family business. Mark Madoff commented in a 2000 interview: "What makes it fun for all of us is to walk into the office in the morning and see the rest of your family sitting there. That's a good feeling to have. To Bernie and Peter, that's what it's all about."

Homes and Stuff, Then and Now

Finally, in the spirit of the chapter title "Queens Kid Makes Good," it's a good juncture to fast-forward a bit through Madoff's early digs in Roslyn, New York, to the broad assortment of homes and toys he accumulated in some of the more posh locales in the country and abroad. This glimpse is based on facts submitted to the SEC in January 2008 and published in the "Investigations" blog of the *Washington Post*.

Montauk

It is well documented that Madoff and his young family liked to spend summers in Montauk in the eastern part of Long Island. For many years they would rent a place and stay for a few weeks in the summer, with Bernie reportedly commuting into Manhattan by seaplane when necessary. In 1981 the Madoffs finally bought a place of their own in the East Hamptons, located at 216 Old Montauk Highway. Madoff and family used it for family occasions, and he is well known for throwing extravagant parties there for his employees including one on the weekend following the Fourth of July. According to the *East Hampton Star*, the home is worth about $3 million and costs about $17,000 a year in property taxes.

Manhattan

In 1984, Madoff and his family moved into a sprawling duplex on Manhattan's Upper East Side. Later, in 1990, he purchased a posh penthouse, 133 East 64th Street, No. 12A, near Madison Avenue, in one of the most desirable parts of Manhattan just over two blocks from Central Park, for $3.325 million according to county records. Reportedly Madoff's neighbors have included NBC's *Today* show host Matt Lauer. Madoff served as chairman of the building's co-op board. Today the property is estimated to be worth $7 million, and it's where Madoff is currently living under twenty-four-hour supervised house arrest after posting $10 million in bail. Madoff also owns his place of business, a three-floor office co-op in the desirable oval-shaped red-granite Lipstick Building, located on Third Avenue in midtown Manhattan, worth between $3 million and $5 million.

Palm Beach

Either as a look-ahead to retirement, or perhaps to get closer to more potential "clients," in 1994 Bernie and Ruth decided to buy a fancy mansion in posh Palm Beach, Florida. It's a prime spot, located at 410 North Lake Way. It's not known why, but Ruth is listed as the sole owner. The five-bedroom, seven-bath home is 8,700 square feet and was purchased for $3.8 million, estimated today to be worth $9.4 million according to county records.

BEACH TOWN CONTRAST: COMPARING PALM BEACH TO FAR ROCKAWAY

If it isn't already clear how much Bernie Madoff's standard of living rose during his working life (honest or dishonest) of forty-eight years in the investing business, the comparison between his latter-day Palm Beach residence and his Far Rockaway roots speaks for itself:

	Far Rockaway	Palm Beach	U.S. Average
Population	58,206	18,412	—
Growth since 2000	2.3%	64.9%	5.9%
Median age	33.4	66.1	37.6
Median household income	$30,667	$101,290	$44,684
% of households earning < $75,000	84.5%	41.5%	71.2%
Median home age	43 years	33 years	27 years
% of homes valued at $1M or more	0.6%	38.6%	1.9%
% of population with four-year degree	9.4%	31.3%	15.2%
% Jewish	10.7%	14.7%	2.2%

Europe, Anyone?

Madoff wasn't to be denied his overseas hideaways, either. Among the collection: a "small villa" overlooking Cap d'Antibes on the French Riviera, yacht included; and what's reported to be a small but expensive office at 12 Berkeley Street in the Mayfair area of London, where he operated and held capital in a British subsidiary known as Madoff Securities International.

Toys and Games

One can only look with tongue-in-cheek at one of Madoff's prize possessions, a fifty-five-foot, thirty-seven-ton wooden fishing boat, built in 1969 by high-end boatbuilder Rybovich & Sons. Purchased in 1977 for $462,000, Madoff keeps this boat in Palm Beach. *Sports Illustrated* once called these boats "the last word in snob appeal." That he nicknamed it "Bull," in hindsight, seems appropriate.

Moving on to the country clubs, it's well known that Madoff is a member of the Palm Beach Country Club (initiation fee $300,000, plus dues) and the Glen Oaks Country Club in Amagansett on Long Island (not quite so high a price tag). Between the two, Bernie evidently had plenty of opportunity to sharpen his golf score and pitch for clients.

Finally, we know about the jewelry collection (valued at approximately $1 million) that he attempted to give to his son while awaiting trial. Apparently the collection includes quite a few vintage watches and fancy Tiffany baubles. He was well known for sparing no expense when it came to personal possessions—which would also explain his $29 million Embraer-145 regional jet.

Madoff clearly made himself a rich man. Without listing the specifics, federal court documents peg his assets at somewhere between $200 and $300 million. Whether or not the term *self-made* applies here, or whether it should be applied to ill-gotten wealth, it's probable that Madoff made plenty of money "the old-fashioned way," simply through trading securities and serving in various management and leadership capacities. That the Ponzi scheme came along at all may have been a carefully calculated maneuver to get ultrarich, or it may have simply been a way to preserve what he already had. It isn't known yet, and may never be.

The next chapter explores how Madoff built his legitimate wealth and personal "brand" through his business, Bernard L. Madoff Investment Securities. It's a story of forward and opportunistic thinking about the securities markets and their legal and technological evolution. It's also a story of mostly legal—if quite aggressive—business dealings.

CHAPTER 3

Building the Madoff Brand

The owner's name is on the door.
—*Bernard L. Madoff Investment Securities website*

From day one in his professional career, which started at age twenty-two, Bernard L. Madoff was a player. A player in the still-pretty-old-fashioned, good-old-boy-dominated securities industry. Madoff came to town (Wall Street, actually) in 1960 with the infamous $5,000 in seed capital and started trading stocks. He was apparently pretty good at it, ready and able to get into markets for individual stocks. Ready and able to buy and sell to make a profit.

As he successfully bought and sold stocks in the small corner of the market he played in, he quite clearly had a vision that other players should be able to do the same thing, easily and without barriers. This vision eventually led to the creation of the electronic virtual market known as NASDAQ, a technology-based, democratized market available to limitless numbers of players with easy access and low trading costs. Given the technology and legal climate of 1960, Wall Street leaders could hardly have foreseen the highly sophisticated form that this would eventually take, but that didn't stop Bernard Madoff.

He made a lot of money trading securities, probably slowly at first. Specific financial records, like most factual evidence of Madoff's early days, are scarce. He became a bigger player in the markets, and then a pioneer and leader in building the

NASDAQ stock market model. In doing so, he built a solid brand for himself in the securities industry.

Somewhere along the way, he used his market acumen and his industry "brand" to move beyond trading stocks and into managing money and making investments on behalf of others. How much, when, and for whom isn't exactly clear. He had good friends and mentors along the way, like clothing magnate Carl Shapiro, who befriended him, treated him like a son, and apparently invested with him almost at the outset—only to lose millions when it all collapsed.

This chapter describes how he became a big player and a trusted and respected name in the securities industry.

The BMIS Business

So what was the early business of Bernard L. Madoff Investment Securities? Initially, it was to trade stocks, to buy and sell, and to be a market player. Like any dealer handling any commodity—be it antiques, cars, or fruits and vegetables—the goal was to buy low and sell high, to be a "dealer" in the market, to help *make* a market as any dealer would in any open-air market around the world. Only instead of bananas or Victorian armoires, it's shares of stock we're talking about.

With the advent of highly accessible, open, electronic stock markets of the current age, becoming a dealer—often referred to in the industry as a *market maker*—has become quite simple. Remember day traders? Low-cost, PC-based electronic trading platforms, which became widespread at the end of the 1990s, gave perfectly ordinary individuals direct access (or fast indirect access) to the physical and virtual electronic trading floors of the New York Stock Exchange, the National Association of

Securities Dealers Automated Quotations system (NASDAQ), and other securities markets.

Individuals could become dealers, buying low and selling high in the marketplace, standing shoulder to shoulder with the big boys—the Goldman Sachses, Merrill Lynches, and J.P. Morgans of the world. The early goal of day traders was to capture the margin heretofore reserved for these big guys: essentially, the eighths and quarters representing the difference between the "buy" (or "bid" or *wholesale* price) and the "sell" (or "ask" or *retail* price of a stock). Some dealers (traders) relied on making this "spread" over and over again (they were known as "scalpers), while others, who really thought they knew where a stock was headed, tried to profit from intraday moves in the stock price. Although that spread ultimately dropped from eighths and quarters to pennies, there was still enough margin—enough profit—to go around.

But back in 1960, becoming such a market player was not so easy. Neither the computerized, networked, electronic trading platforms nor the easy, direct access to markets existed. So what was Madoff going to do with BMIS?

Apparently—and like most of what Madoff did, it's a bit obscure—he entered the markets anyway, despite the lack of tools available to the modern-day player. He was apparently quite cynical about the existing market mechanisms—how closed they were, and how they were controlled by an old-boy network of deep-pocketed trading firms in cahoots with the specialists handling the trades on the NYSE and other exchange floors.

Evidently he had a grand vision of changing this old pattern, of entering the market by any means possible, to provide some competition and get in on the profits being made by the big boys. Now, keep in mind—this was back in the day when fewer than 10 percent of American individuals owned stock, and NYSE market share volumes might have reached 3.2 *million* shares per day on a busy day, compared to the 3, 4, or even 5 *billion* shares per day observed in 2008. Back in those days, there simply weren't as many players in this game, and it wasn't as big a game, either.

Out of this vision was born the subsequent and very prescient vision of the electronic open-air market, with open access, multiple dealers, and electronic trading that eventually evolved into the NASDAQ market, today the world's biggest stock market by most measures. Madoff was a big player in this vision, and eventually served as the non-executive chairman of the NASDAQ market in the early 1990s.

Stock Trading in the Pink

But back to 1960. How did Madoff enter the market and become a player in those early days of paper, telemetry, and vacuum tubes? He first did it through what's known as the "pink sheets."

What are the "pink sheets?" The pink sheets were—well— pink sheets of paper listing quotations for stocks from dealers. Each quotation would list the dealer's name, the stock, and a bid and ask price. The *bid* price was the price the dealer would pay for shares you own; the *ask*, or "offer" price, was the price they would sell you shares for. Again, the difference, or *spread*, represented the profit (the retail markup) the dealer would make on the security. Pink sheets were printed daily by the National Quotation Bureau.

Back before the days of NASDAQ and electronic stock trading, many stocks were bought and sold from dealers on the pink sheets. It worked kind of like this: Say you wanted to buy 100 shares of XYZ Corp. You phoned your broker, or dropped into his swanky downtown office in person if you had the time (and were wearing a proper coat and tie). After discussing the merits with your broker, he would fill out a "ticket"—an order for 100 XYZ—and send it, sometimes in one of those vacuum-tube transport systems, to the "back room." A back-room clerk would get the ticket and figure out where the market was for XYZ—from NYSE, or one of the over-the-counter (OTC) markets served by individual dealers in securities. For more-active securities, the clerk might refer to a list of dealers and call one of them for a quotation. For a less-active stock, the clerk might refer to the pink sheets for a quote, and possibly follow up by phone to verify the quote. Then, in most cases, they would wire the order to the dealer and the transaction would occur.

In those days, pink sheets were quite a legitimate way to buy and sell smaller companies not big enough to be listed on the NYSE, and that list included a lot of companies. Over time, electronic quotation and ordering systems began to automate trading for more-active OTC stocks. The pink sheets became sort of a back burner for very inactive stocks—or stocks that didn't meet SEC requirements to be traded on a traditional exchange. They were a backwater, or worse, a repository for shady, noncompliant, or worthless companies. In the last few years the pink sheets have been revived into a more-legitimate market known as the OTCQX (see www.pinksheets.com).

OTCQX specializes in handling some of the traditional companies too small to list, but has also picked up a new niche—perfectly good foreign companies that choose not to go through painful U.S. Securities and Exchange Commission and Sarbanes-Oxley (financial accountability) compliance. Some are household names, like Europe's Adidas or BASF (the German chemical products company). And of course, today the pink sheets are no longer pink sheets of paper—it is an electronic exchange with a web-based information portal that delivers the latest quotes and company news for companies traded on the OTCQX.

Madoff Goes Pink

If you're wondering about the link between Bernard Madoff and the pink sheets, here it is: Bernard Madoff, sensing the opportunity to make money trading stocks, and possibly sensing the massive eventual democratization of markets with electronic trading, started trading securities on the pink sheets when he started his firm in 1960. Madoff rightly saw, before others did, that electronic stock markets would make it much easier for small dealers to profit by trading stocks. One can only wonder whether he foresaw the coming of day trading, where thousands of citizens from all walks of life would use electronic tools to become, essentially, dealers in the market.

Initially, like other pink-sheets dealers, Madoff apparently made a living trading smaller stocks not listed on the NYSE. Eventually, as will be described below, Madoff started competing directly with the big exchanges, trading stocks manually and then electronically for broker clients. At the same time, he brought his brother Peter into the business and started building the technology base that would eventually help define NASDAQ as we know it today.

Making Money an Eighth (or More) at a Time

In the early days, a securities dealer made money by making a market, or becoming a dealer, in a select set of securities. The dealer would represent himself by posting quotations in the marketplace—a bid (or buy) and an ask (or offer) price. As described above, Madoff posted these quotes primarily on the pink sheets, but probably used phone calls and other forms of communication to disseminate quotes.

Under this scenario, the dealer makes money by capturing the spread between the bid and the ask price. This is still the case today, where thousands of dealers in the NASDAQ and other electronic markets, as well as the auctioneer "specialists" on the NYSE, capitalize on the spread to make profits and drive their business.

If you look today at a typical quotation, you'll see a bid and an ask price just like in the old days, along with a *size* quote representing the number of shares for sale or desired to be bought at that price. But the difference between the bid and the ask is typically one cent; for instance, as this is written, Starbucks (ticker symbol SBUX) quotes a bid of $9.88 and an ask of $9.89. So there is exactly one cent per share to be made by a dealer on each trade. That isn't much, but given the average daily volume of about 14 million shares for SBUX, there's money to be made.

Rewind to the old days. The old days were different in two key ways. One is the unit of trade, which instead of pennies, was "eighths"—that is, one eighth of a dollar or 12½ cents. For many years, at least into the late 1990s, and for most stocks, an eighth was the smallest unit of change—and the smallest spread—for a stock. In the 1990s, one-sixteenth increments (called "teenies") became more common, and, starting in 1999, the markets moved toward penny increments, going 100 percent that way by SEC mandate in 2001.

The idea was to give customers (investors) a better deal. Dealers (market players) didn't like it initially, for it cut into their trading margins significantly. But as more people got involved in the markets, and they were more willing to trade more often (precisely because they *didn't* have to pay a large

DAVID VERSUS GOLIATH, OR GOLIATH VERSUS DAVID?

Were penny increments really designed to help small investors? Maybe; maybe not. More-cynical observers held the view that penny margins were a concoction of bigger market players—the J.P. Morgans and so forth—to cut the profits of the little-guy dealers in the market—the day traders—and hopefully to get rid of them and the competition they represented. Particularly given the influence of big Wall Street firms on the SEC, this theory could well have merit.

spread), everyone ended up making their money anyway, and "retail" market participants—regular, everyday investors—came out ahead, just as the SEC had intended.

What does this have to do with Madoff? In 1960, and for twenty to thirty years after that, the minimum spread was 12½ cents. And that minimum was the rule for actively traded, high-volume stocks, because there were a lot of dealers and lots of competition in the market. But for smaller stocks with less volume and fewer active dealers? The spread could easily expand to 25 cents, 50 cents, a dollar, and occasionally higher. Madoff likely made a lot of money capturing these spreads, even though his longer-term vision of electronic trading and more-democratized markets eventually drove the trading increments, and thus the spreads, downward.

For a Few Dollars More

Bernard Madoff probably could have supported his family quite well by trading securities on the pink sheets, by becoming a competent and respected independent dealer in the securities he handled. Over time he would have built his niche and prospered by capturing the spreads as they came in.

But apparently that wasn't good enough for Bernard Madoff.

He saw, quite correctly, that there were larger sums of money to be made by playing a bigger role in the securities industry. He also saw ways to make more money than merely the spread allowed by the market and its competing dealers. He also saw that by computerizing and automating smaller trades, he could focus on larger ones—thereby helping to create an automation model that eventually spawned a revolution in all markets.

Bernard Madoff was a pioneer with big ideas, and some good ones, at a time when markets and investing were about to evolve rapidly. Right ideas, right place, right time. And, not surprisingly, some of Madoff's methods sailed quite close to the boundaries of the law, or at least, ethical trading practice.

Front-Running

Suppose you're a securities dealer. Shortly after lunch one day, you hear that a large pension fund or institutional investor is looking to pick up, say, 300,000 shares or so of Microsoft. That fund or investor may be a client of yours, or you may have just heard a rumor through the grapevine, or you may have seen some revealing trading activity already taking place.

What might you do? You might go out into the marketplace and pick up as many shares of Microsoft as you could, at the lowest possible prices, to fill this order in a timely way— not to mention profitably, when it finally came in. You would do it quietly and hope nobody else in the market has heard the good news. You would pounce on unsuspecting sellers with orders in the market at favorable prices. You might even go to other clients to try to talk them out of their shares—for there's a lot of spread to be made on 300,000 shares, and if you can pick up the goods cheap, so much the better for the spread. You hope to make this spread, or at least, you hope for a nice run-up in the price of the shares you just picked up for you own account.

Picking up shares—trading for your own account as a dealer or for some favored client, anticipating the "fill" of an incoming order—is called front-running. Front-running is illegal if it's based on private information—that is, information not available to the public. Which would likely make most front-running, including that done by Madoff, illegal. While the SEC and other enforcement bodies have tried to crack down on it over the years, it still happens to this day. It's likely that Bernie Madoff made millions over the years by front-running orders in the market.

Payment for Order Flow

As an independent dealer in the market, what you want most is to get lots of orders for the securities you deal in. Madoff, like many dealers well into the 1990s, got smart about this and began to "pay for" order flow. Essentially, this meant giving a small kickback—a fee—to larger security firms like Charles Schwab or Merrill Lynch, for sending orders your way, or possibly to order routing middlemen who consolidate orders and route them your way. Either way, as a dealer, you pay for the chance to make money fulfilling a stock order.

Payment for order flow seems like a natural outgrowth of the dealer competition that, in the long run, makes markets work better and makes prices more competitive. That's all well and good. But the problem, at least as seen by many Main Street and Wall Street investors, is that payment for order flow can get in the way of an investor receiving the best price or execution of their trade. That is, instead of routing orders to the dealer or to the outstanding order representing the best price, the order is routed to the dealer paying the kickback. So the customer doesn't get the best price.

There have been numerous studies, some quite academic, on this subject— specifically, are retail customers really hurt by payment for order flow? The consensus answer seems to be no, by and large, especially for customers with long-term investing goals in mind. Active traders, on the other hand, learned to avoid brokers who accepted order-flow payments, and many brokers catering to active traders made it a point to tell their customers that they didn't participate in this practice.

Bernard Madoff apparently became a poster child for payment for order flow, becoming widely known in the industry for paying a penny per share to anyone who would bring him an order. In the 1990s, the SEC decided not to take a stand on the practice, and that turned Madoff loose, although it is almost certain he did a lot of it during earlier years. An article in the *Financial Times,* commenting on the ramifications of this SEC "look-the-other-way" inaction, estimated that at one point in the 1990s, Madoff may have grabbed as much as 10 percent of the entire NYSE floor-trade volume by paying for order flow.

That's huge.

Trading Away from the Floor

Madoff initially made his mark, and made his money, by trading non-Exchange-listed, or non-NYSE-listed, stocks over the counter—first through the pink sheets, then, as technology evolved, by phone, wire, and eventually, computer. But he also saw—and grabbed—an opportunity to trade big stocks with the big boys by starting his own trading shop for New York Stock Exchange stocks.

How the NYSE Works

Up to and through most of the 1970s, if you were a U.S. company that anybody had heard of, it was likely your stock was traded on the New York Stock Exchange—the so-called Big Board, famously in existence since 1792 and now residing in the Greek Revival monstrosity at the corner of Wall and Broad Streets in lower Manhattan completed in 1903.

If you were a corporate nobody in the 1960s and 1970s, your shares didn't make the grade to make it onto the Big Board, and were traded over the counter by dealers like Bernard Madoff. Over the years, that changed. Driven in part by the innovations that Madoff pioneered, the OTC dealer network became consolidated into the computer-driven NASDAQ electronic stock exchange, and that exchange proved so successful that some of the biggest names in the market went and stayed there, like Microsoft, Intel, Oracle, Google, and others. In fact, Madoff reportedly helped convince those companies of NASDAQ's merits during his tenure there as chairman.

The NYSE had descended, largely intact, from its early days as an outdoor auction market in the 1790s. As implied, the auction market is controlled by an auctioneer, known as a *specialist* in NYSE terminology. The specialist is a person there to find a price to match buy and sell orders, and thus to complete transactions. The specialist also acts as a dealer sometimes, filling orders through his or her own account, which, naturally, is really the account of a specialist firm, a company that specializes in putting specialists on the NYSE floor. The NASDAQ, by contrast, is a *dealer* market, not controlled by any single auctioneer but in aggregate by all participating dealers.

Unlike NASDAQ, where the number of dealers in a stock is unlimited, every listed stock on the NYSE has a single specialist—one and one only. That specialist works with the orders on the book, and with floor brokers (representatives of major brokerage firms), walking the floor with more, usually larger, orders. The specialist is chartered by the NYSE with the task of keeping "orderly" markets, and the specialist firm is paid not only by profitable trading from their own account, but special fees brokers might pay for special kinds of orders, like so-called *limit orders* specifying a price. These fees and trades might account for only a penny or two per share, or even per transaction, but at 3 billion shares a day, it adds up.

It's a cozy situation: Specialists have control and a steady flow of income from their tightly restricted activities. But what if outside third parties should happen to be allowed to trade NYSE stocks? What if the specialist system were chucked altogether in favor of an electronic system taking the single human out of the process? Trading started to bypass the single human in the 1970s with the advent of computers and competitive, off-market trading. That single human took an even smaller role in 2005 with the advent of the parallel electronic NYSE trading system known as the NYSE Hybrid Market.

Not surprisingly, Mr. Madoff was Mr. Johnny-on-the-spot when the off-floor trading got big for NYSE stocks.

The "Third Market"

The NYSE has a large and rather complex rule book, well beyond the scope of this book. One of those rules, the so-called Rule 390, prohibits NYSE *member* firms from trading NYSE–listed stocks in any outside market; that is, they must be traded on the NYSE floor through its specialists. That's a good thing for the specialist firms, because it helps them protect their business.

Merrill Lynch, Goldman Sachs, and J.P. Morgan can't execute trades that are normally the bailiwick of the specialists.

But Rule 390 also turned out to be a good thing for Bernard Madoff.

Not being an NYSE member—far from it, actually—Bernard Madoff was quite obviously qualified to trade NYSE stocks, and quite obviously saw a lot of money to be made in doing so. So he set out to make markets in NYSE stocks as an independent dealer, using paid-for order flow to help bring in orders. He developed excellent relationships with brokers, including the new discount brokers like Charles Schwab, spawned by the so-called "May Day" changes of May 1, 1975, that gave birth to discounting and broader broker competition.

Greater numbers of orders were routed to regional exchanges—like the Cincinnati or Philadelphia or Pacific Stock Exchanges, or to independent dealers like Bernard L. Madoff Investment Securities—by brokers simply looking to get a better deal or to avoid having to pay fees for limit orders. Or, they were looking to collect order-flow payments vital to making money in light of reduced trading commissions. Brokers saved money—and made money—by coming to BMIS.

According to a 1989 article from the *Forbes* magazine archives "Living off the Spread" by Richard Stern, Madoff made markets in the 250 largest trading stocks on the NYSE. And, according to Lynn Lanz Doran's 1999 Georgetown University research paper, "Market Making in the Third Market for NYSE–Listed Securities," third-market activity "is dominated by two particular dealers, Trimark Securities, Inc. and Bernard L. Madoff Investment Securities."

Stern tells us that Madoff wouldn't disclose which specific firms were sending him orders, so as not to "offend the Big Board or its specialists." But Stern goes on to say that "over

100 firms are doing business with Madoff. . . . each morning, Bernie Madoff's 20 traders sit in front of computer screens on the 18th floor of a mid-town Manhattan building [the Lipstick Building]. When they go home in the evening, the 20 will have handled execution of about 2% of the volume in NYSE–listed stock—sometimes as many as 5 million shares."

One small broker-dealer is quoted by Stern as saying: "Not only do I save 1¾ cents on a limit order [the limit order fee], Madoff gives me a penny . . . that's a 3-cent [per share] turnaround as far as I'm concerned. Or $30 on a 1,000-share order."

And, again from Stern, "He [Madoff] won't say how much his firm makes, but the word is that despite hard times on The Street, Madoff is very profitable. During the last few years, even through the tough years of 1987 and 1988, he added about $8 million a year to the firm's capital position, which recently was $50 million according to SEC documents."

The business grew to involve more trading in NASDAQ stocks and more activity in the so-called "after-hours" market— that is, the markets used mainly by institutions and active traders to trade stocks before and after market close. According to a 2000 interview in industry rag *Wall Street & Technology,* in that year "Bernard L. Madoff Investment Securities is a leading market maker in off-exchange and after-hours trading of U.S. stocks, including all companies in the S&P 500 and 200 leading NASDAQ stocks. . . . Madoff Securities has over *$300 million* [italics added] in firm capital and currently ranks among the top 1 percent of U.S. securities firms."

And according to a *Barron's* article in 2001, Madoff's firm was one of the three top market makers in NASDAQ stocks and the third-largest firm matching buyers and sellers of NYSE–listed securities.

WHAT'S IN A SYMBOL?

The NASDAQ is basically a giant electronic quote board on which all dealers in a stock can quote their best bid and ask prices. And if their quote is better than everyone else's, they'll get the business. So, how does one identify a dealer on NASDAQ? Answer: through their four-digit "Market Participant ID" or MPID. There are literally thousands of MPIDs. Some are household names, like J.P. Morgan Securities, shown as JPMS, or Merrill Lynch (MLCO) or Credit Suisse First Boston (FBCO). Some are smaller firms, like D. A. Davidson and Co. (DADA) and Raymond James & Associates (RAJA).

And some MPIDs, once quite familiar to active traders, are no longer found. Like Bear, Stearns & Co. (BEST) and Lehman Brothers (LEHM). And now, MADF, which simply stood for Bernard Madoff. For any trader using so-called Level II NASDAQ quote screens up until December 11, 2008, MADF quotes were quite familiar and right in there with the big boys.

So, through mostly legal means, Bernard Madoff became a very, very successful market player.

The Software-Driven Market

As had become the pattern, Madoff clearly saw even more opportunity. To make markets, trade fast in those markets, and keep costs down, he saw that automation and computerization were key. His brother Peter became the firm's technology expert. It's unclear when BMIS fully computerized its operations, but it is clear that they were pioneers in this field. Madoff's firm apparently became one of the first firms to automate by developing software to read consolidate quote feeds from market networks.

Madoff's firm had also worked with the Cincinnati Stock Exchange back in the 1970s to help them create a fully automated electronic stock exchange to give him a clearer path to play in third market and intermarket trading. He reportedly spent $250,000 to upgrade that exchange's computers and worked with the CSE over the years to expand its (and his own) business.

According to the 2000 *Wall Street & Technology* interview, Peter further enhanced software to match national best bid and offer prices and automatically execute orders for up to 5,000 shares, and to "offer price improvement if the spread was higher than the minimum increment [12½ cents for most stocks]." These systems helped BMIS work fast, offer better prices, and to focus on larger, more profitable orders coming into the firm. Eventually, the system design influenced the so-called Intermarket Trading System, linking NYSE, OTC, and regional markets together. And BMIS started using the network to list their own quotes on the Cincinnati Stock Exchange, making it a favorite stock shop for brokers and other dealers.

In the late 1980s when Richard Stern of *Forbes* visited Madoff's offices, his comments were quite vivid: "Visit the offices of Madoff Investment and you may be taking a walk into the future of stock trading. Unlike in most trading rooms, where negotiations are still largely done by telephone, the phones hardly ring. When they do, it's for orders of over 3,000 shares, which are negotiated . . . 95% of orders are handled by their computers."

And, of course, continuing his pattern, Madoff didn't stop there, either.

Stern goes on to observe that "Madoff's computer operation is far more sophisticated than one designed solely to cut costs." As Madoff himself explained: "A key to market making is the ability to hedge positions." And so Madoff and his team went on to design computer models to show his traders how to hedge a position just taken—how to buy or sell some other kind of security, perhaps a derivative security like an option or futures contract—to mitigate the risk of a trade.

It is unknown where and when Bernard Madoff started handling other people's money using similar techniques in a "hedge-fund" sort of arrangement, but it's easy to suspect that this activity gained some speed with the advent of these computer systems.

Inside Jobs

Throughout his career, with a then-solid reputation as one of Wall Street's prominent pioneers, leaders, and traders, Bernard Madoff also took leadership positions in prominent trade organizations. He served in what was then known as the National Association of Securities Dealers (NASD), a self-regulatory industry group chartered under the Securities and Exchange Act of 1934 (now known as FINRA—the Financial Industry Regulatory Authority). He also served more recently in several roles in the NASDAQ Stock Market, the automated stock market founded by NASD but divested from it in 2001.

He also served as vice chairman of NASD, a member of its board of governors, and chairman of its New York region, according to the SEC. He also held several roles in the NAS-DAQ stock market board of governors, serving on the executive committee and as chair of its trading committee and was chairman of the board for several years.

NASDAQ Stock Market records filed with the SEC for 2005 show Bernard Madoff and his cronies serving in several capacities. Madoff himself served as an industry representative on the nominating committee for its board of governors. His son Mark served as the chairperson of the Exchange Listed Securities Subcommittee. And one of his firm's employees, David Kugel, served on the Market Operations Committee until 2008. And as noted in chapter 2, Andrew Madoff served on the Technology Advisory Council. It's worth noting (with some relief) that no Madoff people were on the Legal and Compliance Advisory Committee.

Madoff also served as chief of the Securities Industry Association's trading committee in the 1990s and in the early 2000s, representing brokerage firms in talks with regulators about trading rules for electronic-trading and new network technologies.

Whether these roles as a governance good guy for so many years helped immunize Madoff from SEC and other investigations is unclear. One can only wonder.

Giving Back: Philanthropy and the Roots of Community Involvement

Bernard Madoff was an active, energetic securities business guy, to be sure. But as time went on and his net worth rose, Madoff did start to give back through a rather large assortment of charitable contributions and service. Whether it was to clear his own conscience or to get more involved in the community and ethos of the wealthy for nefarious purposes is not known. It was probably some of both. What is clear is that his whole family was involved, and it was all part of building the Madoff brand.

The family has had two encounters with lymphoma—one when Madoff's son Andrew was diagnosed in 2003, and another when his nephew Roger died of the disease in 2006. The Madoff family donated some $6 million for research, and Andrew remains active with the organization today.

Madoff was also heavily involved in Jewish circles in New York and elsewhere. He has served as chairman of the board of the Sy Syms School of Business at Yeshiva University since 2000, and as treasurer of the school's board of trustees since 1996, both until his December 2008 arrest. He is also known to have given large sums of money to the school.

Mr. Madoff was also involved in New York civic organizations, including the city's Cultural Institutions Group, and he served on the board of the New York City Center, a prominent theater.

There is also a foundation known as the Bernard L. and Ruth Madoff Family Foundation. According to the record on www.grantsdirect.com, at the end of 2007 it had assets of $19,125,455, and had given fourteen grants between $25,000 and $100,000 in 2006, mostly to Jewish educational, cultural, and health charities, with some 78 percent of the recipients in Florida. The assets of the foundation have been frozen.

Madoff was also a big contributor to the Democratic Party and New York senator Charles Schumer.

Madoff left his mark on the philanthropic world. But clearly he left a much bigger mark on the evolution of stock markets and stock trading, one that for the most part was legitimate if aggressive. He was a true pioneer of today's modern off-floor electronic trading practices, and left his signature four-character MADF on quote boards and "prints" (trades) everywhere. But as we all know, beyond stock trading, he was to leave a far larger mark on the private investing world, with his thousands of clients standing helplessly near Ground Zero when his Ponzi scheme blew up.

CHAPTER 4

Blind Trust: Recruiting the Best and the Brightest

I know Bernie—I can get you in.
—Mike Engler, friend and recruiter for Bernie Madoff

Who could say no to Bernie?

There in front of you, a soft-spoken, gentle, kind, mild-mannered man with a boyish face, a cute smile, a quintessentially Semitic nose, and facial lines. A guy who would seem just as at home in his garden or in his study in a bathrobe as in an office moving hundreds of millions around each day. A guy who might be just as likely to have a glass of milk with dinner as a double martini. A guy, who seems even more one of the crowd and comfortable should he happen to have his spunky, active, attractive, affable wife Ruth at his side.

You've known of his reputation for years. A super investor, a steady investor, a "let me take care of you" kind of guy. A solid reputation and basis for trust. Credentials. Positions of power and authority in the complex financial world. And common experiences. You probably had many of the same experiences growing up. You probably have much the same perspective on money and wealth and the lifestyle that goes with it.

You probably went to dinner together. You probably attended some of the same social functions, some in pursuit and support of common charitable interests. You gave to the same charities. You went to the same synagogue. You played golf or went boating together. You followed the same sports teams. You read the same magazines. When not in Florida or New York, you traveled to the same places. You shared favorite stories about Wall Street and the financial, political, religious, and social issues of the day.

And so, when the chance came to invest in what you know, invest in who you know, with someone of your own creed and character—why not? Especially because, as you so well know, it's a rather exclusive community that gets the privilege to do so. You have enough money. You have the social standing. You, too, can invest with Bernie Madoff. Why not? What have you got to lose?

We now know how *that* story ended.

The rest of this chapter takes aim at Bernie Madoff's "other life" as a money manager—what he sold, and how, through his own efforts and those of promoters and so-called "feeder funds" around him, he created the "blind trust" necessary to draw his innocent victims into the scheme.

Becoming a Money Manager

To understand how Madoff got started in the field of money management, we must rewind a bit back into Madoff's early days as a trader. Somewhere during those days, probably in the early 1960s, Madoff started managing investments for other people. There is no solid account of how, when, for whom, or how much was involved in Bernie Madoff's first steps into managing money for others. Some accounts indicate that it might have begun with his old friend and mentor, Carl Shapiro. It may have also included a few small institutions, charities, or trusts. There isn't much record to go on.

To understand Madoff's new sideline, one must understand

that the private investment fund like the one Madoff started is actually a *hedge fund*—a largely unregulated pool of assets from private investors set up to protect investors from market disruptions—or, more commonly today, to beat average market returns.

By Any Other Name, Still a Hedge Fund

Ordinary investors have thousands of investing choices, from individual stocks to bonds to mutual funds and Exchange-traded funds offered as "regulated" securities. Whether a specific investment or a "fund" of investments, like a traditional mutual fund, these securities must comply with certain laws enacted by the federal government and generally enforced by the Securities and Exchange Commission.

Many investors wisely seek to "leave the driving to someone else"; that is, they don't feel comfortable or sufficiently informed to make investments, they lack confidence. Or, they just want to spend their time doing something else, like practicing medicine or enjoying retirement. These investors want someone with professional expertise to select individual investments and to build a "diversified" portfolio designed to maximize gains while reducing risk.

Such investors invest in funds—professionally managed portfolios of stocks and other kinds of investments. They choose (or should choose) these funds based on their investing objectives and success, their costs, and the quality and track record of their professional advisers.

Traditional Mutual Funds
Ordinary retail fund investors typically invest in traditional mutual funds. These are "investment companies"—investment

pools designed to achieve certain investing objectives, usually to capitalize on growth, income, or some combination of the two. They were chartered by and are governed by the Investment Company Act of 1940. The Act is very specific about how investors are treated, how the fund discloses results, and how investors are paid by these funds. Compliance is strong, for the Act is vigorously enforced by the SEC. There are about 9,000 mutual funds in existence today, and they have become a mainstay of Main Street, especially 401(k) and other retirement plan investing.

If you're a typical retail investor, you'll probably have to settle for the fairly ordinary returns these funds generate. They're largely safe but tend not to outperform the market. Still, they're better than the alternatives of low-paying cash investments. (Well, indeed those cash investments did better in 2008, but that was a notable exception to the long-term trend.) They're better than not knowing what you're doing and getting stuck with the wrong investments—like Enron, Fannie Mae, or Washington Mutual.

But suppose you're fortunate enough to have a lot of "investable wealth." A million or more; tens of millions, even better. You aren't content to just perform with the market. And you'd rather run your business or skipper your boat than pick individual stocks. You want a little spice in your investing life. You want to run with the big boys, earning better-than-average returns. You want 10, 15, or 20 percent rather than the 5 percent everyone else is settling for. After all, you deserve it; you've worked hard, you're a member of the privileged class, and you want to invest the way other privileged people do.

At least until recently, you might have chosen a hedge fund.

The Hedge Fund Exemption

In the interest of not meddling too much in the world of private wealth and capital, the 1940 Act has two commonly used exemptions to exclude certain types of funds from close regulation. They are found in Sections 3(c)(1) and 3(c)(7) of the Act. Those exemptions gave rise to what are known today as hedge funds.

Hedge funds are private investing pools whose governance is limited primarily to two areas: who can invest and how they're sold. The first hedge fund was started in 1949, and in the beginning they did what the name suggests—they helped investors "hedge" against market downturns or other unforeseen events, because rules and predominant investing strategies made it difficult for ordinary funds or individual investors to do so.

So-called 3(c)(1) funds are limited to 100 or fewer investors, and can only be marketed to investors with more than $1,000,000 in investable assets, or verifiable income exceeding $200,000 a year. The 3(c)(7) funds can have an unlimited number of investors but each must have $5,000,000 in investable assets. The 3(c)(1) fund securities do not have to be registered with the SEC; 3(c)(7) funds only have to register their securities with the SEC if they have more than 499 investors.

Importantly, there's no requirement for the managers of either type of fund to be registered or otherwise qualified or credentialed with the SEC, nor with any other regulatory body or trade group like FINRA (formerly NASD). Neither type of fund can be "offered or advertised to the general public."

An Accident Waiting to Happen

So these funds are left to do what they want, and the managers can charge some pretty hefty fees for doing so. Common was the "2 and 20" compensation rule, where the manager is guaranteed a fee of 2 percent of the fund's net asset value plus 20 percent of the investment gains over a specified amount. That's a pretty powerful incentive.

Further, hedge funds, not being subject to regulation, are allowed to sell short, borrow money, and invest in "derivative" instruments like futures and options to enhance returns. Effectively, they are leveraging their portfolio, controlling, say, $10 million in assets with, say, $2 to $5 million in equity. Great when things are good, not so great when things go bad.

And so the picture becomes clear: Wealthy investors are chasing high returns while trusting private managers in rather exclusive private investments. Managers with few boundaries chased the highest returns possible to get the biggest fees, able to use leverage and other tools to fan the fire.

More fuel for the fire came from federal policies to ward off recession, expanding credit and lowering interest rates. As this happened, greater numbers of investors looked for alternatives to the paltry returns generated by fixed-income investments and mediocre mutual funds; those that could piled into hedge funds.

As 2007 unfolded, suddenly a lot of hedge funds had lots of investors and not much to invest in, so they started investing where they could. The oil story—China, "peak oil," etc.— became quite compelling, and hedge funds piled in. They chased mining, machinery, and fertilizer stocks. As 2008 went into the history books, we know what happened with most of those investments; many hedge funds are now in a bad way or have closed altogether. According to a December 2008 *Business-Week* article, "[E]xperts predict anywhere from 30 percent to 70 percent of hedge funds will disappear in 2009."

It should be noted that while there are a lot of aggressive and shady hedge funds out there, quite a few funds are managed by legitimate investment companies. The largest hedge fund is managed by J.P. Morgan and Co.; others in the "top 10" are managed by Goldman Sachs and Barclays. Some estimate that hedge funds account for as much as 30 percent of

---

SO YOU THINK YOU DON'T OWN HEDGE FUNDS?

According to a report from Open CRS, a congressional research think tank, corporate pension fund involvement in hedge funds is on the increase: "The proportion of U.S. corporate-defined benefit pension funds investing in hedge funds has increased to 24% in 2006, up from 19% in 2004 and 12% in 2000." But the good news is, in aggregate, they don't invest that much: "Although statistics vary, total corporate pension fund assets allocated to hedge funds in 2006 was 2.1%."

And why do pension funds invest in hedge funds? Simple. For pension funds to earn enough returns to pay current pensioners and grow enough to cover your pension, they need healthy returns, perhaps 6 to 8 percent over the long run. When fixed-income investments pay 1 to 5 percent, as they did in the 2007–2008 time frame, pension fund managers need to find something to boost their average return. Enter the hedge fund. And don't think it's just corporate pension funds, either. California's giant CalPERS (California Public Employees' Retirement System) public pension fund famously invested over $1 billion in hedge funds in 2002, and the city fathers of New York caused quite a stir in 2007 with plans to invest in hedge funds. But again, there's good news: Poor 2008 performance culminating with the Madoff scandal has brought most of these funds to reconsider their strategies when it comes to using hedge funds.

---

all stock and bond trading. It's also interesting to note that the top-earning hedge fund managers, according to *Institutional Investor* magazine, earn over $1 billion a year.

So what does all of this have to do with Bernie Madoff? Madoff managed what was, for all intents, a hedge fund. But instead of promising huge "home-run" returns to investors, his promise—and his track record, whether actually achieved or

WHAT ABOUT REGULATING HEDGE FUNDS?

The SEC has been concerned about hedge funds for years, and doubtless after the Madoff incident, they are even more concerned. Although they blew it on the Madoff situation, they really did try to rein in hedge funds a bit—or at least, to add a thin shell of regulation and compliance.

As a first action, the SEC attempted to require hedge fund managers and advisers to register with them, as any public fund manager or financial adviser dealing in securities must do today. They issued a rule change in December 2004, requiring hedge fund advisers for firms managing in excess of $25 million and more than fifteen investors to register by February 2006. In a broader statement, the SEC said it was "adopting a risk-based approach to monitoring hedge funds as part of its evolving regulatory regimen for the burgeoning industry." But alas, a hedge fund manager successfully challenged the change and it was overturned and sent back by a court for review in June 2006.

When it comes to hedge funds, the SEC continues to operate with few tools at its disposal, apparently overwhelmed at the prospect of monitoring some 8,000 hedge funds currently in existence.

How that will change remains to be seen—there's more to come on this topic in chapters 5 and 10.

not—was steady 10 to 15 percent returns. No regulation, no disclosure, no rules—and no questions asked.

A Master of Marketing

So what Bernard Madoff ran on behalf of all his clients, whether with good intentions or bad, pretty much fits the definition of a hedge fund. As evidence was gathered and the facts (or lack of them) become known, what is readily apparent is that Madoff was a master marketer of his investing services and his investment product.

Now, what does it mean to be a master marketer? In business school they teach that marketing consists of the "four Ps"—product, price, promotion, and place. The *product* is what you sell; the *price* is what you sell it for, and how it compares with competitors; *promotion* is how you create visibility; and *place* is where and to whom you sell it. Any marketing strategy consists of a carefully planned mix of the four Ps.

For an investment product such as that marketed by Mr. Madoff, it's more useful to look at the mix slightly differently; actually, one P and three Ms: product, message, messenger(s), and marketplace. It is fascinating to observe how Madoff controlled the product and the message to create blind trust in his dealings. It is also fascinating how Madoff defined and used his marketplace and a network of messengers to successfully deliver the message.

The Product: "A Jewish Bond"

To sell a product, there must be something compelling about it—some set of features or attributes that make people want to buy. Although the record is slim about how Madoff described his investment product, it's likely that in the beginning, he simply leveraged his knowledge and standing in the securities industry to convince clients he could invest their money, too. He also used his reputation in the Jewish and charitable communities to manage their assets, sometimes on a voluntary basis. While there are pamphlets describing his trading business, the record is devoid of any brochure or other specific description of his funds, his investing strategies, or even his results. And because he operated under the compliance radar, no prospectus or statement of results was required anyhow.

As time went on, however, Madoff was able to show a strong track record. He apparently did this through rather crudely produced client statements, said to be printed with an old dot-matrix printer until the very end. There was no electronic access to his past performance through his website (surprising for a guy who pioneered electronic stock trading!). The record was one of steady returns, 8 to 12 percent, in up or down markets. In fact, the returns were steady enough, and the name sufficiently trusted—especially in Jewish circles—to earn the nickname "a Jewish Bond."

As was reported in a *Washington Post* story shortly after the scandal broke, "A hedge fund run by Madoff, which described its strategy as focused on shares in the Standard & Poor's 100-stock index, averaged a 10.5 percent annual return over the past 17 years." And: "This year, amid a general market collapse, the fund reported that it was up 5.6 percent through November, while the S&P 500-stock index fell 38 percent." Indeed, the fund was said to have lost money in only five months over one twelve-year period, starting in 1996.

Because disclosure requirements were minimal to non-existent, little is known about the specific investing methods

Madoff used, or claims to have used. In a 1992 interview with the *Wall Street Journal*, he described his strategy: In the 1970s, he had placed invested funds in "convertible arbitrage positions in large-cap stocks, with promised investment returns of 18% to 20% . . . [and] beginning in 1982, he began using futures contracts on the stock index, and he said he was in index puts [a form of options contract] during the 1987 stock market crash."

According to documents and interviews that have surfaced since the scandal broke, his primary strategy—or at least, his stated strategy—was to invest in S&P 100 core stocks (larger U.S. companies) and to employ relatively simple option strategies to enhance returns. Those strategies, and whether they could have really been deployed or not, are explored further in chapter 6.

What is quite clear is that nobody knew very much about what Bernard Madoff was really selling as a hedge fund investment.

The Message

"Putting lipstick on a pig," a popular Wall Street slang phrase, refers to creating a positive spin on an investment or investment product to draw more customers in. We've all heard the hype at one time or another from brokers, advisers, securities analysts, and others about how we can't lose—how this stock's been a winner for years—how that fund will be a winner for years to come.

None of Bernie Madoff's investing clients received this sort of hype. Instead, the message that came through over and over again was one of exclusivity and trust. If you invested with Madoff, you'd be one of the very few who were privileged to do so.

It would be a once-in-a-lifetime opportunity. Don't miss this chance to get on board.

How exclusive? Here are just a few anecdotes from Madoff clients and those around him.

The minimum investment rose persistently. Associated Press writer Allen Breed interviewed a Palm Beach accountant by the name of Richard Rampell. According to Rampell, over the years, the minimum investment went from $1 million to $5 million to $10 million, and that "as returns stayed steady . . . a little bit of mystique grew around Madoff at the club." Rampell added: "It was almost like you were getting let into the club of investors, and everybody wanted to be in . . . [it] was like, 'Oh, wow! You've got a Madoff account.' "

There are numerous accounts of Madoff telling investors, "I'll get you in when I can." And some of his messengers (to be discussed shortly) hyped up the fund with comments like Mike Engler's at the beginning of this chapter: "I know him—I can get you in." Some investors were even afraid to withdraw funds, even earned income, for fear of not being allowed to reinvest in the fund.

It's plain to see that this message was completely different from the usual investment hype—outlandish returns, buy low and sell high, and so forth. Madoff himself avoided the hype and created a fund, or an image of a fund, with steady and solid but relatively moderate returns. There wasn't much information about it; people were meant to learn how wonderful and steady it was through word of mouth. It was to become another manifestation of the Madoff brand, a brand that represented trust, exclusivity, and the fact that you had "made it" in the circles in which it was known.

It is felt by many crime and Ponzi scheme experts that if Madoff had promised outlandish returns, say, 20 percent, or

IN THE DARK, IN PLAIN SIGHT

Nobody has ever seen a full-page ad in the *Wall Street Journal* or *New York Times* for Madoff's fund. Quite the opposite, in fact. While Madoff was quite present in the marketplace with his trading operations, the money management part of his business was by and large a well-kept secret. It did not appear on the Bernard L. Madoff Investment Securities website in any form. In fact, the kind of thing that did appear on Madoff's website has been preserved by www.archive.org's "Wayback Machine," in Appendixes A and B.

To preserve the aura of exclusivity—or worse, to perpetuate the scam—the product and the operations that supported it were kept pretty much a secret. According to a story published by Bloomberg writers Oshrat Carmiel and Mark Clothier, Madoff "kept his money management operations on a separate floor from the trading operations . . . [and] some potential investors said he refused to share details of his operation."

The physical structure of the Madoff offices also raises eyebrows. The offices occupied the seventeenth, eighteenth, and nineteenth floors of New York's midtown Lipstick Building. According to investigative interviews conducted by Carmiel and Clothier: "The more public market-making and proprietary trading units were on the 19th and back-office functions on the 18th. The advisory operations were on the 17th floor, which wasn't linked to the others. . . . [T]here was little interaction between the groups, [and] . . . the units used separate computer systems."

And Madoff didn't just cordon off his investment advisory activities from the public or certain employees. In the interview, employees recall Madoff's sons, who ran the trading units, saying that "their father kept them in the dark about the advisory unit." And, "While Madoff seldom appeared on the 18th and 19th floors during the workday, he was known to inspect during the evening for sloppy desks or window shades that weren't fully drawn."

very fast returns on their investments, people would have been more suspicious and the fraud would have thus been uncovered sooner. Madoff's modesty kept the scheme under the radar for much longer than most such schemes.

Potential investors wanted to get in; Madoff or his promoters would make people wait in line one way or another, so they felt even better about it once they'd made it into the exclusive club. It was like a new movie release—the longer the lines, the more people want to get in, regardless of how good the movie turns out to be.

And as we found out, Madoff turned out to be a really bad movie.

The Trusted Messenger

As described in the beginning of this chapter, Madoff was a low-key, easygoing, soft-spoken guy who fit in perfectly with the clients he sought. He was Jewish (like they were), interested in and involved with the same community service and charitable organizations. Over time, as his brand became more widely known and respected, he became a real dance-card favorite—anyone going to any party wanted a chance to meet with him, to talk with him, to interact with one of the masters of Wall Street.

BusinessWeek's Robert Tanner interviewed hedge-fund advising firm co-founder Charles Gradante, who attended Palm Beach social events with Madoff. "He wasn't the kind of guy that walked into the room and filled the room with his presence," and, "If you had to pick one of the nicest guys on Wall Street—and there aren't too many—he would've been one of them. He was not a ruthless, tycoon type." Tanner also interviewed stockbroker Joyce Greenberg, who, along with family members, had invested with Madoff. "The man was very low

TRUST, BY ANY MEASURE, ISN'T ABSOLUTE

Okay, you can analyze almost anything to death and put almost anything into numbers. Here's proof. From an article by Charles H. Green, founder and CEO of Trust Associates, Inc., a leading consultant in the field of individual and corporate trust building. Most of what follows is paraphrased.

The Trust Equation describes the components of trustworthiness:

T = (Credibility + Reliability + Intimacy) / Self-Orientation

Of course, any such recipe also serves as a template for reverse engineering, providing helpful guidelines for a con man. Measuring Bernie Madoff by this equation shows just how successful he was at engendering real trust.

Let's add it up:

Credibility: Chairman of the board [of the NASDAQ Stock Market], along with an elite list of clients. Not just anyone could buy in—you had to be approved by the big guy. Exclusivity adds prestige and credibility. Score: 9 out of 10.

Reliability: The best part of Madoff's con: Don't go for the big money. Instead, become known for steady returns. Always being a bit better than average means always staying under the radar. Score: 9 out of 10.

Intimacy: Described as a gentleman, friendly, generous, amiable; the last person one would have suspected. Score: 8 out of 10.

Self-Orientation: Who would suspect a philanthropist, someone who gives to religious causes, generous with his own money? A low score (low self-orientation is good): 2.

Trust Quotient score: (9 plus 9 plus 8) / 2, an impressive 13 out of a possible 15.

Message: As Green put it, there is ". . . no such thing as trust without risk; and Madoff was an awfully talented con man."

Whether or not that was his original intent remains to be seen, but there's no question that Madoff succeeded in creating trust like few others before him.

key . . . he didn't try to sell us anything," Greenberg recalled. He made them wait a week before he took their money. From another Tanner interview with a member of the Palm Beach Country Club, for an Associated Press article: "I will say this to you: [Bernie and Ruth] were nice, nice people. I knew them for 30 years. I never, ever would've believed it."

Relatively few people asked, but if they did, they rarely got an answer from Madoff about how he invested or made them money. Madoff told one investor, nebulously, "I make money when the markets go up; I make money when the markets go down." But he failed to explain exactly how he did this.

And finally, Madoff added to the feeling of trust and comfort through his actions. He was apparently very responsive when his investors wanted to cash out. According to one report, he paid all requested redemptions, many in the millions, quite promptly, with no questions asked.

Moderate returns, steady hand, great people skills, taking care of his clients when they needed it—all part of the Madoff brand as a money manager. And all played in such a way as to build trust and keep the tough questions at bay.

Pretty simple, right?

The Marketplace

The Madoff fund and the Madoff message and the Madoff man himself are scary enough in their smooth and compelling but simultaneously mysterious ways. But Bernie Madoff's understanding of his market and the "penetration strategy" he used to infiltrate his marketplace are beyond scary—off the charts, really.

Madoff had an intimate understanding of his investors and how to work with them. He also knew how to deploy others to get clients on board. Madoff himself infiltrated the Jewish country club circles, and he cast a far wider domestic and international net through so-called feeder funds and trusted promoters, some of whom were members of other family networks.

Whether or not his original intentions were good, and whether it was deliberately planned or simply evolved to fit the need, Madoff put together an undeniably effective marketing strategy.

They Call It "Affinity Fraud"

The term *affinity fraud* has been around for a while, but it's safe to say it's been talked about a lot more since December 11, 2008. Affinity frauds prey on groups—religious, ethnic, professional, or other like-minded organizations—usually to sell some kind of investment or membership in something. The fraudsters usually are (or pretend to be) members of the group, and sometimes work their fraud through the group's leadership. The leaders can be (but are more often not) aware of the scam.

The scam exploits the trust and bonds found within the group; there is a sense that joining in is a win-win, benefiting both you and the community. The group provides a ready and willing market for the scam. The many potential victims and the relatively few questions asked make an affinity group an effective and efficient place to market.

Perpetrators of affinity fraud have preyed on innocent groups like African Americans or members of a particular church. Most have been small-time operations, and exposure can be slow in coming because tight communities are fairly closed and law enforcement can be difficult. An article published by the SEC in 2006—*Affinity Fraud: How to Avoid Investor Scams that Target Groups in 2006* (www.sec.gov/investor/ pubs/affinity.htm)—sheds some light on the subject.

Bernard Madoff definitely wasn't a small-time operator, and he played the "affinity" card like an expert.

The Country Club Circuit

As country clubs go, the Glen Oaks Country Club in Old Westbury, New York, would strike most as pretty much the average country club in the environs of a big city. It has three well-groomed golf courses on hilly terrain and a nice clubhouse, but it's not the fabled Winged Foot of U.S. Open and other tournament fame. It lies near the Long Island Expressway about 20 miles east of Manhattan.

It also lies about 5 miles east of Bernard Madoff's 1970s and early 1980s residence in Roslyn, New York.

As country clubs go, the Palm Beach Country Club is in a whole different class. It straddles the barrier island on which Palm Beach is located, with the Atlantic Ocean on one side and the Intracoastal Waterway on the other. It was originally built in 1916 by Florida East Coast Industries, a flashy railroad and real estate company operated by tycoon Henry Flagler, who was responsible for opening up much of Florida's east coast to tourism and luxury living.

Would Bernard Madoff have prospered there in its early days? Hardly. The original club was famously anti-Semitic, and old-money WASP families enjoyed their winter stays all the more with the club at hand. Jewish members were not welcome, despite their growing numbers and prominent wealth in the area. So in 1952 a group of investors bought the club, remodeled it, and today, it is one of the top clubs in the country.

Reportedly, initiation fees are $300,000, and the club is known as much or more for its lavish social and charity events as for its golf.

Bernie and Ruth Madoff spent quite a bit of time at both clubs, but especially at Palm Beach. They socialized, they ate, and they talked with dozens of close friends and fellow

WHAT'S IN A GOLF SCORE?

Ordinarily, a book about a famous investor, whether in good standing or ill repute, wouldn't include a description of his or her golf scores. But Bernie Madoff's are more interesting than most.

Madoff posted a 9.8 handicap, registered with the Florida State Golf Association at the Palm Beach Country Club. Pretty darned good for a sixty-year-old; all those years hitting baseballs in Queens sandlots must have paid off. But nothing to write home about (or write a book about, either), as a 10 handicap won't get you onto the PGA tour.

But if you look at the actual scores, it gets more interesting. The handicap is based on 20 scores, 18 of them from 1998. Eighteen of the scores are between 82 and 87, with only one 80 and one 89. In the eighties, every time. Thirteen of the 20 scores are between 82 and 85.

Now, outside of Tiger Woods and Vijay Singh, how many golfers do you know who are this consistent? Madoff may have been good, but one has to wonder if this level of consistency is possible. Could there have been a few balls kicked out from behind trees? Could he have fudged his scores?

Now, think for a minute: If he fudged consistency in his golf scores, couldn't he have done the same with his investment returns, too?

members about business and money and each other's charitable interests. Many of these members were executives or themselves managers of large funds or charities. Business deals were made while waiting for each other to tee off or putt, or in the locker room or spa.

As many as a third of Palm Beach Country Club's three hundred members are said to be Madoff investors.

Expanding the Marketplace: Beyond the Golf Links

Madoff was known to be a member of other—as many as four other—golf clubs in addition to Glen Oaks and Palm Beach—but the recruiting drive hardly stopped at the golf club.

Although golf clubs were probably Madoff's favorite venue, given the relaxed atmosphere and pleasant surroundings, he was also a regular at local restaurants in Palm Beach, particularly the Palm, a fancy steakhouse. He knew he could go to the Palm and be surrounded by friends and clients.

But he operated in other places too.

As time went on, particularly into the 1990s and 2000s, Madoff expanded his reach to court large numbers of new investors. The record isn't clear about his intentions—whether he simply wanted to expand his investment advisory business and profit from that, or whether he needed these new investors to feed his Ponzi scheme. But as the 1990s wore on, he brought on an ever larger and more diverse set of investors.

More important, he started to expand beyond his own circle of influence in the country clubs, accomplishing this in two phases. First, he courted charities, mostly local and regional Jewish charities in New York and Florida. He would become a donor, then a board member, and then eventually, he'd be selected to manage some or all of its endowment. In the second phase, he created a network of so-called "feeder funds" and promoters to bring in more investors.

Expanding the Marketplace: Charitable Intentions

Growing out of his country club contacts, Madoff appears to have deployed his personal touch and expanding reputation into the charity and foundation circuit to bring on the first wave of growth. Charities and educational institutions, large and small, from New York's Yeshiva University to its Ramaz Jewish Day School, invested with Madoff. Madoff also managed charitable foundation interests for such notables as Steven Spielberg, publisher Mortimer Zuckerman, and Nobel laureate Elie Wiesel.

Madoff's relationship with Yeshiva University and its Sy Syms School of Business is probably typical. He started as a generous donor, attending its social functions and annual Hanukkah dinner. In 2000 he became chairman of the board of the business school, and in 2001 he made a major donation to that school. That year he also received an honorary degree; Yeshiva's trustees then elected him treasurer in 2002. Yeshiva and Madoff became financially entwined when prominent Jewish financier J. Ezra Merkin joined the board and became chairman of its investment committee. That led to a university investment in Merkin's hedge fund, Ascot Partners, which in turn invested in Madoff's fund. The university lost $110 million.

The *Jerusalem Post* estimates that Madoff cost Jewish charities some $600 million and has led a few prominent ones like the Chais Family Foundation and the Picower Foundation to close their doors altogether. Chapter 8 examines the impact on the Jewish community and organizations in more detail.

Expanding the Marketplace: Following the Feeders

Madoff's impact on Jewish organizations and the Jewish community is profound in its breadth; that is, one man had a tre-
mendous impact throughout the community. But Madoff's
longer and financially deeper tentacles spread in other directions through a network of funds, fund managers, and promoters who unwittingly (for the most part) funneled huge amounts
of money from around the world into his operation.

Funds-of-Funds

In the world of hedge funds and private investing, it's common for some funds to act as "funds-of-funds." A *retail* fund
deals directly with the client, discussing investment objectives
and finding investments to meet those objectives. The funds-
of-funds will then place the client's money into a series of
investments, some or all of which are in other funds, usually
hedge funds. The idea is to save the client the trouble of finding and researching individual funds, and to provide some
diversification should any of the purchased funds run into
trouble.

It turns out that some pretty prominent funds-of-funds simply turned over large chunks of cash to Madoff. They've since
become known as "feeder funds" for the way they pulled assets
into Madoff's network. Being a feeder fund isn't illegal per se,
but investigators are now wondering whether these funds acted
in good faith—and did their due diligence—in vetting and select-
ing Madoff's fund (more about this in chapters 6 and 10).

Crime within a Crime?

Beyond the staggering losses, investors everywhere are shocked
at the chutzpah of some of these funds for charging large

"FEEDER FUNDS TOP THE LIST"

The *Wall Street Journal* published a complete list of victims of the Madoff scandal on January 7, 2008. Eight of the ten largest victims—all listed below except Fortis and HSBC—are feeder funds. (The two exceptions lent money to Madoff investors but did not invest directly.)

- Fairfield Greenwich Advisors, $7.50 billion
- Tremont Capital Management, $3.30 billion
- Banco Santander, $2.87 billion
- Bank Medici, $2.10 billion
- Ascot Partners, $1.80 billion
- Access International Advisors, $1.40 billion
- Fortis, $1.35 billion
- Union Bancaire Privée, $1.00 billion
- HSBC, $1.00 billion
- Nataxis S.A., $554 million

Chapter 7, "Collateral Damage," takes a closer look at the fallout; a more complete list of investors and their losses appears in Appendix D. Source: the *Wall Street Journal*.

fees—sometimes 1 to 2 percent, sometimes the "2 and 20" fee structure common to hedge funds—for simply passing funds on to Madoff. As long as due diligence is served and disclosure is proper, it's legal. But with good reason, some consider this the crime within the crime, and some victims, like the New York Law School, have brought suit for damages.

The rest of this chapter gives a few examples of how the feeder network worked; it is by no means a complete analysis of the feeder network.

Local Connection: Ascot Partners

Few would have thought that Jacob Ezra Merkin was anything but a financial good guy. His roots go way back into Orthodox Judaism; he was known to be a prominent Jewish theologist, and he became the president of the Fifth Avenue Synagogue. As a financier and investor, he became general partner in a $5 billion family of hedge funds known as Gabriel Capital L.P. He was a well-known proponent of the value-investing style made most popular by Warren Buffett, who himself once said that the biggest risk in investing is "not knowing what you're doing." He ran Yeshiva University's investing committee and its nearly $2 billion endowment. And he became the chairman of auto-financing giant General Motors Acceptance Corporation (GMAC).

A pretty impressive track record, for sure. But during his tenure at Yeshiva, Merkin got to know Bernie Madoff. After Merkin directed $200 million of Yeshiva's money into one of his own hedge funds, Ascot Partners, Merkin then moved almost all of Ascot Partners' investments—some $1.8 billion— to Bernie Madoff. No questions were asked, and Yeshiva apparently did not have a conflict-of-interest clause in its rules.

The rest is history, including the hefty fees Merkin collected along the way as Ascot fund manager.

Local Connection: Fairfield Greenwich

Ascot and Ezra Merkin furnish a relatively simple example of how the affinity network worked. Fairfield Greenwich, a family of funds (funds-of-funds, really), provides a far more complicated and intriguing case study, not to mention one that resulted in the single largest Madoff loss of $7.5 billion.

Fairfield Greenwich came together in the 1980s when a bank executive by the name of Walter Noel started an investment firm in 1983. He merged with a small brokerage firm run by a lawyer, Jeffrey Tucker, formerly a specialist with the SEC's enforcement division. Fairfield built itself into a rather prestigious fund-of-funds. The prestige came from two places. First, Walter Noel's wife, Monica, was part of a prominent family in Switzerland and Brazil, not to mention their tony hometown of Greenwich, Connecticut. Her family name, Haegler, had cachet in foreign circles. And Mr. Tucker inspired confidence through his record in regulatory compliance. And the funds—particularly the largest, known as the Sentry Fund—placed well, especially in international circles. Some 95 percent of its assets are reported to come from overseas, 68 percent from Europe, according to a December 2008 *New York Times* article.

Mr. Tucker knew Mr. Madoff, and that apparently inspired investments in Madoff's fund as far back as the early 1990s. Fairfield Greenwich was proud of its record of steady returns even in down markets, in fact boasting of 11 percent returns over fifteen years, with only thirteen losing months. These numbers played well with European investors.

This story is fairly consistent with other feeder-fund stories, but does introduce a new twist. Fairfield Greenwich recruited its large base of mostly international investors through a special set of promoters. Partners in the firm, partners in crime, as it were—and partners by marriage.

Walter and Monica had four daughters, who were apparently qualified to attract husbands from some of the best and the brightest in international financial circles. The eldest daughter, Corina, married a Colombian named Andrés Piedrahita; based in London and Madrid, Piedrahita would end up recruiting many European and prominent Latin American investors for Madoff, directly and through Banco Santander, mentioned below. Daughter Lisina married Yanko Della

Schiava, the son of prominent European magazine editors, and Alix married Philip Jamchid Toub, the son of Said Toub, director of Saronic Shipping of Switzerland. Completing the picture, Marisa married Matthew Brown, the former mayor of the wealthy enclave of San Marino, California. All four sons-in-law were "placed in service" to the firm, becoming partners in marketing its product.

And market it they did. Fairfield then placed its $7.5 billion with Mr. Madoff, collected fees, and the rest is history. Or will be history, as regulators and courts decide just what Fairfield's responsibility was in the matter.

Cohmad as Hell: Robert Jaffe

Robert Jaffe was a dapper dresser and a smooth talker, recall Palm Beach residents who knew him. He and his wife, Ellen, went to all the best parties in style. He was chairman of the $90 million Palm Healthcare Foundation.

He was also a neighbor of Bernard Madoff, living some 1,000 feet down North Lake Way in a $17 million mansion. And apparently he was a lot more than a neighbor, too. And more than a director of a foundation, for that matter. He was also a vice president and principal of the New York-based Cohmad Securities Corp.

The "mad" in the name stands for Madoff. Investigators are trying to figure out the relationship between Cohmad Securities Corp. and Bernard Madoff Investment Securities.

At the elite Palm Beach Country Club, however, most view Jaffe as Madoff's emissary. One Palm Beach Country Club member told the *Palm Beach Post:* "He was the man you went to to get to Madoff. You had to grovel."

Jaffe "made one to two points [percent]" on the deal, according to Richard Rampell, which Jaffe explained as "common practice in the business." But naturally, Palm Beach residents, like the investigators, wonder just what he did to earn that fee, and what he knew about Madoff.

And if that wasn't enough, Jaffe's wife just happens to be the daughter of the ninety-five-year old clothing magnate Carl Shapiro, the biggest individual victim of the scandal. We can only guess that Jaffe's stock isn't very high with his father-in-law or the rest of the family right now.

A French Connection: Access International

Headline: December 23, 2008: MADOFF INVESTOR FOUND DEAD OF SUICIDE. This was the first known casualty of the scandal, and it happened in a pretty high place. Dead was a Mr. René-Thierry Magon de la Villehuchet, a dapper Frenchman known for his wealth and prestigious family roots. In his posh New York office, he took sleeping pills before slitting his wrists; in an apparent gesture of kindness toward the custodial staff, he set it up so his blood would drain into a couple of wastebaskets.

Villehuchet happened to be a founder of Access International Advisors LLC, a fund-of-funds that had invested $1.4 billion with Madoff. Not only did Access funnel extensive wealth from Europe into Madoff's coffers, 20 percent of the loss came from his own personal wealth. Friends and associates speculate that his suicide was more a matter of responsibility to his clients than despondence over his personal loss.

A Latin Connection: Banco Santander

Banco Santander SA, a large bank holding company based in Santander, Spain, has grown into one of the world's largest, with almost $1 trillion in assets. It has also grown into one of the best brand names in the banking business, particularly in Europe and Latin America.

And now, Banco Santander is also recognized as a feeder firm, having invested and lost some $3 billion of its clients' money with Bernard Madoff, along with about $25 million of its own funds. Banco Santander does about 30 percent of its business in Latin America, but its losses are especially large, putting a crimp in its once-sterling reputation there and impairing expansion plans.

Now it appears that promoter Andrés Piedrahita of the Fairfield Greenwich family and fame was heavily involved in making the rounds and bringing in client funds, as well as managing some funds on Banco Santander's behalf.

An Austrian Connection

The European tour hardly stops with Banco Santander. There are many small European banks and investment funds involved, too, many courted and recruited by the promoters described above. One standout is an Austrian bank known as Bank Medici; although relatively small, its ties to Madoff were large, amounting to some $2.1 billion, virtually all of its invested assets.

Bank Medici was founded in 1984 and run by a descendant of a wealthy banking family, Sonja Kohn. It sold two funds to investors around the world (in fact, 93 percent outside Austria). One of those two funds, unfortunately known as the Herald USA fund, won an annual award in Germany given to hedge funds for "providing consistency in turbulent times." The times turned out to be more turbulent than they expected.

Sonja Kohn is now working with the Austrian government to salvage her bank. The government has appointed an auditor to supervise in the meantime. Along the way, Kohn denied *New York Times* reports of being "in hiding" from burned Russian investors, maintaining that Bank Medici had institutional clients only, not once-wealthy individual investors of the type who might be out for revenge.

Connecting to the Rest of the World

Not surprisingly, the tentacles spread farther than Europe and Latin America. New revelations are announced almost daily. The Abu Dhabi Investment Authority, recruited by Fairfield Greenwich son-in-law and "agent" Philip Toub, may be out $400 million.

And Asia was clearly viewed as another "global opportunity." Fairfield Greenwich set up a partnership with a company called Lion Capital in Singapore in 2004, known as Lion Fairfield Capital Management. The firm attracted money from some large Asian life insurers, among others. Another fund known as Stellar US Absolute Return came online in 2006 to feed funds into Fairfield Greenwich's Sentry fund. Thus another layer had been added to the network: feeder fund to feeder fund to Bernard Madoff hedge fund.

Little wonder that so many foreign investors were caught by surprise.

As should be quite clear by now, people didn't know what they were investing in, but assumed they were investing in something good. Along the way, a few folks—investors and proprietors of competing funds—got curious, and a few brief investigations did take place. But like the individuals who fell into the scheme, the SEC apparently also couldn't figure out what people were investing in, but also assumed it was okay. The cost of the SEC's blind trust turned out to be enormous. The next chapter tells that unfortunate story.

CHAPTER 5

One Step Ahead of the Regulators

You get hundreds and hundreds of letters and e-mails; there's no guarantee the SEC is going to catch any given wrongdoer.

—Laura Unger, former SEC commissioner

The SEC blew it.

The Securities and Exchange Commission heard the dogs barking, but they didn't find the burglar. In particular, they heard the loud bark of one prominent bloodhound from Boston by the name of Harry Markopolos, who pretty much sniffed out the whole scandal over the course of eight years, beginning in 1999—to no avail.

According to the *Wall Street Journal,* Bernard Madoff Investment Securities LLC was investigated by the SEC and other regulators at least eight times in sixteen years. He was interviewed directly by the SEC twice. So why didn't anything happen? How was it possible for Madoff to stay one step ahead of the law?

The Case for the SEC

In the SEC's defense, they have a tough job, and the task of sniffing out a Madoff is by no means straightforward. The SEC has about 3,600 employees, including clerical and support staff, yet it must monitor tens of thousands of securities, tens of millions of securities transactions, and some 10,800 registered brokers and financial advisers.

On top of that, the matrix of rules and laws they must enforce is exceptionally complex, and the sheer volume and pace of securities trading has grown exponentially in recent years. The Internet has added to securities fraud and has made it harder to keep up and to investigate. Finally, as a Senate Finance Committee report noted, "[L]ightly regulated hedge funds under pressure to deliver extraordinary returns and increased use of complex trading strategies all present new opportunities to profit from, and hide, unlawful activity."

The end result is an agency that, while having plenty of authority, apparently didn't have the bandwidth—or process discipline—to deal with it all. They should not be excused from the burden of dealing with a Madoff, for as will be seen, the dogs were barking loudly. But these factors may explain in part why the fraud wasn't detected.

Then, of course, there's the cozy relationship that was established between Madoff and the SEC over the years, through his long stint as a trading firm and then with agencies like the NASDAQ Stock Market, which work closely with the SEC. Some even point to the connection—and marriage— between his niece Shana, who managed Madoff's legal compliance activities, and Eric Swanson, a former assistant director in the SEC's compliance office (they met in 2003 at a conference and married in 2007). Madoff was by all means a smooth talker and relationship builder, and it could well be that he simply fooled the SEC, or at least deflected their attention elsewhere.

Either way, it points to a longer-term need for the SEC to step up enforcement and not turn a blind eye to anyone, no matter who they are. That need will only grow as market- and hedge-fund turmoil continues to increase.

The SEC and What It's Supposed to Do

Before examining the Madoff inquiries, it helps to briefly examine and understand the SEC itself. Much of what follows in this section comes from the SEC's own website, www.sec.gov.

How the SEC Came to Be

In the early days, before the Great Crash of 1929, there was little support for federal regulation of the securities markets. Proposals to prevent securities fraud and create better financial disclosure didn't fly. Then along came the crash that blindsided the 20 million investors who came into the market in the 1920s. Public confidence was destroyed, and Congress, as it would have today, held hearings.

Those hearings led to the two laws described below: the Securities Act of 1933, and the Securities Exchange Act of 1934, which created the SEC. As the SEC puts it, the main purpose of these laws "can be reduced to two common-sense notions":

- Companies publicly offering securities for investment dollars must tell the public the truth about their businesses, the securities they are selling, and the risks involved in investing.
- People who sell and trade securities—brokers, dealers, and exchanges—must treat investors fairly and honestly, putting investors' interests first.

Interestingly, the SEC consists of five presidentially appointed commissioners, with staggered five-year terms. No more than three of them can belong to the same political party, and one is designated by the president as chairman of the commission, the agency's chief executive.

The Job, in a Nutshell

The SEC oversees the key participants in the securities world, including securities exchanges, securities brokers and dealers, investment advisers, and mutual funds. The SEC wants to promote the disclosure of important market-related information, to maintain fair dealing, and to protect against fraud. As described on the website, the SEC's responsibilities are to:

- interpret federal securities laws;
- issue new rules and amend existing rules;
- oversee the inspection of securities firms, brokers, investment advisers, and ratings agencies;
- oversee private regulatory organizations in the securities, accounting, and auditing fields; and
- coordinate U.S. securities regulation with federal, state, and foreign authorities.

These activities lead to a considerable amount of enforcement action, but one wonders if it's enough in light of recent events and the growth and speed of the markets it must watch. According to the agency's 118-page 2008 Performance and Accountability Report, there were 671 enforcement actions brought against individuals and companies in 2008 for securities law violations, including insider trading, accounting fraud, and providing false or misleading securities information. Only 13 percent of those cases concerned "investment advisers and investment companies." The 671 cases filed stemmed from some 4,545 pending investigations.

Investors themselves are a major source of tips that lead to enforcement action. According to the SEC's 2008 Annual Report, it received some 81,000 investor inquiries during the year.

That's a big load for 3,600 staff members.

The Securities Law Book

Largely in response to the 1929 crash and subsequent fallout, Congress passed a series of laws to regulate the heretofore largely unregulated securities industry. The following four are the most important and have a direct bearing on the Madoff case:

- *The Securities Act of 1933*—sometimes known as the "truth in securities" law—requires disclosure of financial information for securities brought to public sale; it also prohibits "deceit, misrepresentation or fraud" in the sale of securities.

- *The Securities Act of 1934* created the SEC and empowered it to register, regulate, and oversee brokerage firms, and firms involved in transferring and clearing securities transactions. It also endowed the SEC with the authority to extend its reach through so-called self-regulatory organizations (SROs) like FINRA (formerly NASD) and the exchanges themselves. It also required regular corporate financial reporting.

- *The Investment Company Act of 1940* regulates companies, including mutual funds, set up to invest or trade securities, and who sell their own shares to the investing public.

- *The Investment Advisers Act of 1940* regulates investment advisers, requiring that firms or sole practitioners compensated for advising others about securities investments must register with the SEC and conform to regulations designed to protect investors. A 1996 amendment requires only advisers who have at least $25 million of assets under management or who advise a registered investment company to register.

These laws provide a framework, but aren't absolute in nature; the SEC can and does have the authority to add rules to these laws in order to close gaps and accommodate new technology and methods.

Arms of the (Securities) Law

The SEC is a large and complex organization, but much of it is organized in the following four groups, three of which loosely align with the major securities laws:

- *Division of Corporation Finance* primarily oversees proper disclosure of regular financial information to the public, like annual and quarterly reports and other required filings, and thus centers its activities on the 1933 law.
- *Division of Trading and Markets* concerns itself with "maintaining fair, orderly and efficient" markets. As such, this division makes sure exchanges, brokers, and others involved in trading securities follow the rules, especially those set forth in the 1934 law.
- *Division of Investment Management* ensures proper registration and disclosure for funds, investment advisers, and investment managers—primarily the 1940 laws.
- *Division of Enforcement* investigates violations and takes civil or administrative action when appropriate.

You may be wondering why this quick tour of the laws and the administration of those laws are included here as part of the story. Bernie Madoff knew the SEC system quite well from years of working and complying with it, and, as will be seen, his familiarity may have allowed him to fend off the SEC, or at least slide between the cracks a little more easily than others might have done.

It's time to change the channel to cover certain investigations involving Bernie Madoff.

SEC: A GOOD PLACE TO WORK—OR NOT?

Much has been made of the idea that the best people for the regulation and enforcement jobs at the SEC are also qualified for the best Wall Street jobs, which pay a much higher salary. This may be the case, but according to its 2008 report, the SEC is quite proud of itself as a place to work. One metric is the staff turnover rate, measured as the percentage of active employees who leave the agency each year. In 2008, that figure was 6.2 percent; in the years 2005 to 2007, it was 8.3 percent, 8.5 percent, and 8.4 percent, respectively. The agency notes that "the trend in recent years has been toward turnover significantly lower than it was in the previous decade," and claims that it is "an exceptionally positive indicator for staff morale and the agency's success in its mission to be an 'employer of choice.' "

In another internal metric, the agency measures itself as being one of the "Best Places to Work in Government," stating as part of the objective: "By offering competitive pay-for-performance and benefits systems that rival those offered by the private sector, the SEC aims to be an 'employer of choice' in the federal government." Indeed, by survey, they achieved a "third-best place" standing against a "top five" objective.

So maybe, at least by their own measures, the SEC is a good place to work. But perhaps the desiccation of the once-so-lucrative Wall Street jobs and the economy in general is reducing the brain drain and improving employee satisfaction. One wonders which "story" is closer to the truth.

Early Investigation: Avellino & Bienes

Once upon a time, there was a small feeder fund operating in New York and Florida, promising high returns, collecting funds, and investing them with Madoff. It started out as a small New York accounting firm known as Avellino & Bienes and grew to become an investment firm, converting 100 percent to that purpose in 1984, "in a partnership with Bernie Madoff." It was called on the carpet in 1992 by the SEC, acting on a tip.

According to the SEC complaint, Avellino & Bienes had apparently been feeding funds to Madoff for years, possibly as long as thirty years, back to 1962. By the late 1980s, A & B actually had its own feeder funds, at least two smaller firms, funneling funds into it. The promoters had advertised "curiously steady" returns of 13.5 to 20 percent to investors and sold $440 million of unregistered securities to 3,200 investors.

The SEC's primary issue with A & B was the lack of proper securities registration per the 1933 Securities Act. The outcome was simple and reached by settlement: The firm was shut down in 1993, an $875,000 fine was paid, and A & B and the other two feeder funds were required to return the funds to investors. That return of funds happened quickly and easily, "over a weekend." It seems that Madoff had the funds handy and hadn't yet sunk them too deeply into the Ponzi scheme (if the scheme was even under way at the time).

For his part, according to a 1992 *Wall Street Journal* interview, Madoff didn't know the funds had been raised illegally, and added that "his performance tracked the 10-year performance of the S&P 500, hardly notable."

Apparently, the SEC "examined [Madoff's] books soon after," but found no reason for further action. According to a *BusinessWeek* story, "When investigators learned the money had been funneled to a Wall Street titan, Madoff, they became less concerned about outright fraud . . . The Madoff connection 'was a good thing' for the firms, says a person close to the SEC investigation . . . Nothing improper was found [in Madoff's books]."

So one wonders how much further the SEC might have gone if Madoff's name hadn't been involved. Did SEC become too focused on the more black-and-white issue of securities registration, leaving a much larger elephant in the room? Most experts agree that if the SEC had dug deeper, they may have found discrepancies between reported and actual fund returns, which would have led them still deeper, perhaps taking care of the problem right then and there. But that didn't happen.

An interesting footnote: Lee Sorkin, the attorney retained by Avellino & Bienes for the case, is currently representing Madoff.

1999: Trading Practices under the Glass

In 1999 and 2000, Bernard Madoff got another visit from SEC examiners. The subject this time was apparent violations of the so-called "limit order protection rule." This rule, implemented in stages in the different markets throughout the 1990s, prevented market makers like Madoff (the trading side of his business) from hiding customer orders in the market. Here's how it worked: Suppose Madoff wanted to quote a bid for XYZ shares of 20¾ and an offer of 21. That means he would pay $20.75 for shares to a customer desiring to sell, and charge $21 a share to a customer wishing to buy, giving a healthy 25-cent spread (or markup).

Now suppose another customer was willing to pay 21⅞, or $20.875 per share—a better deal. If that offer—submitted by the customer as a *limit order*—was submitted to or through Madoff's firm, it would be to Madoff's advantage to keep it off the market and not display it. It also prohibited market makers from displaying better prices in "off" markets than in their primary market, usually the NASDAQ. Either way, the customer wouldn't get his order filled as soon as he might have, if at all, and Madoff would preserve his profit. This scenario was more likely to happen in less-active stocks with fewer dealers in the market. The limit order protection rule forbade this practice.

In response, Madoff "outlined new procedures to address the findings" and moved on. As the inquiry concerned the trading part of his business, and was probably handled by the SEC's Division of Trading and Markets, it didn't come close to exposing the scandal.

2004: Trading under the Glass Again: Front-Running

By this time, more people in the industry were becoming suspicious of Madoff, both for his trading and investing practices. In 2001, two publications—*Barron's* and a hedge-fund industry trade publication known as *MarHedge*—published articles implicating Madoff in a front-running scheme, not only for himself but for favored clients (see chapter 3 for an explanation of front-running).

In 2004 these issues led to a brief investigation by the Washington staff of the SEC, who, after "finding no evidence of [front-running]," turned the matter over to the SEC's New York office.

2005: Getting Closer: A Peek at the Investment Advisory Business

The New York office doesn't seem to have known what else to do with this tip, but continued to pursue it. But along the way, they also broadened the investigation to include the investment advisory arm. In 2005, the New York staff interviewed Bernie Madoff, his brother Peter, sons Mark and Andrew, and his niece (and attorney) Shana, questioning whether the firm was big enough to require registration as an investment adviser. A firm that "offers advice" to more than fourteen clients is required to register with the SEC and undergo periodic reviews.

According to the SEC investigation, Madoff's investment advisory business had sixteen clients and managed some $8 billion—a small fraction of the funds apparently in Madoff's control even at the time. And, Mr. Madoff apparently "would not acknowledge" that these accounts were really investment-advisory business, because he made his money by taking commissions for trades, not fees or a percentage of products, as is typical for hedge funds.

He went further to avoid the front-running allegation by showing that the trades involved were executed outside the United States and outside of trading hours, making it impossible to front-run the active-dealer market. The findings, according to the SEC, "somewhat alleviated" their concerns about front-running. Here we see a Bernard Madoff intimately familiar with both the rules and the SEC itself, and using that familiarity to push the envelope with respect to both trading and investment-advisory compliance.

Harry Markopolos and His Twenty-Nine Points of Light

Harry Markopolos was a quiet, "bookish" math whiz and accountant with a master's degree in finance from Boston College. He was working for a small Boston investment firm called Rampart Investment Management. He got assigned a new task.

His bosses at Rampart wanted to know how to match Bernard Madoff's double-digit returns, so in 2000, according to a *Boston Globe* account, they asked him "to deconstruct Madoff's strategy to see if he could replicate it."

Markopolos couldn't.

Again and again, Markopolos studied Madoff's methods and stock and option trades, feeding the information into a computer analysis and covering all reasonable scenarios. He still couldn't replicate Madoff's results. He noted that Madoff seemed to make money in all market conditions, up or down. He couldn't make that outcome work, either. "You have to have some losses—you can't dominate all markets all of the time," Markopolos said.

Markopolos got suspicious of Madoff's legendary secrecy, even with his own clients, and decided that Madoff was "either running a Ponzi scheme" or making an unusually large amount of money from front-running. He began "funneling memos and tips" to the SEC's New York office (which had jurisdiction) through an SEC worker in the Boston office. He apparently began some of that communication in 1999, before conducting the detailed analysis, and continued it even after leaving Rampart in 2004, up through April 2008, just before the Madoff scheme blew up. Reportedly he sent a note to the SEC's new director of risk assessment, detailing his concerns about Madoff.

According to the *Globe* account, Markopolos was primarily motivated "by the pure intellectual challenge of cracking a Wall Street legend." Encouragement from his Boston SEC contact also played a role. The tidbits funneled to New York did not result in an investigation, but apparently did expand the above-reported 2005 investigation to a degree.

Markopolos apparently got pretty frustrated with the SEC in 2005, and sat down and crafted a nineteen-page memo entitled "The World's Largest Hedge Fund Is a Fraud." In the *Globe* interview, he commented: "I felt like I was an army of one," and "I wasn't good enough to outmaneuver the SEC, the press wasn't listening to me, and I had no other avenue."

The now-famous memo gave twenty-nine brilliantly derived and communicated reasons why Madoff's operation was a fraud. As it turns out, he was right on the money. The rest of this section touches on Markopolos's major premises and his twenty-nine points.

The Premise

Markopolos spells out his suspicions quite clearly in the opening part of his memo. There are two possible scenarios that involve fraud by Bernard L. Madoff Investment Securities. Again, this was written in 2005, three years before the scandal broke.

> *Scenario # 1 (Unlikely): I am submitting this case under Section 21A(e) of the 1934 Act in the event that the broker-dealer . . . depicted is actually providing the stated returns to investors but is earning those returns by front-running customer order flow. Front-running qualifies as insider trading since it relies upon material, non-public information that is acted upon for the benefit of one party to the detriment of another party.*
>
> *Scenario # 2 (Highly likely): Madoff Securities is the world's largest Ponzi Scheme. In this case there is no SEC reward payment due the whistle-blower so basically I'm turning this case in because it's the right thing to do. Far better that the SEC is proactive in shutting down a Ponzi Scheme of this size rather than reactive.*

Markopolos goes on to editorialize a bit more, claiming that the Madoff family was running what amounted to "the world's largest hedge fund, with estimated assets under management of at least $20 billion to perhaps $50 billion." No one was sure of the exact figures, but Markopolos was confident that it was operating underground, which he found appalling. He goes on to say that no one is exactly sure of the size of the entire hedge-fund industry, so it was only a matter of time before a fraud this huge was perpetrated, since these funds are not regulated properly. Markopolos indicates that if he had to guess, he would say that about $30 billion was involved.

Markopolos notes that Madoff's hedge fund was not organized like a regular hedge fund but acted and traded like one. However, Madoff offered a different component to investors. He would accept investments from third party funds (FOFs) or, in many cases, run their investments for them, charging commissions. As we'll see, Markopolos questions why Madoff would do this when he could earn a lot more than just commissions by managing their assets for a full fee.

The Red Flags

Markopolos wastes no time in laying out his suspicions. The twenty-nine "red flags" could hardly implicate or incriminate Madoff any more clearly. Here are a few:

Red Flag #1: Money on the Table: Organization and Fee Structure

Markopolos wonders why Madoff was organized the way he was, and why he reportedly settled for commissions for managing assets instead of charging typical hedge-fund management fees. He also questions whether a registered investment adviser can even charge such commissions. Through a rather complex mathematical calculation, he concludes by asserting that Madoff was running a Ponzi scheme because he left so much money on the table—as much as 4 percent of the value of the assets he managed. Unless he was charging more than that in commissions without disclosing it—an unlikely scenario.

Red Flag #3: Secrecy

Although Markopolos may not have been familiar with the wealthy Jewish circles Madoff operated in, he still wonders why Madoff was so secretive. As he puts it: "Why the need for such secrecy? If I was the world's largest hedge fund and had great returns, I'd want all the publicity I could garner, and would want to appear as the world's largest hedge fund in all of the industry rankings."

He goes on to ask why Madoff, who would be the world's largest hedge fund manager if he wanted to make that claim, wouldn't brag like all the other hedge funds, venture capital firms, and others with assets under management. Good question, for bragging rights are important on Wall Street—if you have anything legitimate to brag about.

Red Flag #4: Trading Strategy Doesn't Hold Water

As many writers have noted since, and as will be further examined in chapter 6, the options contracts that Madoff supposedly used to expand returns didn't exist in sufficient quantities to actually provide the hedge and income he claimed. Markopolos estimates that Madoff was managing between $20 and $50 billion; Fairfield Sentry Ltd. alone had invested $5.1 billion with BM (a number that grew, probably with investment returns, from 2005 to over $7 billion). Markopolos says that Madoff's claim of only using OEX (Standard & Poors 100 Stocks index) options was impossible to substantiate, especially since he claims to only trade them on the over-the-counter (OTC) markets. There wouldn't be enough options to trade in this market. He observes that the total OEX options outstanding amounted to $9.107 billion in market value when he investigated, hardly enough to generate the claimed income on $20 to $30 billion in invested assets.

Red Flag #6 follows Red Flag #4, and perhaps states it more clearly:

> *At my best guess level of BM's assets under management of $30 billion, or even at my low-end estimate of $20 billion in assets under management, BM would have to be over 100% of the total OEX put option contract open interest in order to hedge his stock holdings as depicted in the third-party hedge funds marketing literature. In other words, there are not enough index option put contracts in existence to hedge the way BM says he is hedging. And there is no way the OTC market is bigger than the exchange-listed market for plain vanilla S&P 100 index put options.*

Red Flag #5: Trading Strategy Doesn't Hold Water, Part II

In Markopolos's letter, Red Flag #5 naturally comes before Red Flag #6, but #6 was moved up in this analysis because it follows the logic of Red Flag #4.

If Madoff had hedged his portfolio with "put" (right-to-sell) options, as he said he did, they would have been far too expensive and would have cut drastically into his returns, especially during market downturns. It was a "too unbelievably good to be true" scenario. Markopolos emphasizes the fact that Madoff had experienced only seven small monthly losses in the past fourteen years. To achieve the returns he claimed, he couldn't have done it all with options, and most likely couldn't have done it with stocks, either, for individual stocks simply haven't returned that much that consistently. "Mathematically none of BM's returns listed . . . make much sense. They are just too unbelievably good to be true," quips Markopolos.

Red Flag #7: Too Big to Be True
Following the options trading a step further, Markopolos maintains that neither of the big brokerage firms Madoff would have traded with (UBS and Merrill Lynch) would have done so given the size and credit risk; he adds that these firms should be contacted for their trading records to see if Madoff's trading was possible. Markopolos adds, "If any other brokerage firms' equity derivatives desk is engaged in a conspiracy to cover for BM, then this scandal will be a doozy when it hits the financial press, but at least investors would have firms with deep pockets to sue."

Red Flag #10: Like His Golf Scores—Too Consistent to Be True
Markopolos can't believe the steady positive returns, and maintains that like Madoff's golf scores (mentioned in chapter 4), they were most likely impossible to achieve. There must have been at least one bad hole somewhere on the card. Markopolos notes:

> *It is mathematically impossible for a strategy using index call options and index put options to have such a low correlation to the market where its returns are supposedly being generated from. This makes no sense! The strategy depicted retains 100% of the single-stock downside risk since they own only index-put options and not single-stock put options. Therefore, if one or more stocks in their portfolio were to tank on bad news, BM's index put would offer little protection and their portfolio should feel the pain.*

More to the point: Markopolos questions the reported seven small losses in fourteen years as "too good to be true," and likewise, the fact that BM never lost money two months in a row. "Either BM is the world's best stock and options manager that the SEC and investing public has never heard of—or he's a fraud," warns Mr. Markopolos.

Red Flag #12: Order-Flow Tricks Couldn't Support His Returns

Markopolos raises the possibility that Madoff might have been making his returns from front-running and other trading games, but casts doubt on it here, noting that while BM did have access to his customers' order flow through his broker-dealer, he was only one of many; it would have been impossible for him to predict the market's direction to such an extent that he would show monthly losses so rarely. Markopolos claims that the rest of Wall Street experiences losses more regularly than BM, and asks how BM's trading experience could have been so much better than the rest of the large firms. Again, it causes him to suspect that BM is a fraud.

Red Flag #14: Could He, or Would He, Eat Losses?

Not likely, or even possible, unless he's a Ponzi scheme, and it would be illegal anyway unless disclosed clearly. Markopolos details the fact that Madoff subsidized down months so that his investors could show a low volatility of returns—another example of securities fraud—and scolds these funds-of-funds for not reporting Madoff to the SEC or other industry regulators.

Red Flag #17: Avoiding the Auditors

Not surprisingly, Markopolos shines a light on Madoff's use of an unknown and non-standard accounting firm. He states that a London-based fund-of-funds client once requested an audit during their due diligence, only to be told that only "Madoff's brother-in-law who owns his own accounting firm," reviewed the books in order to "keep Madoff's proprietary trading strategy a secret so that nobody can copy it." Surprisingly, as Markopolos reports, the fund went ahead and invested $200 million of their client's money despite this fact, because the returns were so enticing. Markopolos mentions other phony hedge funds that also depended on fake audits for their success, like Wood River and the Manhattan Fund. By the way, the tiny firm Friehling & Horowitz was listed as Madoff's most recent auditor, but to date the fact that it was owned by Madoff's brother-in-law is unconfirmed. The point: Madoff steered clear of the so-called "big four" accounting firms; suspicious for a firm with such a large asset base.

Red Flag # . . . (Well, You Get the Idea)

Markopolos continues to slice and dice the whole matter and its record. At the end, he gives a two-page, ten-item summary of the "Fall Out" that would occur if the matter were to blow up, including billions in forced hedge-fund redemptions here in the States, as well as a huge impact on European capital markets because of the number of French and Swiss private banks involved.

He predicted that Congress would be in an uproar, leading to hearings in the Senate and the House. This would also lead to changes in the system that would ultimately require more due diligence from investors, brokers, counterparties, and regulators—something that would be "a good thing and long overdue," according to Markopolos. He also notes that critics of the SEC would be silenced. Markopolos adds that he hopes the SEC would be able to increase its powers and receive additional funding to better police the activities of these types of funds. Markopolos goes on to predict that then-New York Attorney General Eliot Spitzer would probably decide to investigate first, before the SEC, thereby causing further embarrassment to the SEC.

So far, the Eliot Spitzer part is the only part he got wrong.

In reading Markopolos's lengthy and prescient analysis, one can only wonder why the SEC didn't take more action than it did. They probably looked at Markopolos as a relative nobody compared to the fame and credibility of Madoff. They may have been too busy to really dig into the case, or they may have been worried there wasn't enough factual evidence, or that it may have been too hard to retrieve. They may have been afraid or intimidated by Madoff, or they may have simply trusted him.

What really happened isn't yet clear, although it's likely to become more so as Congress and the SEC's own leadership try to dig back into what really happened and discover the reasons why.

2006: Finally, a Registered Adviser

The SEC did, at least, reportedly meet with Mr. Markopolos in late 2005 in New York. That review and the nineteen-page letter did lead to opening an enforcement case—a more serious effort than a mere examination. Mr. Markopolos must have felt that maybe, finally, his analysis would get its day in court.

The SEC also interviewed Bernard Madoff, along with officials from the Fairfield Greenwich Group, the largest of the feeder funds (described in more detail in chapter 4). But the case never did have much punch. Consider the "Case Closing Recommendation Narrative" published by the SEC in November 2007:

The staff opened this case on January 4, 2006, to investigate (1) whether Bernard L. Madoff Investment Securities LLC ("BLM"), a registered broker-dealer, provided investment advisory services to large hedge funds in violation of the registration requirements of the Investment Advisers Act of 1940 and (2) whether BLM engaged in any fraudulent activities in connection with these services.

Markopolos gets some lip service:

The investigation was prompted, first, by a letter from an "independent fraud investigator," a person who had previously provided helpful information to the enforcement staff at BDO alleging that the returns reported by BLM's hedge fund clients were the result of a fraud perpetrated by BLM. Second, in the course of a preliminary inquiry into these allegations, the staff learned that, during a recent examination of BLM by NERO's broker-dealer examination staff, Bernard Madoff, the sole owner of BLM, did not fully disclose to the examination staff either the nature of the trading conducted in the hedge fund accounts or the number of such accounts at BLM.

Then, "Conclusions Reached:"

The staff found no evidence of fraud. The staff did find, however, that BLM acted as an investment adviser to certain hedge funds and high net worth individuals in violation of the registration requirements of the Advisers Act. The staff also found that FGG's (Fairfield Greenwich) disclosures to its investors did not adequately describe BLM's advisory role and described BLM as merely an execution broker for FGG's accounts. As a result of discussions with the staff, BLM registered with the Commission as an investment adviser, and FGG reviewed its disclosures to investors to reflect its advisory role. . . .

Then,

We recommend closing this investigation because both BLM and FGG voluntarily remedied the uncovered violations, and because those violations were not so serious as to warrant enforcement action.

No evidence of fraud? Apparently nobody read Markopolos's letter, or took it seriously, or bothered to do the work to investigate.

Just a couple of minor corrections to minor registration and compliance infractions . . . kind of like issuing a ticket for an expired drivers' license—and nothing more—to a driver responsible for crashing into a bus and killing thirty people.

The SEC may regret this "miss" more than any other.

Where Was FINRA?

FINRA stands for Financial Industry Regulatory Authority, which changed its name from the more familiar NASD (National Association of Securities Dealers) a few years back. FINRA is one of the SROs—self-regulatory organizations— backed by the SEC and chartered with providing some front-line regulatory effort, as well as education, certification testing, and other services.

FINRA examines broker-dealer statements every two years. In 2007, their investigation of Bernard L. Madoff Investment Securities LLC did reveal some irregularities—one being that it apparently made no trades for his investment fund! Now, it's true that his investment fund might have placed trades through other brokerages, but why would it have (1) paid commissions, and (2) possibly accepted inferior executions and prices by using other brokerages?

The undeniable implication here is that Madoff wasn't actually placing any of the thousands of trades his statements said he did—a clear indication of fraud. The question is: Why didn't FINRA take this any further?

Now, in their defense, and probably in the SEC's too, the folks who examine trading activity probably aren't concerned about the accuracy of fund statements and vice versa (remember, these two things fall under separate organizational silos, at least at the SEC). But you'd think someone would have noticed, especially in light of the Markopolos letter and other inquiries.

Those who oversee the regulatory process are wondering where FINRA was in this whole matter. Quite plausibly, FINRA trusted Madoff too far, just like everyone else.

Mea Culpa, and What's Next for the SEC?

Something clearly went wrong. The laws and regulatory processes administered by the SEC and its SROs clearly let this "black box" operation of Bernie Madoff's slip through the cracks. The question is why—and what should be done about it?

And there's plenty of egg on plenty of faces to go around.

Shortly after the scandal broke, on December 16, 2008, outgoing SEC chairman Christopher Cox noted that he was "gravely concerned about the apparent multiple failures" of his agency, in not digging deeper into years of warnings about Madoff. And, the SEC will now have to investigate "all staff contact and relationships with the Madoff family and firm, and their impact, if any, on decisions by staff regarding the firm."

Congress Points Its Finger

Congress didn't waste any time getting involved. The House Financial Services Committee held a hearing on January 5, 2009, to lay out the facts about what happened in an attempt to understand it, and to try to uncover whether the scandal, and missed oversight, reflected "deep, systemic problems" at the SEC.

Some called for an outright restructuring or reinvention of the SEC. Rep. Paul Kanjorski (D-Pa) said that "Clearly our regulatory system . . . failed miserably and we must rebuild it now." Spencer Bachus (R-Ala) called for a regulatory structure "for the twenty-first century," but later stepped back from the idea of a completely new configuration. "What we may have in the Madoff case is not necessarily a lack of enforcement and oversight tools, but a failure to use them."

Indeed, this is probably closer to the truth. Did the SEC carry out its mandate? Could they have made a more complete, more thorough, more objective effort to examine Madoff's broker-dealer and investment management businesses? It certainly seems that way. Mary Schapiro, then the head of FINRA, has said that the agency only had the authority to look at Madoff's trading business and not the money management business. But some question that and think it should have been looked at as one business. Schapiro also maintains that FINRA received no tips on Madoff.

The outcome of the assertion will prove interesting, because Mary Schapiro has now become the head of the SEC.

New Leadership

If one suspects a lack of coordination between FINRA and the SEC, and lack of proper follow-through on investigations they jointly oversee, then the nomination of Schapiro might help soothe those concerns a bit. She has publicly said that she'd "take the handcuffs" off the agency's enforcement division by looking closely at "procedural hurdles." She has also vowed to deliver more oversight of hedge funds.

We'll have to wait and see what all of this means.

Still, the Nagging Question Why

So why didn't the SEC "discover" the fraud and act on it? Did relationships between the inspectors and inspectees get in the way? Is the SEC simply stretched too thin to give due diligence to all of its enforcement obligations? Is the SEC sufficiently objective to consider all possible outcomes of an investigation, not just the ones its inspectors may anticipate going in?

These answers will become clearer as the investigations—and the civil and criminal complaints against Bernard Madoff—move forward.

CHAPTER 6

"It's All Just One Big Lie"

It's a stunning fraud that appears to be of epic
proportions.

—*Andrew M. Calamari, associate director of enforcement,*

SEC New York office

Theodore Cacioppi, Special Agent, Federal Bureau of Investigation, showed up at Bernard Madoff's posh Upper East Side penthouse at 8:30 a.m. on December 11, 2008, to make the arrest. It isn't clear if he had a written complaint at the time of the arrest, but by the end of that day, the complaint, case number 08-MAG-02735, was complete. The approval for the complaint came from Marc Litt, Assistant U.S. Attorney. It was filed before the Honorable Douglas F. Eaton, U.S. Magistrate Judge, Southern District of New York. The complaint was for a "Violation of 15 U.S.C. §§ 78j(b), 78ff; 17 C.F.R. §240.10-b-5." That's one count of securities fraud, in plain English.

Or, as described in the complaint (which appears in its entirety in Appendix C):

BERNARD L. MADOFF, the defendant, unlawfully, willfully, and knowingly . . . did use and employ manipulative and deceptive devices in violation of [the act listed above] by (a) employing devices, schemes, and artifices to defraud; (b) making untrue statements of material facts and omitting to state material facts necessary in order to make the statements

*made . . . and (c) engaging in acts, practices, and courses of
business which operated and would operate as a fraud and
deceit upon persons, to wit, MADOFF deceived investors by
operating a securities business in which he traded and lost
investor money, and then paid investors purported returns
on investment with the principal received from other, different
investors, which resulted in losses of approximately billions
of dollars.*

The complaint had been written based on Cacioppi's interviews with "two senior employees of Bernard L. Madoff Investment Securities LLC" in the days immediately prior to the arrest. What those two employees—who are not identified in the complaint but are likely his sons, Mark and Andrew—told Mr. Cacioppi appears later in this chapter.

The complaint was a last-minute culmination of a remarkable and fast-brewing series of events. Yet when the news of the arrest broke on December 11, 2008, most of the world—especially the one outside the tight-knit Wall Street investment community and his mostly Jewish New York and Florida brethren—had scarcely heard of Bernard Madoff.

What were the events that led up to the arrest? Did he leave a wide swath of clues as to his demise, or was it a secret to the end? How have the wheels of justice turned since? And was it always "just one big lie"?

The Clues

By definition, as with all Ponzi schemes, the collapse of the Madoff scheme was inevitable. It was just a question of when. But also like most Ponzi schemes, the clues, especially in the hands of a master operator, aren't so obvious. And Madoff was a master operator who took advantage of his investors' trust in him. He kept the details of his operation under wraps until the very end. Only a few days before his arrest, apparently under great personal stress and strain, did he decide to remove the curtain of deceit. The opening of that curtain has been compared by some to the Wizard of Oz finally revealing his true character and nature after existing—and succeeding—in a world of utter myth.

But few criminals can cover their tracks completely. As investigators, clients, and others close to Madoff are now starting to piece together, there were a few clues, a few tears in the curtain, that started to form in the year or two before the scandal broke.

The Well Runs Dry

A Ponzi scheme survives as long as there's enough fresh money coming into it, or if good things happen to increase the value of whatever principal might lie within. It appears that new funds did continue to arrive, but they were harder to come by in recent years. More obviously, the cranky investment markets of 2007, and especially 2008, not only stopped the investment gravy train of steady returns enjoyed through 2006, but also undermined the confidence of his investors as well. It was a series of withdrawal requests for $7 billion that finally broke the camel's back.

The Foundation Cuts Back

According to statements available at www.grantsdirect.com, The Bernard L. and Ruth Madoff Foundation received a grant of $25,000,000 in 2000, probably from its founders. From those funds and their earnings, the foundation contributed generously, mainly to health-related causes in Florida. In 2000, it gave $220,000. That increased to $599,776 in 2001 and $521,750 in 2002; then, with no explanation, donations jumped to $6,453,433 in 2003, and $5,578,564 in 2004. A foundation, by the way, is required to give away a minimum of 5 percent of its assets each year; these figures far exceeded that.

Then, again without explanation, the grants dropped to $303,700 in 2005, rose to $1,277,600 in 2006, then dropped through the floor to $95,000 in 2007. Operating and administrative expenses, which had never exceeded $23,000 and generally were under $10,000 through 2006, suddenly rose to $135,020 in 2007.

Could these figures represent an attempt by Madoff to throw as much cash overboard as possible in 2003–2004? Could he have suddenly seen the end at hand and virtually stopped giving in 2007, even as he appropriated $135,000 to cover his own expenses? One wonders.

The foundation's assets have been frozen by the courts as the case proceeds.

Failing More "Smell Tests"

As time went on, especially after the year 2000, more signs of trouble appeared. Although they individually appeared quite benign, taken together and in hindsight, if anyone had done so, they might have pointed the way to the fraud. In an eerie way, it's like the clues that might have thwarted the September 11, 2001, terrorist attacks, if anyone had bothered to piece them together.

As shown in chapter 4, Madoff greatly expanded his reach into overseas markets, primarily through feeder funds and the network of promoters like Andrés Piedrahita.

Another report suggests that Madoff reduced his minimum investment amount to $50,000 from over $1 million shortly after the 2005–2006 SEC investigation.

One wonders, with all of Madoff's "success," why he suddenly needed to reach so far out for funds. Apparently, he still maintained his aura of exclusivity with his traditional, local clientele, continuing to tell investors that the fund was "closed" until near the end.

Veryan Allen, a writer on hedge funds and alternative investments with a "background in computational analysis and statistics," questions a lot of what went on in the declining days of the scheme. First, he wonders quite appropriately why Madoff isn't a member of the Forbes 400 list of the world's wealthiest; after all, if he were really running a $50 billion hedge fund with the success he advertised, he'd be collecting billions for his efforts if one recalls the usual "2 and 20" compensation scheme.

He then compares the returns of the Fairfield Sentry fund (the largest feeder fund) with another fund advertising the same basic strategy, the so-called "split strike conversion" option strategy described later in this chapter. That fund, known as the Gateway Fund, grew a dollar into $4 between 1993 and September 2006. Fairfield Sentry, on the other hand, had much the same trajectory until 2000, growing to about $2 that year. Then it fell back to about $1.50 in the 2001 slump, and only recovered to about $2.50 before falling back again.

So, Fairfield Sentry investors were not earning what they should have been for the kind of investment they were told they had.

Not that they or many other investors in Madoff feeder funds were told much. In fact, a lawsuit involving the Austrian Bank Medici and Madoff asserts that toward the end, Madoff "specifically forbade managers who gathered assets for him from mentioning his name in their marketing literature and other reports." Quite a reversal from his cozy country-club-circuit days.

It's also interesting to note that apparently those who had invested directly with Madoff enjoyed steady—not declining—returns in 2001, as they had seen in earlier years. That was despite a significant downturn and an overall increase in volatility in the markets.

Allen then quite rightly questions the fact that there was no outside administrative firm or custodian involved in handling Madoff's investments. We're still left to wonder exactly who did handle Madoff's administration, and how, including how the monthly statements now known to be fictitious were ever produced.

The Auditors Didn't Smell Too Good, Either

And then there's the small, three-person accounting firm known as Friehling & Horowitz, supposedly Madoff's auditor, located in a thirteen-by-eighteen-foot office in a small suburban office complex thirty miles north of New York. Hardly one of the "big four" firms (or whatever the number is now) that a firm with the ostensible size of Madoff's would retain. Nope; in fact, F & H told the American Institute of Certified Public Accountants (AICPA) that it doesn't conduct audits; this is probably a good thing, since only one member of the three-person firm is actually an active accountant.

The firm signed off on Madoff's annual financial statements through October 31, 2006. A four-page report dated December 18, 2006, attested that the financial statements of Madoff's securities firm were "in conformity with accounting principles generally accepted in the United States."

The growing use of feeder funds was one reason the insufficiency of these audits didn't come to light. The feeder funds, Fairfield Greenwich and others, used more conventional household-named firms like PricewaterhouseCoopers. They signed off on their audits of the feeder funds without examining the books or audits of the funds they held downstream. Apparently this is normal. From a *Time* magazine interview with Cindy Fornelli, executive director of the Center for Audit

---

GETTING IN ON THE 132ND FLOOR

The number of court cases arising out of the Madoff affair is staggering, and will continue to grow. One filed during the first week of January 2009 points to Madoff's continued nefarious dealings with investors almost right to the day the scandal broke.

The case was brought by Martin Rosenman of Great Neck, New York, proprietor of a family heating-oil distribution business and the president of Stuyvesant Fuel Service, a heating-oil distributor in the New York area. In typical fashion, Rosenman had apparently been referred to Madoff by a friend.

Rosenman apparently called Madoff in his office on December 3, eight days before the case broke. He wanted to invest $10 million. As reported by the *New York Times*, from the legal complaint, Madoff told him that "the fund was closed until January 1, 2009, but that Rosenman could wire money to a BMIS account where it would be held until the fund opened after the New Year." The money was then wired to a BMIS account at J.P. Morgan Chase on December 5.

Mr. Rosenman was notified by BMIS on December 9 that the money had been "received and invested." That was two days before the arrest. As we will see, that was just as Madoff was starting a last-ditch campaign to pay out dwindling funds from the firm to select recipients. However, true to form, no record of that money being "invested" has been found. Rosenman's attorney believes that Madoff was simply collecting the money to "make the final distribution he wanted to make."

Quality, we learn that "it is not the responsibility of the accountant for a capital-management firm to audit the underlying investments of the firms it invests in."

And so it went.

Opaque to the End

If you had your funds invested with Bernard Madoff, you probably didn't know much about your investments. As reported in chapter 4, the Madoff firm statements were old-fashioned and cryptic, printed on an old dot-matrix printer. Most hedge funds in this day and age offer their statements on websites, some with downloadable files to help investors track their investments. The irony, of course, is that Madoff and his cohorts pioneered electronic trading and other early applications of technology to the investing space.

A couple of months into the investigation, it was revealed that no trades were recorded by BMIS on behalf of its hedge-fund customers, even though apparently some trades did appear on client statements. How this happened—and who pulled it off—is still a mystery. Peter Madoff, the firm's computer expert, isn't currently a target of the investigation (he's helping out with it, instead), but his role makes one wonder. It's doubtful that Bernie Madoff put on the green eyeshades and created the fabricated statements himself in the wee hours of the morning.

Another, somewhat related mystery finds its way forward in the quarter-end and year-end statements produced by the firm. Apparently BMIS took each investor's investment, sold it off, and converted it to Treasury securities. Nice and safe; pull some money off the table, lock in some gains.

But is this what really happened? An examination of securities filings showed that the firm held less than $1 billion in shares through most of the year. That was the explanation for why so few securities were shown as owned, but where was the cash? It isn't clear. Furthermore, if Madoff had really sold off the bulk of the shares, wouldn't that have triggered nasty capital gains taxes for his investors? There's little record of those gains being produced, let alone any complaints from angry investors stuck with big tax bills.

The Final Days: Bailout and Confession

While the earlier clues were subtle, the later ones were not. The ship was starting to take on water.

A $250 Million Bailout

Sometime around December 1, 2008, just ten days before the scandal broke, Bernie Madoff asked his old pal, mentor, and father figure, ninety-five-year-old clothing magnate Carl Shapiro, for some cash—$250 million, in fact.

It isn't known exactly how Madoff framed this request. Hard to imagine asking such a close friend for $250 million over lunch at the country club; just what would you tell him it was for? Especially when they figure you to be a pretty successful guy? It isn't known for sure whether Madoff indicated that this would be a loan or an investment, but apparently he promised to pay it back quickly, with interest.

The funds were never paid back. They served to double poor Mr. Shapiro's losses in the debacle to some $545 million, the largest individual loss known to date.

Bubbling to the Surface

Most likely under extreme duress, Bernard Madoff began telling two of his "senior employees" some pretty strange things.

Those senior employees, who we can only assume were his two sons, thought them strange enough to get the FBI, specifically Theodore Cacioppi, involved. They contacted the FBI on the evening of December 10, 2008, the night before the arrest. Cacioppi interviewed the two senior employees, and that interview formed much of the basis for the FBI complaint.

There is no better account of what was going on with Madoff and his firm than what his senior employees told Cacioppi, which is documented in Item 4, sections (a) through (e) of the federal complaint (shown in full in Appendix C):

> *a. The Senior Employees are employed by Bernard L. Madoff Investment Securities LLC, in a proprietary trading and market making capacity. According to the Senior Employees, BERNARD L. MADOFF, the defendant, conducts certain investment advisory business for clients that is separate from the firm's proprietary trading and market making activities. According to the Senior Employees, MADOFF ran his investment adviser business from a separate floor in the New York offices of Bernard L. Madoff Investment Securities LLC. According to Senior Employee No. 1, MADOFF kept the financial statement for the firm under lock and key, and stated that MADOFF was "cryptic" about the firm's investment advisory business.*
>
> *b. In or about the first week of December [2008], BERNARD L. MADOFF, the defendant, told Senior Employee No. 2 that there had been requests from clients for approximately $7 billion in redemptions, that he was struggling to obtain the liquidity necessary to meet these obligations, but that he thought he would be able to do so. According to the Senior Employees, they had previously understood that the investment advisory business had assets under management on the order of between approximately $8–15 billion. According to a form ADV filed by MADOFF on behalf of Bernard L. Madoff*

Investment Securities LLC with the SEC on or about January 7, 2008, MADOFF's investment advisory business served between 11 and 25 clients and had a total of approximately $17.1 billion in assets under management.

c. On or about December 9, 2008, MADOFF informed Senior Employee No. 1 that he wanted to pay bonuses to employees of the firm in December, which was earlier than employee bonuses are usually paid. According to the Senior Employees, bonuses have been traditionally paid in February of each year. On or about December 10, 2008, the Senior Employees visited MADOFF at the offices of Bernard L. Madoff Investment Securities LLC to discuss the situation further, particularly because MADOFF appeared to the Senior Employees to have been under great stress in the prior weeks. At that time, MADOFF informed the Senior Employees that he had recently made profits through business operations, and now was a good time to distribute it. When the Senior Employees challenged his explanation, MADOFF said that he did not want to talk to them at the office, and arranged a meeting at MADOFF's apartment in Manhattan. According to Senior Employee No. 2, MADOFF stated, in substance, that he "wasn't sure he would be able to hold it together" if they continued to discuss the issue at the office.

d. At MADOFF's Manhattan apartment, MADOFF informed the Senior Employees, in substance, that his investment advisory business was a fraud. MADOFF stated that he was "finished," that he had "absolutely nothing," that "it's all just one big lie," and that it was "basically, a giant Ponzi scheme." The Senior Employees understood MADOFF to be saying, in substance, that he had for years been paying returns to certain investors out of the principal received from other, different investors. MADOFF stated that the business was insolvent, and that it had been for years. MADOFF also stated that he estimated the losses from this fraud to be at least

121

*approximately $50 billion. One of the Senior Employees had a
personal account at Bernard L. Madoff Investment Securities
LLC in which several million had been invested under the
management of Madoff.*

    *e. At MADOFF's Manhattan apartment, MADOFF
further informed the Senior Employees that, in approximately
one week, he planned to surrender to authorities, but before
he did that, he had approximately $200–300 million left,
and that he planned to use that money to make payments to
certain selected employees, family, and friends.*

Holy cow. Now it all comes out, in Technicolor. The lies,
the deceit, the corruption. The separate, clandestine, mysterious ways of the advisory business. The pending $7 billion in
withdrawals, which finally sank the firm in a bad market. The
fictitious SEC filings, vastly understating the size and length of
the scheme's tentacles. The totality of the scam, the admission
it had been a Ponzi scheme, and that it had "been insolvent for
years." The final, futile attempts to pay bonuses and distribute
money to "select employees, family, and friends"—which were
probably to be funded from Shapiro's loan/investment, not
coincidentally matching the "$200–$300 million" he claimed to
have available.

Madoff already had the checks cut, some $173 million, sit-
ting in his desk drawer. They were found after the arrest. Again
we are left to wonder—just like his fictitious client statements,
who cut these checks? It's hard to envision Bernie Madoff
doing it himself with QuickBooks.

The Arrest

One can only imagine the John Grisham-esqe scene. Theodore Cacioppi and another agent meet early on the morn-

ing of December 11, 2008, perhaps at the Dunkin' Donuts at the corner of 56th and Lexington Avenue. Hot coffee in large paper cups, two glazed and two maple donuts, and a wad of napkins.

"Hey, Joey, this guy's going down. He really pulled a big one. His boys told me the whole story, and it's fucking unbelievable. I'm going to find out if he's home. At this point I'm not expecting any crap from the guy; he's already spilled the beans. Let's make sure we write down everything he says, and that the NYPD boys do their thing with the evidence. Hope you got some sleep. It's gonna be a long day once the shit hits the fan with the press."

They straighten their ties, put on their New York uniform-black topcoats, and head out into the December cold for the ten-block jaunt to 133 East 64th Street, Number 12A, on the Upper East Side.

Bernard Madoff apparently decided not to wait the "approximately one week" to surrender to authorities. Or maybe that was decided for him. At any rate, the morning after the senior employees met with Cacioppi, the arrest went down, apparently without complications.

The complaint, apparently submitted to the court later that day, was amended to capture the details of the arrest. Again, the document itself furnishes the best record of what happened that day:

> *On December 11, 2008, I spoke to BERNARD L. MADOFF, the defendant. After identifying myself, MADOFF invited me, and the FBI agent who accompanied me, into his apartment. He acknowledged knowing why we were there. After I stated "We're here to find out if there's an innocent explanation," MADOFF stated, "There is no innocent explanation." MADOFF stated, in substance, that he had personally traded*

and lost money for institutional clients, and that it was all his fault. MADOFF further stated, in substance, that he "paid investors with money that wasn't there." MADOFF also stated that he was "broke" and "insolvent" and that he had decided that "it could not go on," and that he expected to go to jail. MADOFF also stated that he had recently admitted what he had done to Senior Employee Nos. 1, 2, and 3.

Whereupon the complaint ends with the following quaintly worded phrase: *WHEREFORE, the deponent prays that BERNARD L. MADOFF, the defendant, be imprisoned, or bailed, as the case may be.*

Wearing a striped shirt and dark trousers, Bernard Madoff made his first appearance in federal court in Manhattan later that day.

The Proceedings

The criminal case was set up as *U.S. v. Madoff,* and it was filed on the docket of the United States District Court for the Southern District of New York as Case # 1:08-mj-02735-UA. The plaintiff is listed as Marc O. Litt of the U.S. Attorney's Office, with two lead attorneys from the private sector. The presiding Judge Magistrate would be Douglas F. Eaton.

The civil case was set up as *"Securities and Exchange Commission v. Madoff et al."* on the civil docket of the same court, Case # 1:08-cv-10791-LLS. The cause was "15-77 Securities Fraud." The filing date was December 11, 2008, and the presiding judge was Louis L. Stanton.

The prosecutors and SEC litigants joined together on the investigation of details, and both cases moved forward immediately. The private attorneys handling the suits have been approached by "dozens" of other potential clients to handle their suits, and several have already been filed.

On December 11, Judge Magistrate Eaton set up bail of $10 million, secured by the Manhattan apartment and other properties, with travel documents surrendered (including Ruth Madoff's, as well). Travel was to be restricted to the areas covered by the southern and eastern districts of New York and Connecticut, but this was later changed to house arrest when prosecutors warned of Madoff's potential "harm or flight."

Originally ordered to have electronic monitoring and a 7:00 p.m. curfew, the ruling was changed to simply being barred from leaving the apartment except for court appearances. Not too surprisingly, some death threats were received, so to keep tabs on Madoff, and to protect him as well, the building is now monitored by security guards and video surveillance—much to the chagrin of his neighbors.

The civil case also became official on December 11. On December 12, a receiver, Lee Richards of Richards Kibbe & Orbe LLP, was assigned to handle all "assets and accounts" of Bernard L. Madoff Investment Securities LLC. At about this point, most content on the BMIS website was removed and replaced with the notification of receivership described in the introduction to this book, which has been since updated.

The next step was to issue a temporary restraining order and freeze assets, and to direct "defendants to provide a verified accounting immediately, [including] but not limited to a verified written accounting of Madoff's interests in BMIS and all other entities," and to prohibit "the destruction, concealment, or alteration of documents. . . ." Madoff was also ordered to furnish a list of clients and a list of personal assets.

The firm was ordered to liquidate under the Securities Investor Protection Act of 1970, under the auspices of the Securities Investor Protection Corporation (SIPC). The SIPC would allocate any resources still left in the firm to investor claims, plus likely pay direct investors according to the SIPC insurance for losses up to $500,000.

Irving Picard from the SIPC was appointed by Judge Louis Stanton to take over as trustee. At this point the case was being handled like a bankruptcy, and claim packages were mailed to known customers, broker-dealers, and known creditors in early January of 2009. Apparently more than 8,000 such forms were mailed out. It was the first that some clients had heard of the matter. Picard was also assigned the task of selling the trading and market-making business, the proceeds of which would be used for distribution to creditors and defrauded investors.

Selling the trading business was the relatively straightforward task, although no buyers came forth immediately. Experts placed a value on that business of $200 to $400 million, and an investment banker was retained to manage the sale. Less straightforward was the untangling and valuing of what's left of the investment management business. According to Stephen Harbeck, president and CEO of the SIPC, the "utterly unreliable" records will "take six months to sort out." The firm's assets and trading activities are frozen by SEC order, but salaries on the trading side are still being paid.

The Dragnet

Although some question whether the $7 million penthouse where Mr. Madoff is cordoned off would qualify as "having him where we want him," at least for now, the authorities have full control of the man and his activities and can proceed with the case.

Less clear is who else was involved.

Busy at the Typewriter?

As this text has brought up a few times, it just doesn't seem possible that Bernard Madoff could have pulled this whole thing off by himself. It would have been too big for one person, especially when one considers the administrative tasks. Tallying month-end figures, preparing statements, tax statements, SEC filings—how did all of that get done, and who actually performed the tasks? In fact, one attorney representing some of the firm's clients observed that "someone had to create the appearance that there were returns," and that "there must have been a team buying and selling stocks, forging books, and filing reports."

Mark, Andrew, Ruth, and Peter

The investigators first took a look at the family members—wife Ruth, and sons Mark and Andrew, who have been involved with the firm for years. To date, investigators have found no clear evidence of wrongdoing, and all three have cooperated with the investigation.

According to the attorney's statement, "Mark and Andrew Madoff are not involved in the firm's asset management business, and neither had any knowledge of the fraud before their father informed them of it on Wednesday, [December 10, 2008]." The prosecutors and the SEC seem to be going along with that for now.

The innocence of Ruth Madoff is a little less clear. Many wonder how she could have not known about the scheme, and how she could have unknowingly recruited clients up to the very end. Prosecutors have seen some evidence that she was involved in disbursing funds, but have not to date found anything specific enough to press charges. It could be that she has more value as a witness than as a coconspirator, and at least one report suggests that her potential indictment may be used as a lever by prosecutors to secure a plea deal.

Some observers perceive her as a victim; as a *New York Times* article puts it: "One day she was married to a stock-market genius; the next she was married to one of history's greatest con men."

Although Ruth Madoff has surrendered her passport, in the initial post-arrest period she was permitted to live with Bernie and leave the apartment at will. Her assets were frozen, and the two homes she held title to were used to secure the $10 million bail, but she was granted an undisclosed monthly allowance.

And then there's Peter Madoff, Bernie Madoff's brother— longtime partner, and legal and technology expert in the business. At the end, he was a senior managing director and the chief compliance officer for the firm. Were his long tenure and deep involvement in the operations of the firm confined to the trading side of the business? One wonders, but for now, prosecutors are focused on one issue: Since he was apparently told about the Ponzi scheme the day before the arrest, did he have a duty to disclose this knowledge? Prosecutors are also more interested in getting his help in unraveling the firm's mysteries and clarifying the case than in prosecuting him, although other legal investigations and actions are likely to end up at his doorstep.

Frank DiPascali

Like Bernard Madoff, Frank DiPascali grew up in Queens, although he was eighteen years his junior. Shortly after graduating from high school (not the Far Rockaway High School Bernie attended), a neighbor introduced them. Frank DiPascali started with Bernard L. Madoff Investment Securities in 1975, researching stocks for the trading operations. He became an assistant to the firm's operational guru, Peter Madoff, and in 1986, he was named the director of options trading. DiPascali "oversaw options trading for Mr. Madoff's investment-advisory operations," according to another Madoff employee interviewed by the *Wall Street Journal.* That would have put him center stage in the investment fund's primary stated strategy.

In 1996, he became chief financial officer (CFO) of the firm. Now, one would expect a CFO to have intimate knowledge of all activities in a firm such as BMIS, but his role and knowledge of the plot remain a mystery. Like Madoff himself, he seems to have sheltered himself in a shroud of secrecy. He only communicated to clients and others by phone and fax, apparently avoiding e-mail. An SEC memo brought to light by the *Journal* said that "he didn't know who was responsible for processing and settling trades in the investment-advisory side of the firm," and that his answers were "evasive and incomprehensible" during an interview on the firm's premises shortly after the arrest.

DiPascali was said to be involved in the firm's redemptions. Not surprisingly, prosecutors have taken great interest in what he did and what he knows about where the money went and the firm's operations in general.

The firm's accountant, David G. Friehling of Friehling & Horowitz, will also become part of the investigation; whether any indictment or accusation comes of this remains to be seen.

Ezra Merkin

One also wonders about the role of J. Ezra Merkin, the prominent Jewish philanthropist, investment adviser, and hedge-fund manager who ran Ascot Partners into the ground with a

$1.8 billion investment with Madoff. Merkin also had smaller amounts invested from two other funds.

In the early phases, the main investigation treated Merkin more as a victim than a coconspirator, taking interest in what he knew about the Madoff fund and its operation. But the New York Attorney General's office is also investigating Merkin's practices with the nonprofit endowments he helped to manage, including disclosures, fees earned, and other conflicts of interest. They have subpoenaed Merkin and his funds, and are broadening their investigation to include fifteen nonprofit foundations that supposedly were touched by Merkin. The investigation will examine appropriate due diligence on the part of those funds, which collectively lost some $100 million of their endowments to Madoff's scheme.

The Recovery

Just as complex, if not more so, than the case against Madoff himself is the determination of any settlement for his investors and creditors; put succinctly—it's a mess.

So is there anything left? What funds are still available to pay out to cheated investors? Whose claim takes precedence—direct investors, feeder funds, or investors who invested through feeder funds? How will the recovery be handled among the many separate lawsuits being filed? Can investors expect recovery from the SIPC, the government agency charged with protecting investors from brokerage firm failures (but not investment losses)?

Madoff has produced a list of his assets and a list of his clients per court order, but these lists have been kept under wraps by the court. They may be keeping the asset list confidential for fear that foreign creditors and regulators may seize the assets, many of which may have been transferred overseas.

Fraudulent Conveyance

One of the stickiest issues in the case concerns the potential responsibility of investors who cashed out of the fund prior to the uncovering of the fraud. Of course, if they knew about the fraud, they could be held liable to return their profits and even some of their initial investments. But if they didn't know about the fraud, they still could be liable under an obscure bankruptcy provision called *fraudulent conveyance.*

Fraudulent conveyance typically prevents the illegal transfer of property to another party to "defer, hinder or defraud" creditors (per *Forbes* Investopedia). The mainline case is where a debtor donates or redeems assets away to protect them from creditors. But the provision can also cover so-called "good faith" transfers where certain creditors—the ones who withdrew early—come away with preference. The statute of limitations on such transfers is six years. The courts must decide whether the doctrine applies, and if so, how to apply it. The court may try to find out from those who withdrew whether they had some inkling that the firm might not be the best place to invest, or whether it was a more-innocent cash withdrawal simply to use for other purposes. The recovery of profits is fairly well established in law; the recovery of initial principal paid out may now even be possible based on a 2007 court case involving the Bayou hedge funds. Worse, investors who get snared in this recovery probably paid taxes on it, although they may be able to recover those taxes.

SIPC Insurance

The Securities Investor Protection Corporation protects brokerage account investors for up to $500,000 in losses from failed brokerage firms. But the securities or cash must be missing from the accounts, not just lost in bad investments. It appears that those who invested directly with Madoff—the country club circle and beyond—may have some hope of recovery, but it may take a while; and the half million to be recovered pales in comparison to amounts that most originally invested. Less clear is what happens to investments moved to Madoff through

---

BAIL OR JAIL?

Bernard Madoff is known to like jewelry and other juicy personal effects, and apparently he had quite a collection of them. He really ticked off the U.S. prosecuting attorney Marc Litt and others when he mailed five packages of these belongings–approximately $1 million worth–on December 24, 2008, to certain family members, including sons Mark and Andrew and brother Peter. Mark and Andrew reported their father's mailing to Litt. The mailings apparently included some pretty nice stuff. As reported by *USA Today,* one package ". . . contained 13 watches, one diamond necklace, an emerald ring and two sets of cufflinks–items estimated to be worth more than $1 million. Two other packages contained a diamond bracelet, a gold watch, a diamond Cartier watch, a diamond Tiffany watch, four diamond brooches, a jade necklace, and other assorted jewelry."

Litt viewed this action as a sign that Madoff might not be cooperating so much with prosecutors, and asked for a court hearing in early January 2009 to consider revoking bail because the mailing of these belongings violated the agreement to freeze assets. The government wanted Madoff in jail. At the hearing, the now-presiding Judge Magistrate Ronald L. Ellis continued the bail, but required Madoff to make an inventory of personal items and to have it checked by authorities every two weeks. He also required a search of any items mailed or otherwise removed from the apartment. The restrictions apply to Ruth Madoff, too.

feeder funds. Will they be treated as bad investments or a bro-kerage failure? And is a feeder fund considered one investor, entitled to one $500,000 payment, or many investors (the indi-viduals who invested in the feeder fund) each of whom could be entitled to a payment? The courts will have to decide.

One thing is for certain: It will take years to sort out what's there to be had and who gets what. The real winners will be the attorneys and tax accountants who end up delivering the main case, and especially the hundreds of side cases, to their conclusions. Stephen Harbeck, SIPC CEO, put it well in a *Fortune* interview: "I don't think the extent of the losses is going to be known for months. This is a completely different order of magnitude than anything that has gone before it, certainly in terms of brokerage firm failures or any other kind of financial institution fraud. This is a monster."

The Plea Bargain

As the case moved forward into January 2009, the thirty-day postponement of a hearing made it apparent that Madoff and his attorney Lee Sorkin were working with government pros-ecutors on a plea deal in which Madoff would plead guilty in return for some leniency. The fraud charge carries a maximum penalty of $5 million (not too harsh for the likes of Madoff) and a twenty-year jail term (pretty harsh for a seventy-year-old man). It clearly would be in the best interests of Madoff to settle, and it might be in the best interests of the government to work something out and shift attention to mopping up the aftermath—and to attend to measures that would prevent such a thing from ever happening again. As this book goes to press, the outcome of the plea bargain is unknown.

Could It Have Really Worked, Anyway?

"It's a proprietary strategy. I can't go into it in great detail." Bernard Madoff is known to have made this statement many times to many people.

And his strategy may not have passed many "smell tests" if he had gone into that detail. What little Madoff has disclosed about his strategy points to a relatively simple trading scheme involving "baskets"—portfolios—of big-name companies, stock indexes that represent those companies, and options derivatives used to earn some income and hedge against strong downside moves. The supposed strategy was fairly basic.

Numerous financial experts—Harry Markopolos, most loudly and clearly—have expressed total doubt as to whether the "strategy" could have worked in anything but the best of conditions.

Following is a fairly high-level explanation and an example of the alleged Madoff strategy—and why it probably couldn't have worked.

The OEX Base

On January 21, 2009, the Standard & Poor's 100 Index, also known as the OEX, closed at 397.63. It was up 16.31, or 4.28 percent—a pretty good day in a pretty bleak year. Pretty bleak year indeed; exactly twelve months earlier, the index had been at 612.88, after hitting a high of 728.03 just a few months before on October 10, 2007. Typically the OEX moves within about a 100-point range in any given year. The year 2008 was an exception—and a doozy.

The OEX is an index created by the Chicago Board Options Exchange to track the price movements of a subset of the better-known S&P 500 index, which contains generally the

500 largest and best-known companies in the U.S. The OEX, or S&P 100 index, is a selection of the top 100 stocks from the S&P 500. Companies in the OEX represent about 45 percent of all the market capitalization—that is, stock market value, in the U.S.

Why do we care about the OEX? It's because Bernard Madoff claims to have made his money trading S&P 100 stocks and buying and selling *options* on the index.

The Option Kicker

So what is an option, anyway? Without getting too technical, it's the right to buy, or sell, a certain security on or before a certain date at a certain price. The date is called the *expiration date* and the price is called the *strike price*. The *right* is bought and sold as a contract; typically each contract represents 100 shares or underlying units.

There are two types of option contracts. The first represents the right to buy a certain security at a price—a *call* contract. The second is the right to sell a certain security at a certain price—a *put* contract. Option traders would buy a call contract if they expect the underlying security to go up, because the option would allow them to buy that security at a lower price at or before expiration. It works if the option finishes the expiration period in the money; that is, the security price rises above the strike price.

They would buy a put contract if they expect the underlying security to go down, because at expiration, if the security were below the strike price, they would profit because they could sell the security at the strike price.

The contract is bought and sold on an options exchange. The buyer pays a price known as a *premium* to the option seller. The premium is driven by several factors, including the volatility of the underlying security (more volatile means greater chance of meeting or exceeding the strike price) and the amount of time until expiration (more time means more possibility to meet or exceed strike price).

The best way to illustrate this is by example.

Suppose shares of XYZ Corporation sell for $100. You think they might go up, so you think about buying a call option. An option expiring in a month with a strike price of $105 costs $4, so you pay $400 ($4 times the 100 shares in the contract) for the option. If the stock goes to $112, the option contract says you can exercise (or buy) the shares, for $105. So you make $7 profit, less the $4 you paid for the option, or $3. Why is this a good deal? Because you didn't have to lay out $10,000 for 100 shares of the stock. You laid out $400 and earned a $300 profit, a 75 percent return on your investment in one month.

Now turn this around the other way. You own 100 shares of XYZ already, bought for $100. You see that you can sell that call for $4, pocketing $400 for the transaction. Now, if XYZ stays below $105 before expiration, that $400 stays in your pocket as profit. If it goes to $112—well, it still stays in your pocket, but you sell the stock at $105, the strike price. The difference between $105 and the $100 you paid—$5, times 100, or $500—also becomes your profit. But the stock is gone, and while you captured $900 in profit, you could have had $1,200 if you hadn't sold the option.

This transaction is called a *covered call sale*. You sell a call, and it's covered because you own the underlying security, and you can sell it if the option finishes in the money.

Now, time to move to puts. Suppose you buy XYZ for $100. In case the bottom falls out of the stock market, you want to be able to sell it for a minimum of $95. To guarantee this, you can buy a $95 put option, the right to sell your stock at $95, for a certain premium. Since stocks can rise to infinity but only fall to zero, typically the put is a little cheaper than the call. In normal market conditions, it might be $3—although in times of turbulence (like late 2008), puts can be more expensive than calls. The $3 premium is like buying insurance on your investment.

The Madoff Method

Bernard Madoff claims to have used a *split strike*, or *collar option* strategy. Rather than using individual stocks like XYZ, he claims to have bought an assortment—a *basket*—of shares representing a portion (not all) of the OEX index. Then he sold an OEX index covered call against them to raise cash, and, for the sake of insurance, he bought a put.

During friendlier market times of relatively steady increases, seen during the 1990s and mid-2000s, this strategy could have produced a decent profit. Unless the market really lurched forward, he would have collected the $400 call premium in the example, plus sometimes the $500 gain on the rise in the price of the stocks—if they rose enough to be called away—less the premium he paid for the insurance put in case the market went down. In our example, $500 + $400 in gains, less $300 paid for the put, or a $600 profit.

One Big Lie? Probably

There are several problems, as many journalists and financial experts, including whistle-blower Harry Markopolos, have pointed out (see chapter 5).

First, since the OEX is an index and thus isn't as volatile as most individual stocks, the OEX option premiums are relatively smaller than those for stocks. Indeed, when the OEX closed at 397.63, the four-week expiration call at 405 sold for

$13.30 ($1,330 extended), and the four-week expiration put at 390 sold for 16 (or $1,600 extended). So selling a call and buying a put equally out of the money would actually lose money! But market sentiment was pretty weak at the time.

In more-normal markets, the option prices might be reversed, but the profit opportunity—$1,600 minus $1,320—is still weak: a $280 profit. To "cover" the trade, Madoff would have to put up $40,000 in capital to buy the underlying stocks. That's a return of about 0.7 percent in four weeks, or just over 9 percent for the year. Not bad, so it seems.

But that assumes relatively stable stock prices. The reality is that a down month would derail that gravy train. Having bought the put option, there is some downside protection, but if the portfolio declined to the equivalent of the OEX at 390, that's $763 lost, wiping out three months of gains. And if the portfolio went up to the equivalent of the OEX at 405, that's a nice gain, but to keep the trade going, Madoff would have had to come up with more capital, putting more at risk of another downturn.

To make this complicated story short, analysts simply haven't been able to replicate Madoff's returns, or anything close, with real-market examples over the years. CNBC *Mad Money*'s Jim Cramer went a little further, loudly proclaiming: "The strategy stunk," and that his own analysis showed that it would have generated a return of *negative* 2.6 percent since the year 2000, not the *positive* 80 percent return Madoff claimed.

Aside from this analysis, there are three major showstoppers:

1. If Madoff really had $50 billion invested, or anything close to that amount, there's no evidence he bought enough options to really hedge the position and make the money.

If he had, it would have exceeded the total trading volume for those options during most periods. Several financial experts have made this point.

2. Records have shown little evidence that Madoff bought and sold anything for these investors. He didn't actually do the trades, and probably couldn't, since the option markets weren't big enough to support him. If he had tried to make the trades with insufficient counterparty volume, the prices would have been driven out of sight.

3. According to a 2001 *Barron's* article, Madoff said he only traded thirty to thirty-five stocks out of the S&P 100 index, so he wasn't tracking the index exactly, and it would have been possible for his hedges to fail. That is, the index goes up, but his thirty-five stocks wouldn't track that gain exactly, meaning he'd potentially have to come up with more funds to cover his bets.

So as a result, it's hard to conclude, at least in its latter years, that the Madoff fund was anything but a scam. Some have speculated that he really paid out his returns with front-running and other trading gains. Then, as markets moved away from the scenario of stability and modest gains, he started to lose big-time. Indeed, investigators have suggested that Madoff's strategy may have worked for a while and then failed. At that point it became a Ponzi scheme, only revocable if some kind of home run was hit, if at all. Those sources suggest the Ponzi scheme was probably in effect at least by 2005, and probably earlier.

As the investigation proceeds, more about Madoff and his scheme will become known, and more names of individual players and firms will doubtless surface as either knowing about or playing a direct role in Madoff's scheme. And still much more will come to light in the comments and lawsuits of the hundreds of victims touched in the case.

Switching gears, those victims will be the topic of the next chapter.

CHAPTER 7

Collateral Damage

Bernie Madoff has put a new face on the ugly side of Wall Street.

—David Callaway, MarketWatch

With a blast heard 'round the world, the Bernie Madoff bomb went off on December 11, 2008, as chronicled in the last chapter. Of course there was near total destruction at Ground Zero, where Bernard L. Madoff Investment Securities, for all intents and purposes, ceased to exist.

But outside the few employees involved, few people care about that. The real impact, the real story, lies with the victims—the mostly innocent victims who were affected by the blast. And just like the very worst man-made bomb disasters, the impact will be felt for years to come—for *generations* to come, really.

It's time to redirect the story to the plight of those victims, to understand who they were, what and how much they lost, and the larger impacts on their communities.

The Blast: How Big and Where

Two months after the blast, the size of the bomb was still uncertain. Madoff himself said it was a $50 billion Ponzi scheme. Investigators haven't been able to come up with an exact figure, and it's a pretty tough task. For one thing, it's easy to double-count, as feeder funds and individuals who invested through them may report a loss for the same sum. For another, it's unclear whether investors should count investment gains accumulated over the years—which weren't real—in the loss figures. And, even with Madoff's own court-ordered accounting of clients, it's a huge job to uncover all affected clients and how much they lost.

Without doubt, the blast and the victims list exceeds the eleven to twenty-five clients and the $17.1 billion under management reported to the SEC in January 2008. By the latest analysis tallied from the *Wall Street Journal* and other sources, total losses reported amount to some $35.1 billion—a figure that is likely to approach Madoff's estimate as more accounts of loss surface, and as more of those who lost funds identify how much they have lost.

There appear to be three major epicenters of the blast. The first, and probably the largest, is the wealthy Palm Beach area in Florida, where Madoff and others famously worked the Palm Beach Country Club and other venues for years. It's the talk of the town: Some 124 articles referencing Madoff, from local reporting and wire services, appeared in the local *Palm Beach Post* in the six weeks following the scandal, covering everything from local victims to the effect on local business and the tourist economy. The second epicenter, not surprisingly, is New York, and especially the Jewish financial and philanthropic circles there. The third and most recent center of destruction lies in the high-level financial circles of Europe, and, to a lesser extent, Latin America and Asia. And as we'll see, the shrapnel has spread far beyond these epicenters.

A Short Analytical Tour of the Victims List

Two sources, the *Wall Street Journal* and a hedge-fund blog called HedgeFundBlogger (www.hedgefundblogger.com), have been tracking news reports on specific Madoff losses incurred both by individuals and institutions, including banks, hedge funds, asset managers, charities, schools, and private foundations. Both sources have published lists, identifying the party, what kind of investor they are, and how much they lost. A composite list, drawn from both sources, appears in Appendix D.

At the risk of some inaccuracy created by double-counting, the two lists have been merged as part of the research for this book in an attempt to give the latest and most complete picture of the victims and their losses. What follows is an analysis of that combined list.

As of late January 2009, the combined list has 184 names on it—again, a far cry from the "11 to 25 clients" reported by Madoff. Some 125 of those 184 names had a dollar amount attached; the others are listed as "n/a," meaning not available, not yet assessed, or in some cases, included in other figures reported by feeder funds or other intermediaries. The $35.1 billion figure mentioned above comes from summing up the reported amounts from the 125 names.

If you want to see where the greatest damage happened and how widespread it was, read on; otherwise, cover your eyes and skip to the "Palm Beach Hurricane" section on page 156.

Biggest Losses Overall

The compiled *Wall Street Journal* and HedgeFundBlogger lists were massaged and analyzed by size of loss and type of victim. The first cut shows the Top 10 victims overall by size of loss.

By themselves, the Top 10 account for $25.2 billion, some 72 percent of the funds lost by all 125 victims who reported loss figures. Widespread press coverage and further investigations have turned many of these previously obscure entities—like Fairfield Sentry (Fairfield Greenwich) and Tremont—into household names since the scandal broke. This list-you-don't-want-to-be-on is dominated by feeder funds, hedge funds, and international banks:

TOP 10 VICTIMS BY DOLLAR AMOUNT		
Investor	Investor type	Loss
Fairfield Sentry (Fairfield Greenwich Group)	FOF feeder fund	$7.5 billion
Tremont Group Holdings	FOF feeder fund	$3.3 billion
Banco Santander	bank	$2.87 billion
Kingate Management	FOF feeder fund	$2.8 billion
Bank Medici of Austria	bank	$2.1 billion
Ascot Partners	hedge fund	$1.8 billion
Access International Advisors	hedge fund	$1.5 billion
Fortis Bank Nederland	bank	$1.35 billion
HSBC	bank	$1 billion
J. P. Jeanneret Associates	asset manager	$946 million
	TOTAL	$25.17 billion

Sources: *Wall Street Journal*, HedgeFundBlogger

No two ways about it—these are big, big losses.

By Investor Type

Investment professionals believe strongly in diversification, and there can be no doubt that Madoff wasn't content to rely on one group or type of investor to support his scheme. The next four tables show the top victims in four groups of particular interest: hedge funds, international banks, individuals, and charities.

Hedge Funds, Funds-of-Funds, and Feeder Funds

This group combines single hedge funds and the so-called "fund-of-funds" operations used to funnel or feed investments into Madoff's scheme. The largest names on this list also dominate the Top 10 overall list, and they account for some $14.9 billion in losses.

TOP 10 VICTIMS: HEDGE FUNDS		
Investor	Investor type	Loss
Fairfield Sentry (Fairfield Greenwich Group)	FOF feeder fund	$7.5 billion
Tremont Group Holdings	FOF feeder fund	$3.3 billion
Kingate Management	FOF feeder fund	$2.8 billion
Ascot Partners	hedge fund	$1.8 billion
Access International Advisors	hedge fund	$1.5 billion
Fix Asset Management	hedge fund	$400 million
Man Group PLC (RMF)	hedge fund	$360 million
Maxam Capital Management	FOF feeder fund	$280 million
Pioneer Alternative Investments	hedge fund	$280 million
RAB Capital	hedge fund	$10 million
	TOTAL	$18.2 billion

Sources: *Wall Street Journal*, HedgeFundBlogger

Fairfield Sentry, part of the Fairfield Greenwich Group introduced in chapter 4, is the largest feeder fund and largest loser overall in the scandal. Tremont Group Holdings is a classic "fund-of-funds" arrangement, choosing other hedge-fund investments for its clients. The staggering $3.3 billion loss occurred in two different divisions of Tremont, and may represent as much as half of its assets in play. Investigators and investors alike are questioning Tremont's high fees for simply moving money on to Madoff, and legal challenges loom. The Kingate Global Fund was managed out of the UK. Ascot was managed by J. Ezra Merkin, and Access International was managed by the aristocratic Frenchman René-Thierry Magon de la Villehuchet, who committed suicide on December 23, 2008.

International Banks

As the Madoff story continues to emerge, one of the bigger surprises is how far he reached into the overseas banking sector. Many of these banks were really acting as investment advisers or asset managers, so the attribution of "bank" may actually overlap other categories. That said, some thirty-one overseas banks, twenty-seven of those in Europe, have now reported losses totaling $12.6 billion. The Top 10 accounted for $10.9 billion of that.

TOP 10 VICTIMS: INTERNATIONAL BANKS		
Investor	Investor type	Loss
Banco Santander	bank	$2.87 billion
Bank Medici of Austria	bank	$2.1 billion
Fortis Bank Nederland	bank	$1.35 billion
HSBC	bank	$1 billion
Benbassat & Cie	bank	$935 million
Union Bancaire Privee	bank	$790 million
Natixis	bank	$554.4 million
Royal Bank of Scotland	bank	$492.76 million
BNP Paribas	bank	$431.17 million
BBVA	bank	$369.5 million
	TOTAL	$10.9 billion

Sources: *Wall Street Journal*, HedgeFundBlogger

As described in chapter 4, Spain's Banco Santander was popular not only in Spain and the rest of Europe, but also with wealthy Latin American clients. Bank Medici is the Austrian bank 75 percent owned and run by Sonja Kohn, which had placed almost all of its hedge-fund investments with Madoff. Fortis Bank in the Netherlands doesn't have direct exposure, but apparently Madoff investments were used to collateralize loans, and the situation is similar with Britain's HSBC.

Individuals and Families

On the surface, one might feel less sorry for the banks, hedge funds, and asset management companies that got snookered by Madoff. But behind most of those numbers were individual investors who trusted their funds to these intermediaries.

One feels for those folks, and one really feels for the individuals who were "sold" on Madoff directly—who, in response to his charms and seemingly common background, entrusted him with their funds, and in some cases, their life savings. Some nineteen individuals and "family offices" have come forward with amounts lost; another twenty-one have not specified an amount or are still trying to figure it out.

TOP 10 VICTIMS: INDIVIDUALS		
Investor	**Investor type**	**Loss**
Carl and Ruth Shapiro	individual	$400 million
Ira Rennert	individual	$200 million
Jerome Fisher (Nine West founder)	individual	$150 million
Family of Sarah Chew	individual	$30 million
Phyllis Molchatsky	individual	$17 million
Alicia Koplowitz	individual	$13.7 million
Richard Spring (Boca Raton recruiter)	individual	$11 million
Richard Roth	individual	$10 million
Michael Roth	individual	$7.5 million
Vincent Tchenguiz	individual	$6.3 million
	TOTAL	$845.5 million

Sources: *Wall Street Journal*, HedgeFundBlogger

One must feel for the top entry on this list, ninety-five-year-old clothing magnate Carl Shapiro. Shapiro lost $400 million, some $250 million as the last-ditch loan/investment in the days before the scandal went public. Shapiro had been a friend of Madoff's for years, reportedly helping him start out in the business; he was like a father to Madoff. "It was a knife in the heart" was Shapiro's famous quote when the scandal broke. And his pain wasn't limited to his individual loss; his foundation tops the list of charitable victims, described next. When you combine his personal and foundation losses, the figure of $545 million would have him just miss the Top 10 list of victims overall. It's a staggering amount of money.

Ira Rennert is a well-known investor, businessman, and chairman of Renco Industries, one of the top 100 privately held companies in the U.S. Rennert's company specialized in acquiring and turning around basic industrial businesses like steel and mining companies.

Most of the rest of the list is made up of wealthy individuals who ran into Madoff in the country club circles and elsewhere, or had their funds committed to Madoff through supposedly knowledgeable intermediaries. A few lost nearly their entire net worth, although it isn't known whether that's true of any of the Top 10 list. It should also be noted that some individual investors have amended their loss totals to reflect their original investment, not the fraudulent "gains" reported over the years.

Charities and Foundations

The damage to charities, foundations, and nonprofits is remarkable; one can scarcely believe that Madoff or anyone else would have done this to such well-intentioned organizations. Some eighteen charities have come forth with over $500 million in losses. Many losses were in smaller figures, like $1 or $1.5 million, but for a charity, it's a huge hit. And most of these organizations were aligned with the Jewish faith and tradition.

TOP 10 VICTIMS: CHARITIES		
Investor	Investor type	Loss
Carl and Ruth Shapiro Family Foundation	charity	$145 million
Hadassah	charity	$90 million
MorseLife (elder care facility)	charity	$73 million
Wolosoff Foundation	charity	$38 million
Mortimer B. Zuckerman Charitable Remainder Trust (*New York Daily News* owner)	charity	$30 million
Arthur I. and Sydelle F. Meyer Charitable Foundation	charity	$29.2 million
Madoff Family Foundation	charity	$19 million
Jewish Community Foundation of Los Angeles	charity	$18 million
Foundation for Humanity (Elie Wiesel's charity)	charity	$15.2 million
Lautenberg Family Foundation	charity	$12.8 million
	TOTAL	$470.2 million

Sources: *Wall Street Journal*, HedgeFundBlogger

Again, unfortunately, Mr. Shapiro tops the list. Hadassah, the number-two victim, is typical—a Jewish women's organization which funds and operates health-care, education, and youth programs, mainly in Israel. Not surprisingly, the $90 million loss has devastated its finances, and has put some key medical institutions in Israel in financial jeopardy. MorseLife operates senior living facilities "in the spirit of Jewish traditions and values" in the Palm Beach area. The remaining names are sort of a who's who in the Jewish community—publisher

Mortimer Zuckerman, Nobel Prize–winning writer Elie Wiesel, and so forth. Some well-known charities and foundations are facing closure or have already closed, like the Picower Foundation and the Chais Family Foundation. Also getting a mention—for what it's worth—is Madoff's own foundation, for a cool $19 million.

The destruction in the charitable and nonprofit community is the centerpiece of larger damage to the Jewish community. Effects on the finances—and the psyche—of that community are the subject of the next chapter.

. . . And All the Rest

Hedge funds, wealthy individuals, charities and foundations—these organizations have garnered most of the headlines in the post–12/11 (2008) world of Bernard Madoff's unraveling. Yet damage occurred in other places, too, especially toward the end as the "marketers" of the scheme apparently searched the world over to find fertile pastures to extend the fraud. These other targets included pension funds, schools and universities, and insurers.

Pension Funds

Really, when you think about it, pension funds are a natural victim. Madoff's "brand promise" of safe, steady, above-market returns was music to the ears of pension-fund managers. The obvious need of pension funds for safety drives them to carry mainly low-yielding fixed-income assets. But to actually achieve the investment results necessary to fund their future pension obligations, pension-fund managers need to achieve returns of 6, maybe 8 percent on their portfolios. How do they do this, especially in the easy-credit, low-interest-rate environments experienced since the early 1990s?

Answer: hedge funds, like Bernard Madoff's fund. As noted in chapter 4, 24 percent of U.S. pension funds had some hedge-fund exposure, compared to 12 percent in 2000. Not that pension funds committed 100 percent to hedge funds, but some did more than others. Of the 179 Madoff victims tallied so far, 13 are pension funds, and 9 have reported losses ranging from $3 million to $45 million. The total loss is about $135 million, but this will likely get larger as pension-fund investments through hedge and feeder funds become known. The largest loss was $45 million for Europe's Royal Dutch Shell—not a big hit for an organization that size.

Just behind that, however, is a $42 million hit for the Town of Fairfield (Connecticut) Employees Pension Fund. That's some 15 percent of its total asset base of $290 million. That amount had been invested through Maxam Capital Management, number eight on the Top 10 hedge-funds list above. The town's first selectman, Kenneth Flatto, has assured the 800 or so employees that their pensions are intact, but one wonders. (Incidentally, here we see a modest example of the probable double-counting as the victims and their losses are sorted out.)

More typical is the $12 million reportedly lost out of the $40 billion State of Massachusetts pension fund, again invested through a fund-of-funds operator. And, a little closer to the Ground Zero of Palm Beach, the West Palm Beach Police Pension Fund lost $838,000—a small fraction of its $161 million fund.

Schools and Universities
As with the many charitable organizations he ensnared, one wonders how Madoff could have had the gall—the chutzpah— to bring losses and grief to schools. Like the charities, most schools and universities were within Jewish circles.

With one obvious exception, the losses weren't huge on the scale observed in other areas. But a million here, six million there—these are huge amounts for such institutions. The known victims' list has eight schools with a total loss of $138 million. The "exception" is New York's Yeshiva University, which lost $110 million while under the leadership of Madoff (treasurer and chair of the business school) and his buddy, J. Ezra Merkin (chair of the investment committee).

The Technion-Israel Institute of Technology is located on an attractive 300-acre campus with 86 buildings in an area known as "Technion City" in Haifa, Israel. The university, with 12,000 students and strong technical programs, is known as the "MIT of Israel." Technion lost some $6.4 million with Bernie Madoff.

And what's the connection, one wonders? Apparently, a man named Stanley Chais, now of Beverly Hills, once attended the school and later got an honorary doctorate and served on its board. In the United States, he became chairman of a Beverly Hills investment management firm company known as Brighton Co. Good luck finding anything about this company online; a search on "Brighton Company" returns the city of Brighton, Colorado, and a Massachusetts business specializing in outsourced corporate financial services (not investments). Stanley Chais apparently invested and lost $250 million with Madoff, including the $6.4 million from Technion. And he lost personally, too. Along the way, he founded the Chais Family Foundation—which shut its doors days after the scandal was revealed as a result of Madoff investments.

The Ramaz School in New York is described rather well on its website:

> [T]he Rabbi Joseph H. Lookstein Upper School of Ramaz is a modern orthodox, coeducational yeshivah day school

*spanning grades nine through twelve . . . The Upper School
provides a stimulating educational environment in which
young men and women can develop their commitment to a
life of Torah learning and mitzvot, to the land and country
of Israel, as well as their appreciation for the values and
achievements of Western culture. Most important, we seek to
graduate individuals who embody the values of menschlichkeit,
reflecting moral refinement and ethical sensitivity.*

The Ramaz School lost $6 million with Bernard Madoff.

And finally, there's the New York Law School, which was
taken for some $3 million through J. Ezra Merkin's Ascot Part-
ners fund. Not surprisingly, the school is one of the leaders in
civil litigation to recover its funds. Doubtless, Boston's Tufts
University, which by one report lost $20 million through the
same path, will join in.

Insurers

Insurance companies, big and small, were hardly immune
from the Madoff syndrome. The victims' list contains fourteen
insurance companies, evenly split between Europe and Asia,
all of whom reported loss amounts, the total of which is about
$350 million.

The largest two are Europe's AXA and Swiss Life Holding, who together account for about $214 million of the total.
But in what might have been the last hurrah for Madoff's
recruiters, mainly through Fairfield Greenwich's partnership
with Singapore's Lion Capital, several Asian insurers were vic-
timized, too. The largest Asian loss was Korea Life Insurance
Co. ($50 million); other victims and amounts were mostly
modest, and include names like Mitsui Sumitomo Insurance
Co. ($8.8 million) and Meiji Yasuda Life Insurance Co. ($1.1
million).

Dancing with the Stars

Almost immediately after the Madoff scandal broke, the names of victims started to emerge. The general public was soon glued to its TV sets and newspapers, aghast to learn of some of the high-profile celebrity names involved. Not surprisingly, most were from the Jewish community, and nearly all declined to give any figures or details on their losses, choosing instead to hide behind the carefully crafted words of their agents and advisers. But once again, the story of blind trust created through affinity and community reaches center stage.

Here are a few of the more-prominent celebrity victims:

- Steven Spielberg—The famous filmmaker sponsored a personal and private foundation known as the Wunderkinder Foundation, with gifts of over $1 million a year. The foundation gives, among other things, to popular environmental causes. According to reports, Madoff handled about 70 percent of the fund's assets and income.
- Jeffrey Katzenberg—He's the CEO of DreamWorks Animation SKG Inc., and his Marilyn and Jeffrey Katzenberg Foundation was "extraordinarily damaged" by their Madoff exposure; he's been quoted as saying that the losses were "painful and humiliating," and that it was a "disgrace" that Madoff was free on bail. The foundation listed assets of $22.1 million.
- Eric Roth—A first-tier screenwriter, Roth is best known for award-winning films like *Forrest Gump* and *The Curious Case of Benjamin Button*. He's suing his investment manager—Stanley Chais of Brighton Co.—for "massive losses" incurred in the Madoff scandal. The lawsuit claims that Chais "simply handed over the entirety" of millions that he handled for various clients to Madoff.

- Kevin Bacon and Kyra Sedgwick—One of Hollywood's best-known couples, Bacon starred in *Footloose, Mystic River,* and *Frost/Nixon,* while Sedgwick has had numerous roles in TV and films, including the series *The Closer* and the movie *Born on the Fourth of July.* According to some unconfirmed reports, the celebrity couple has lost everything except their checking accounts and the land they own.

- Zsa Zsa Gabor—Actress and socialite Gabor, along with her ninth husband, Frederic von Anhalt, say they may have lost $10 million, and may be forced to sell their Bel-Air home, cars, art, and jewelry.

- Elie Wiesel—The famous author lost more than $15 million through his Elie Wiesel Foundation for Humanity, nearly all of its assets. More to come on this one in chapter 8.

- Norman Braman—A Miami businessman and former owner of the Philadelphia Eagles, Braman was especially angry and spoke out loudly when the scandal broke, calling Madoff a "first-class crook who should go to jail for the rest of his life." He called the Ponzi scheme the "scam of the century," and added some color about his recruiting manner and technique: "Madoff won over investors, in part, by presenting himself as an extremely caring and accessible guy. If a tragedy occurred in a family, he'd go to the funeral. If somebody caught a cold and he knew about it, a phone call would come." Braman was worth about $1.7 billion according to Forbes.com, but has not disclosed how much he may have lost.

- Fred Wilpon—With another partner, Wilpon runs an investing partnership known as Sterling Stamos, which owns the New York Mets and other New York–area sports teams, along with New York and Florida real estate investments. This entity may have lost as much as $500 million.

- Larry King—The famous CNN talk show host apparently lost over $1 million, although not many details have been disclosed. Perhaps King can't wait to get Madoff on the show, so he can tell all and ask all. Can't wait for that show.
- John Robbins—A well-known author in the food and vegetarian circles, with titles like *Diet for a New America* and *The Food Revolution,* Robbins walked away from the Baskin-Robbins family fortune to "seek a simple life" away from the "toxic mythology" of "self-worth defined by net worth." According to some accounts, he and his wife lost 98 percent of their net worth.
- Henry Kaufman—The John Robbins loss is ironic, but this one may be even more so. The eighty-one-year-old Kaufman, a former chief economist at Salomon Brothers, earned the name "Dr. Doom" in the 1980s with his repeated bearish calls on the market and calls for investor caution. He apparently lost several million.

It won't be surprising if, after the smoke clears, several more prominent names find their way onto the victims' list.

The Palm Beach Hurricane

With the who's who behind us, it's worth a visit to some of the places to capture the stories and moods of those close to the damage. The first stop is Palm Beach, the easternmost city in Florida and luxury capital of Florida's Atlantic "Gold Coast."

Palm Beach is a posh hangout for what could be described as mature, well-to-do adults. Located just off the Gulf Stream, the winters are awesome, and the population triples from 10,000 to 30,000 as the wealthy snowbirds fly in from "up North." New York accents and Jewish ancestry dominate the incoming flocks. The community itself is noted for its comforts and impeccable surroundings, although there is a well-documented undercurrent of intrigue and discontent noted by many, including Laurence Leamer in his new book, *Madness Under the Royal Palms: Love and Death Behind the Gates of Palm Beach* (Hyperion, 2009). From the town's website:

> *Palm Beach is a fully developed community, world-renowned for its extraordinary beauty, quality of life and small-town character. As we envision our future ten years from now, we see Palm Beach remaining true to the inspired legacy of our founders, a Mediterranean-style mecca of stunning architecture and natural beauty, acclaimed shopping, restaurants and hotels, a cosmopolitan culture, and an involved citizenry committed to civic and philanthropic causes and excellence in Town government.*

The quiet ambience of the wealthy leisure class was broken when Hurricane Madoff made landfall in December 2008.

"I'll Dig a Ditch"

Ten days before Hanukkah, the music stopped. Word came through the wires, from New York, about the Madoff arrest and confession. Phones rang. Neighbors talked. There was an air of nervous excitement in the otherwise-placid Palm Beach Country Club.

Laurence Leamer called the revelation of the scam a curse of almost biblical proportions on the elite Jewish community. "It was like the *Titanic*," he explained in a blog after visiting with some of the victims at a society event in Florida. "The ship was sinking, and people were crying and everybody was drunk. [It was] a feeling of incredible shame, embarrassment, of exposure, as if their whole world has been exposed as jerry-built."

The experience of one anonymous Palm Beach resident interviewed by the *Palm Beach Post* is typical. They arrived at their home to find two FedEx envelopes leaning against their door, containing letters from the Westport National Bank, an intermediary, informing the couple "that their money was with Bernard L. Madoff Investment Securities and had disappeared." They, like many others, had "had no idea their money was being invested with Madoff."

For others, there was less surprise. They *did* know their money had been invested with Madoff—but they still couldn't believe their eyes and ears when the news broke.

Gerald Blumenthal's story, also captured by the *Palm Beach Post,* was typical. Blumenthal is a retired Boca Raton ophthalmologist (Boca is about ten miles south of Palm Beach). In the 1980s Blumenthal found Madoff and his steady returns through his wife, who knew Ruth Madoff. The investments seemed to be working, so his adult children, in-laws, and friends also invested—even his grandchildren, according to the account. In all, thirty-five to forty people in Blumenthal's circle invested a total of $30 million.

Everything seemed to be fine when Blumenthal retired in 1993. But in the aftermath of December 11, 2008, the seventy-eight-year-old and his wife got the bad news: Their life savings of $4.5 million was history. "Now my wife and I are in dire straits," proclaimed Blumenthal. "We have to sell our house, and we're doing what we can to cut expenses. I'm looking for work and my wife is also interviewing for jobs." In fact, Blumenthal is seeking to modify a mortgage while he looks for work. "I'll dig a ditch," he said poignantly.

A "War Zone"

Blumenthal has many peers; many residents in the area lost 90 percent of their savings. In fact, there's a bit of a conflict brewing between those who lost and those who pulled their money out—just who's entitled to those funds, anyway, if those who pulled out were simply taking funds from those who entered or stayed in?

Many are left scratching their heads about this issue; they are also wondering how they could have been duped by Madoff's many recruiters and "close associates" who made the rounds in their community. And most are exploring their legal options, retaining attorneys to create or join lawsuits against Madoff or the feeder funds, to recover taxes paid on phantom gains, and to pursue possible recovery, $500,000 maximum, from the Securities Investor Protection Corporation.

Some, like Larry Leif, a Delray Beach resident who lost about $8 million, have "gone public," making several appearances on national media outlets to talk about their losses. Leif, in a December 16, 2008, interview with CNN's Alan Chernoff, was quite direct:

Chernoff (to Wolf Blitzer): Wolf, one investor told me that he feels as if there has been a financial murder in his home. For years, investors of Bernie Madoff felt special. They felt that they were lucky to have money with him. But today, they feel taken.

Leif: I didn't believe it at first. I said, this is impossible.

Chernoff: Larry Leif says he had $8 million invested with Bernard Madoff—virtually all of his money, now apparently gone.

Leif: You know, I was living the American dream. And within a day, my American dream was taken away from me.

Chernoff: It was the late '70s when Leif put the pension of his sporting goods company with Madoff. The money, he says, grew steadily every year—producing annual returns better than 10 percent—so good that Leif has been living off the returns since retiring a decade ago.

Leif: And I used to say that Mr. Madoff was the smartest man on Wall Street. Unfortunately, I have to say he probably still is, to pull this off.

Chernoff: Now Madoff is charged with running a multi-billion-dollar Ponzi scheme, in which he allegedly used new

---

BUSINESS AS USUAL?

Although Palm Beach has had some shady dealings over the years, it's still regarded as one of the top destinations and places to live in the country. Now, given all of the international media attention, is that still the case?

The *Palm Beach Post* decided to find out and interviewed some locals and folks in the know. One was Nancy Del Risco, a tourism consultant and professor at Florida International University's School of Hospitality and Tourism Management. Her response was noncommittal: "It can go either way. It can also go both ways." She added, "It would take more than one unsavory individual to sully a town's image . . . a more likely culprit would be a natural disaster like a hurricane."

Not a very convincing answer.

But one local business does see a strong positive. A consignment shop called Classic Collections has been doing quite well lately. On December 31, a CNBC feature noted the shop's increase in consignment items from Madoff victims, who have been bringing in their belongings to sell. New customers and the shop itself reaped the benefits from the added attention bestowed on Palm Beach. Owner Sally Kimball reported a 25 to 40 percent increase in business during the holidays, and lots of new exposure from other media interviews.

What more could a business ask for?

investment contributions to pay returns to his investors. Victims blame the SEC, which concluded an investigation of Madoff last year without bringing any charges.

Leif: How could the government let me down 100 percent?

It probably feels good, in light of such awful news, to let the regulators know your outrage, to try to help steer others clear of such scams, and to just plain "get it off your chest." Leif went on to interview with CBS, CNBC, and others.

It all leads to one conclusion: The Madoff saga has caused considerable financial and emotional trauma in the area. Palm Beach hedge-fund manager Doug Kass summed it up well for the *Palm Beach Post* on his return to Florida shortly after the scandal broke: "Coming back to Florida, after a week in New York City, feels like being back in a war zone."

A New York Headache

As if New Yorkers needed something else to worry about.

Did New Yorkers need yet another attack from the financial industry, well beyond all the bad stuff that already happened in 2008? Short answer: no. The unraveling of Bernard Madoff's Ponzi scheme sent shock waves through New York philanthropic and real estate circles, not to mention its broad financial realm, including the individual New Yorkers who got caught in the scam.

Most of the hits to the philanthropic world were taken in the Jewish community; some of the more high-profile organizations, like Elie Wiesel's foundation, have already been mentioned, and more will be described in the next chapter, which focuses on collateral damage in the Jewish community.

Some of the victims were in the arts, although it isn't clear how vulnerable they were financially. The Madoffs themselves served on boards and donated to many community organizations. The Madoff Family Foundation recently donated $50,000 to New York's Public Theater, where son Mark is a trustee, and $77,500 to the Lincoln Center Theater, where Mark was also on the board. They gave $30,000 to the Robin Hood Foundation, a popular charity on Wall Street. These are just a few examples, and they don't include the dozens of other individuals and foundations who had money with Madoff, now gone.

Most New York nonprofit entities, many beyond the Jewish and arts circles, are scurrying to tally the damage. The Madoff Foundation donated $15,000 to City Harvest, a hunger program, and $25,000 to Prep for Prep, an organization that provides aid to minority students in New York City schools. Health-care entities were also big recipients: The Lymphoma Research Foundation, the Leukemia and Lymphoma Society, the Gift of Life Bone Marrow Foundation, and the Memorial Sloan-Kettering Hospital all received substantial gifts from Madoff and his family foundation over the years.

The damage is spreading far beyond New York and Palm Beach circles. As an example, the Museum of Fine Arts in Boston and Brandeis University have received substantial contributions from the Carl and Ruth Shapiro Foundation, which had $145 million—some 45 percent of its total funds—invested with Madoff. The shock waves will continue to ripple outward in the days, months, and years to come.

Queens en Prise

Some of the victims were in Madoff's hometown of Queens, and not all are in the Jewish community. One is Ruth's alma mater, Queens College. Bernard Madoff served as a trustee of the

Queens College Foundation and wrote checks to the college every year, and there are plausible but unconfirmed reports that the Queens College Foundation had funds invested with Madoff.

Other hits have surfaced in Queens. The North Shore–Long Island Jewish Health System runs fifteen hospitals and a series of health- and long-term-care facilities, mostly on western Long Island. The nonprofit entity had at least one donor who gave $5.7 million but stipulated that it be managed by Madoff. In addition, Madoff himself has given about $6,000 a year, some $216,000 over thirty-six years. But in a statement, the organization's board of trustees' investment committee denied any involvement with Madoff, either as an investment manager or board member.

The New York Mets play in Queens. Fred Wilpon's Sterling Stamos investment fund owns the Mets, and although they lost $500 million, they say it won't affect the operation of the ball club. Another worry centered on whether the building of Citi Field—the $850 million state-of-the-art baseball stadium in the Flushing Meadows–Corona Park area of Queens—would be affected by the scandal. Citi Field was meant to replace Shea Stadium; would it be finished in time for its April 2009 debut—or finished at all? The answer turned out to be "Yes"; fortunately, it was spared from the Madoff scandal. Incidentally, a greater risk to that facility's finances may come from an examination of the CitiGroup naming-rights deal, which may have been ultimately paid for by federal bailout funds.

Another Blow to Real Estate

Many of the major New York philanthropic names, like Wilpon and Zuckerman, also had substantial real estate investments in the New York area. Beyond these individuals, several local developers and real estate managers invested with Madoff. That, combined with economic and job dislocations produced by the scandal, is making a cloudy real estate market even cloudier.

Some large developers and their owners, like Glenwood Management and Blumenfeld Development Group, are said to have "invested heavily" with Madoff. Their projects—retail developments, apartment buildings—may be on the rocks. And "scores of" individuals touched by the scandal are planning to sell their apartments, or have backed out of deals, according to Curbed, an online New York real estate journal. One Upper East Side broker lost two $2-million apartment sales because of Madoff losses. Now, one might not feel too sorry for individuals buying $2-million apartments, but the damage doubtless goes deeper than that.

Aside from its prominence as a center for entertainment and the arts, New York City's financial and real estate industries are the lifeblood of the city. Any blow to these industries is a blow to the city as a whole, and a hit to its collective psyche. As Curbed put it: "As we're well aware, the big machine didn't need another wrench thrown into it, let alone an atomic bomb. How bad is this thing going to get?"

It remains to be seen what Madoff's long-term legacy will be. While there have been countless financial, political, and other types of scandals in New York's long and colorful history, none have cast a shadow on the city in the long run. This one will probably be no different; however, there's no doubt that it will have a long-lasting and indelible impact on some of its citizens.

Another Victim, Another Story

He's seventy-six, a good-looking retiree with dignified, wavy gray hair and a bushy gray mustache, a thick New York accent, and a ruddy but worried face. His story is a lot like the Palm Beach stories, except that his has taken place in New York. He's Allan Goldstein, a retired business owner in the garment industry, who watched "a few million dollars" evaporate to "absolutely nothing" in the scandal. He testified before the House Financial Services Committee in early January 2009 to help explain what the scandal has done to real people like him. He spoke with NPR's Scott Simon on *Weekend Edition* shortly afterward.

"I used up all my assets over the years to let my Madoff account grow so I could retire with a decent income," Goldstein told Simon. "So I had no assets left except cash and my life insurance policies. I'm having trouble paying my mortgage. My children are helping me out. My house is up for sale."

Goldstein says he was introduced to Madoff Securities by his accountant, who told him Madoff's returns were strong—between 10 and 12 percent in both good years and bad. Madoff's fund, he was told, was a "safe" place to put his money. Now Goldstein is looking for a job, something he didn't expect to be doing in his seventies. He says he needs to earn money just to cover food and car expenses. "I can't keep taking money from my children," he added.

He goes on to talk about his emotions. "The first three days, four days, I was just filled with anger, because I was in shock; I lost all my money. I didn't know what to do or where to turn. And I realized I couldn't go on and live my life consumed with anger. So right now, I don't really care about Bernie Madoff. I don't care if he goes to jail. I don't care if he stays out of jail. It's not going to improve my life one way or the other, so I really don't care." And then, he commented on the regulators and the environment that led to this. He believes it was more than a failure. "I believe [the government was] complicit in this," he says. "There were so many red flags, so many warning signals, so many letters written about this, and they did nothing."

Like so many, he said he "had absolutely no inkling that anything was amiss . . . The statements came every month. Any monies I needed to withdraw were taken out with no problem."

In an interesting side comment, probably reflecting the feelings of many who figured others would have found trouble had there been any, Goldstein speculated: "There were banks, hedge funds who put billions of dollars into this man. They must have done some due diligence—and they also invested their money."

And finally: "It's a horrible situation, and I have to tell you that I receive e-mails every day. There are so many, many people in the same position that I'm in that it's heartbreaking.

FREEDOM FIGHTER GETS FLEECED

The American Civil Liberties Union has fought for years for individual rights and due process. Now it appears that the ACLU has become a Madoff victim.

Not directly, perhaps, as none of its own funds were invested with Madoff. But that doesn't make them immune. Two contributing foundations, rumored to be the JEHT (which stands for Justice, Equality, Human dignity, and Tolerance) and Picower Foundations, who supported their work on "national liberty and reproductive freedom," were clobbered. As a result, the ACLU stands to lose some $850,000 in support in 2009, so it has cut its staff by 10 percent and put out an appeal for other contributors to fill the gap.

If Madoff has "due process" issues during his trial, don't expect the ACLU to come to his defense.

Heartbreaking," he says. "I have my health, and my wife is healthy. . . . We'll get through this somehow."

He'll have a lot of company.

Black Eye for the Financial Profession

The Madoff disaster sent shock waves through the financial advisory profession, which includes a wide range of services: "retail" client financial planners; professional fund advisers; and managers of investment companies, both the regulated ones and the unregulated hedge-fund variety. Not surprisingly, the Madoff scandal has caused a lot of nervousness and anxiety for financial professionals and the customers they serve. There are two main issues:

Issue #1: Fiduciary Responsibility

One issue is the fiduciary responsibility inherent in these professions, which most advisers swear to uphold—at least those in the higher tiers of the profession. Fiduciary responsibility guides these professionals to act in the best interests of their clients; to make decisions suitable for each client's individual needs and risk tolerance; and to always do "due diligence" to make sure good ideas are really good ideas.

The Madoff scandal exposed not only a huge and obvious breach in fiduciary responsibility on Madoff's part, but also a major breakdown on the part of the many advisers, funds, banks, and other conduits to Madoff's scheme.

Issue #2: Fees—for What?

This is really one component of the fiduciary responsibility issue, but it's so glaring that it deserves to be recognized separately. What about the financial intermediaries, the "asset managers" and advisers like Fairfield Greenwich, Bank Medici, Tremont, and J. Ezra Merkin, for that matter, who took large commissions simply to fork the dough over to Madoff? These individuals and organizations made huge money for little more than mailing a check to someone else. Those on a "2 and 20"commission schedule, like Merkin, fared particularly well, but even those on a more typical fund commission of 1 or 1½ percent made millions.

Naturally, this issue calls into question the entire compensation scheme for asset management, although not for the first time.

A Big PR Problem

And, more to the point, the old adage "Who *can* you trust?" has enjoyed no finer hour, at least among the millions of investors who trust others to help manage their money.

The financial advisory profession is feeling the heat, as clients everywhere scurry for answers and ask tough questions of their advisers. A recent poll by *InvestmentNews* asked advisers: Are you worried that the reputation of financial advisers has been tarnished by the $50 billion fraud allegedly carried out by money manager Bernard Madoff?" According to the publication, some 69 percent of the 1,015 advisers polled said yes.

The advisers were also asked whether they saw a public relations issue, and thought their trade groups should "step up their efforts to project a more positive image of advisers in light of the scandal." Some 86.3 percent of advisers polled said yes.

As a result, *InvestmentNews* recommends an industry-wide national ad campaign to educate consumers and restore their confidence. Meanwhile, financial advisers will feel the fallout for some time, as their process and ethics continue to be questioned by a skeptical public (and press, for that matter).

Above and Beyond

Battles don't tell the story of a war, and the devastation described in this chapter hardly provides the complete picture of the Madoff scandal. Many, many more individuals and organizations were affected. The damage is still being assessed, and will continue to be for a long time to come. The tentacles reach deep and wide, and many still don't know how much they lost, or if they lost anything at all. And the courts will decide, through the bankruptcy action and hundreds of individual and class-action court cases, what, if anything, can be done to compensate those who lost money. There is no doubt that this compensation will fall far short of making up for the huge losses they have experienced.

While Palm Beach and New York were the geographic epicenters of the blast, there can be no doubt that the Jewish community was the cultural center of destruction. The next chapter takes a closer look at that impact. The last chapter examines the legacy of the Madoff scandal—what might (or will) happen to the investing world and the regulations and regulatory agencies as the scandal is sorted out. It finishes with some words of wisdom for individual investors, large and small, about how to find shelter from this sort of disaster.

CHAPTER 8

Chosen Again: The Profound Effects on the Jewish World

Jews had more faith in Bernie Madoff than they did in God.

—Laura Goldman, Tel Aviv money manager to Palm Beach Post

Much is known about the financial and geographic centers of destruction from the Madoff bombshell. But we can hardly understand the full story nor appreciate the full impact without taking in the appalling impacts on the cultural and philanthropic core of the Jewish community.

It's well known that Madoff traveled easily and comfortably in Jewish circles, serving on boards of foundations and universities. He was woven into the fabric of the community, both in New York and Palm Beach, and he had a solid reputation among Jews elsewhere, including overseas. But the details of some of these involvements reveal a lot, and continue to leave anyone, Jew or Gentile, wondering: "Just how could he do this?"

Even more astonishing—and more abstract—is the impact on the Jewish psyche and sense of place in the world. Madoff's actions have served to fan the flames of anti-Semitic feelings and commentary around the world, based on the ridiculous-as-usual premise that one person represents the whole community. Yet that's the way things work out sometimes, and many in the Jewish community are left scrambling to deal with it.

This chapter takes a look at how the scandal impacted on the philanthropic fabric of foundations and their recipients, using some of the more prominent organizations as examples. It then moves on to assess how Madoff fanned the flames of anti-Semitism, finishing with a look at the more far-reaching effects on the Jewish identity.

Foundations and Far-Reaching Consequences

Imagine for a moment that you run a small nonprofit health-care agency providing services to the Jewish community. Your organization does the usual fund-raising things—memberships, newsletters, small envelopes to collect $25 here, $50 there. But the bulk of your funding comes from a couple of large foundations created by prominent Jewish citizens—perhaps household names like Steven Spielberg, perhaps not.

The Madoff scandal breaks and you feel for the victims. Then you hear that the very foundations that form the foundation of your existence lost millions. You panic. You wait to hear any day now that those foundations will be cutting back. Or closing altogether.

You have very good reason to panic, and with any luck, you'll be spared. But the chances don't look so good, because so many of these foundations had some or all of their money invested with Madoff. You fear for the life of your organization and its causes. And you fear for your job. With good reason.

As the smoke clears, you realize the impact isn't just today, and isn't just an open-or-shut case with the foundation and its generosity toward you. You realize that there will be long-term impact and damage done to the wealthy individuals who started and continue to maintain the foundations. Many will be unable to give as much, and many good causes will cease to be supported. Many will have to close their doors.

Madoff's bomb left a big crater in the land of Jewish philanthropy. The last chapter estimated *known* charity losses at about $500 million, and *known* individual losses (which usually lead to charity losses) at over a billion dollars. Once the losses are sorted out, it's clear that more damage will be revealed. Michael Charendoff, president of the Jewish Funders Network, believes the losses will amount to at least $2.5 billion, and noted that "it's getting bigger."

And there's more than mere financial loss here. Charendoff described the mood at a recent meeting of the Jewish Funders Network, for the *Boston Globe:* "There was a good deal of anger in the room. These are all people who have committed their lives to Jewish philanthropy, and here this guy went around and partly used this facade of being a Jewish philanthropist in order to identify and exploit his victims."

These wounds will take a long time to heal.

The rest of this section provides a cross section of what happened to some of the more-prominent foundations, how they're dealing with it, and what impact it is having on other organizations and individuals further downstream.

"This One Just Leaves Me Breathless"

Mortimer B. Zuckerman was born into wealth in Canada and came to the United States to become a media and real estate mogul. Once a member of the Harvard Business School faculty, Zuckerman is now the chairman of real estate firm Boston Properties and owner of the *New York Daily News* and *U.S. News & World Report*. His foundation—actually, the Mortimer B. Zuckerman Charitable Remainder Trust—lost about $30 million to Madoff, 11 percent of its value.

Zuckerman, by profession and by faith, is an articulate conservative media commentator and strong supporter of Israeli and other Jewish causes. He has a sense of humor, too; once, when labeled as a "member of the media wing of the Israeli lobby," he replied: "I would just say this: The allegations of this disproportionate influence of the Jewish community reminds me of the ninety-two-year-old man sued in a paternity suit. He said he was so proud, he pleaded guilty."

Zuckerman says he found out by e-mail that his $30 million "no longer existed." He also says he didn't know Madoff, but instead was hooked by J. Ezra Merkin and his Ascot Partners hedge fund (see sidebar below).

THE LETTER

Mort Zuckerman didn't know Madoff, and in fact got tangled up with him through Ascot Partners and its managing director, J. Ezra Merkin. He was quick to make that clear to the press, writing a letter to Andrew Serwer, managing editor of *Fortune,* in response to a January 19, 2009, article ("Will Madoff Get Hard Time?") that appeared on Fortune.com and CNN Money. Zuckerman chided Serwer for his comment about many having missed the signs of Madoff's Ponzi scheme, including the SEC and Zuckerman himself. Zuckerman noted: "I did not invest with Mr. Madoff, had never spoken to him nor heard of him when the scandal broke. It was a charitable trust called the Mortimer B. Zuckerman Charitable Trust that invested in the Ascot Fund run by Ezra Merkin." Zuckerman went on to say that Merkin's fund was entirely invested with Madoff—a fact that was not revealed to him or to most other Ascot Fund investors. In addition, Merkin was receiving $27 million per year to perform due diligence on a wide array of funds—this diversity being at the core of Merkin's "investment philosophy."

Zuckerman has been outspoken about the loss. In an NPR interview he said, "I have to put this kind of bluntly: I made the money, contributed to charity. And to find out this kind of money dissipated is just infuriating, not to mention tragic for the community. This money was devoted to the task of cancer care, education, scholarship, food for the poor—I could go on. And to have these funds lost—this one just leaves me breathless."

Although Zuckerman told NPR that there would be cutbacks, more recently he has stated that all current charitable obligations will still be honored, with no changes. During a forum held at the YIVO Institute for Jewish Research, discussed again later in this chapter, Zuckerman told the group that no one since Julius and Ethel Rosenberg, who gave atomic secrets to the Soviet Union, "has so damaged the image and self-respect of American Jews."

"Not to Care Is Not an Option"

Elie Wiesel was born in Romania and survived Auschwitz to become a well-known journalist and author. His first of more than forty books was a memoir of his death camp experiences. Aside from his writing, Wiesel has been an avid supporter of Israel and Jewish causes. For his literary and human rights activities, he has won the Nobel Peace Prize and received the Presidential Medal of Freedom. He and his wife, Marion, established The Elie Wiesel Foundation for Humanity shortly after winning the Nobel Prize in 1986.

The Wiesel Foundation's mission, according to their website, is "rooted in the memory of the Holocaust," and is meant to "combat indifference, intolerance, and injustice through international dialogue and youth-focused programs that promote

ANOTHER LETTER

Foundations and funds devastated by the Madoff scandal have, of course, had to notify their charity and nonprofit recipients of the event and its consequences. Some of these notifications have been decisive and direct, announcing the termination of support, or even of the fund itself. Others are more of a heads-up, promising to sort things out in the weeks to come, leading to a very nervous wait for the recipients. While most of these notifications have been done privately and without fanfare, the Wiesel Foundation decided to make theirs public, placing it on their website for all to see:

To Our Friends:

We are deeply saddened and distressed that we, along with many others, have been the victims of what may be one of the largest investment frauds in history. We are writing to inform you that the Elie Wiesel Foundation for Humanity had $15.2 million under management with Bernard Madoff Investment Securities. This represented substantially all of the Foundation's assets.

The values we stand for are more needed than ever. We want to assure you that the Foundation remains committed to carrying on the lifelong work of our founder, Elie Wiesel. We shall not be deterred from our mission to combat indifference, intolerance, and injustice around the world.

At this difficult time, the Foundation wishes to express its profound gratitude for all your support.

The Elie Wiesel Foundation for Humanity

One can only imagine the pain of the Foundation, its supporters, and especially its beneficiary organizations.

acceptance, understanding and equality." The foundation runs several programs, many oriented toward Jewish youth.

The foundation lost over $15 million—"substantially all the Foundation's assets" (see sidebar on previous page).

Wiesel was also quite blunt with his comments about Madoff in a *Palm Beach Post* interview: "I don't think any enemy has done so much harm to the Jewish community in America as he has." But he also pledged to carry on his own philanthropy, acknowledging that "not to care is not an option."

Cutting to the Chais

Stanley Chais is the head of Brighton Company, an investment company in Beverly Hills, California. Brighton apparently funneled $250 million of investor money, mostly from wealthy individuals in the entertainment business, into Madoff's fund. A class action suit has been filed. The suit alleges that the Brighton firm was "aware of, or recklessly disregarded, the misuse and mismanagement of investment funds."

But it turns out that Chais is a victim, too.

Chais served on many charitable boards with Madoff, and they became good friends. Chais set up the Chais Foundation in 1985, which supported a host of Jewish educational, literacy, and community-building programs located mainly overseas, in Israel, Russia, and Eastern Europe. Annual gifts totaled about $12 million, and one list revealed that Chais was supporting eighty different and mostly very small agencies and projects. One example is the Jerusalem-based Elul. Dedicated to "Jewish renewal," Elul members study Jewish texts from the Bible through contemporary literature and philosophy. Another is Judapest, a website and chat room for young Hungarian Jews.

The Chais Family Foundation was 100 percent invested with Madoff, and shut down four days after Madoff-related losses left it penniless. "Like everybody else who trusted and invested with Bernie Madoff, he betrayed my trust," Chais said. Once again, the truly bad news is the impact this scandal has had on the eighty agencies supported by the Chais Foundation, now saddled with an unexpected funding hit. It's likely that these funds were irreplaceable. One report estimates that sixty small nonprofits will have to close in Israel alone as a result of the scandal.

The Stakes Grow: The Picower Foundation

On December 19, 2008, eight days after the Madoff arrest, the Jeffry M. and Barbara Picower Foundation announced it was closing its doors.

That announcement sent a huge shock wave through the philanthropic community. Why? Because with over $1 billion in assets, most or all managed by Madoff, Picower ranks as the seventy-first-largest foundation in the country. That's huge.

Founded in 1989 and based in Palm Beach, with an office in New York, the Picower Foundation gave $23 million in 2007 to a variety of causes, mainly for education, healthcare innovations, and Jewish community life, and many important domestic causes stand to lose. Picower gave big to biomedical research, diabetes and brain and cognitive sciences, including a $4 million annual sponsorship of the Picower Institute for Learning and Memory at the Massachusetts Institute of Technology, and several research projects at the Harvard Medical School, some of which are now in jeopardy.

The foundation reached beyond health care to fund organizations as diverse as the New York Public Library, the Children's Health Fund, and the Palm Beach County school district. They also supported about two dozen Jewish service organizations. Interestingly, one 2007 gift went to the Queens

College Foundation—with Madoff's wife Ruth listed as the contact.

As executive director Barbara Picower put it, Madoff's "act of fraud has had a devastating impact on tens of thousands of lives, as well as numerous philanthropic foundations and non-profit organizations."

JEHT: Justice Not Served

JEHT stands for Justice, Equality, Human dignity, and Tolerance. The cleverly named organization was founded in 2000 primarily to promote justice and fair elections. JEHT's own statement about its termination of operations, posted on its website, pretty much tells the story:

> The JEHT Foundation, a national philanthropic organiza-tion, has stopped all grant making effective immediately and will close its doors at the end of January 2009. The funds of the donors to the Foundation, Jeanne Levy-Church and Kenneth Levy-Church, were managed by Bernard L. Madoff, a prominent financial advisor who was arrested last week for defrauding investors out of billions of dollars.
>
> The Foundation was established in 2000. Its name stands for the values it holds dear: Justice, Equality, Human dignity, and Tolerance. It supported programs that promoted reform of the criminal and juvenile justice systems; ensured that the United States adhered to the international rule of law; and worked to improve the voting process by enhancing fair representation, competitive elections, and government transparency.
>
> The JEHT Foundation Board deeply regrets that the important work that the Foundation has undertaken over the years is ending so abruptly. The issues the Foundation addressed received very limited philanthropic support, and the loss of the foundation's funding and leadership will cause

significant pain and disruption of the work for many dedicated people and organizations. The Foundation's programs have met with significant success in recent years—promoting change in these critical areas in partnership with government and the nonprofit sector. Hopefully others will look closely at this work and consider supporting it going forward.

The amount lost hasn't been made public, but the foundation granted $26.4 million in 2006. Its twenty-four employees have been laid off.

The Lappin Foundation: "Business as Usual, Then Suddenly Closed"

The Boston-based Robert I. Lappin Charitable Foundation was a relatively small charity dedicated to financing trips for Jewish youth to Israel, among other Jewish community causes. Founder Robert I. Lappin cut its programs after revealing that the money for its operations was invested with Madoff. Again, a brief website statement tells the story:

> *The programs of the Robert I. Lappin Charitable Foundation and the Robert I. Lappin 1992 Supporting Foundation are discontinued, effectively immediately. The Foundations lost $8 million, all assets, in the Bernard Madoff scandal. The Foundation staff was terminated Dec 12, 2008.*

That was the very day after Madoff's arrest. The Foundation lost $8 million in assets, and apparently Mr. Lappin also had a lot of his own personal wealth tied up with Madoff. The foundation gave $1.5 million a year and had seven employees. To its credit, the foundation is now trying to recover. Posted on their website is a new campaign called "Save Y2I [Youth to Israel] 2009," with a solicitation to donors "for any amount" of money.

In an ironic twist, Robert I. Lappin, who lives and runs his foundation in the Boston area, shares a name (almost) with W. Robert Lappin, the founder, music director, and conductor of the Palm Beach Pops orchestra. "Before this month, I didn't know Madoff existed," quipped the latter Mr. Lappin to the *Palm Beach Daily News.*

Lautenberg: A Political Connection?

One of the wealthiest members of the Senate—or any sector of politics, for that matter—New Jersey senator Frank Lautenberg had invested about $14 million with Madoff, the entirety of his family's charitable foundation. The Lautenberg Family Foundation gave to a wide range of Jewish-oriented religious, civic, arts, and educational programs, mainly in New Jersey. What's interesting is the political tie: According to an Associated Press story, Madoff apparently contributed a great deal to New Jersey campaigns—more than $400,000 since 1986—including $13,600 for Lautenberg's 2008 reelection campaign.

Perhaps Madoff really liked Lautenberg's contribution to government. More likely, he valued Lautenberg's representation—or perhaps he just needed Lautenberg's money. But Lautenberg has decided otherwise for Madoff's support; a Lautenberg spokesman said, "We will be ridding ourselves of [his campaign] contribution."

Going West: The Jewish Community Foundation of Los Angeles

Most—but not all—of the Madoff foundation damage occurred in New York or Florida. But Los Angeles has a large Jewish population, too, and it was by no means spared.

The Jewish Community Foundation of Los Angeles was founded in 1954 to provide "permanent resources for the community." It gives grants—$25,000 here, $50,000 there—to a number of small nonprofits, including local museums, synagogues, and Jewish community centers.

The Foundation disclosed shortly after the scandal broke that about $18 million was invested with Madoff—which had grown to over $25 million on paper—about 11 percent of their assets. Apparently these investments were made in 2004, based on the recommendation of a paid financial adviser from a company called Cambridge Associates. The Foundation's CEO and board chair said in a letter: "Mr. Madoff was highly regarded and his firm has been one of the most prominent firms on Wall Street for decades. We were shocked to learn of this alleged fraud."

Another foundation with a similar name, The Jewish Federation of Greater Los Angeles, said it lost $6.4 million—also about 11 percent of its endowment—as a result of Madoff's scheme. Paul Castro, the executive director of Jewish Family Service, one of the beneficiary organizations that also had some money invested alongside the Foundation, summed up the tough times in an article in LA's *Jewish Journal:* "It's a convergence of factors all at once: The government [California government, another source of funds] is unraveling, the economy is hurting our supporters, and now you have not only the decline on Wall Street but also this fraud. It's a perfect storm." He continued: "We are hopeful, but it is going to be a big challenge. We are focused in on raising the dollars we can just to keep existing operations going."

Taking the Fifth: The Fifth Avenue Synagogue

Back to New York, and this time to a synagogue instead of a foundation.

If you had to pick one physical place—besides Palm Springs and its country club—where you'd be sure to find extensive

Madoff damage, the Upper East Side's Fifth Avenue Synagogue might just be the place. According to a *New York Post* report, members lost some $2 billion in all. Elie Wiesel and businessman Ira Rennert—one of the top individual victims (see chapter 7), with a loss of about $200 million—are two of the most prominent members among a list of dozens of victims.

And little wonder—the synagogue's president is J. Ezra Merkin, the Jewish theologian and investment adviser who lost $1.8 billion through his hedge fund, Ascot Partners, while collecting some $40 million in fees. Madoff himself doesn't belong to the synagogue. Instead, it's likely that Merkin gave Madoff access to his victims (or gave the victims access to Madoff, as the case may be).

"Obviously, it's a black eye for the synagogue," one member told the *Post.* Indeed, it might be quite a while before things return to normal for the congregation's three hundred families.

Back to Gesundheit

Madoff dealt a body blow to a surprisingly large number of foundations, and in so doing, wreaked havoc on the plans, and even the existence, of hundreds of organizations and causes dependent on those foundations. So what's next for these organizations? Almost all are still assessing what's next, although some have already thrown in the towel and closed their doors. As seen, some, like the Robert I. Lappin Foundation, have put out an appeal for others to step up, contribute, and keep things going. But in the 2008–2009 economy, that's a tough sell.

Some nonprofits will get assistance from foundations they haven't previously solicited for funds. In late December 2008, an organization known as the Jewish Funders Network hosted a meeting with thirty-five large foundations, to figure out what

THE FUTURE: BACK TO THE *PUSHKES*?

The Bernard Madoff scandal may reshape Jewish philanthropy for some time to come. In fact, it may return it to a much older tradition of smaller gifts from more givers. On the *Jewish Daily Forward*'s Bintel Blog, former columnist Lucette Lagnado anticipates the decline of the Jewish mega-donor in favor of a more traditional, more "humble" form of philanthropy—wider collections of smaller checks, and *pushkes.*

Lagnado explains that in recent years, Jewish nonprofits have relied on "fewer—but larger—gifts," according to Jack Wertheimer of New York's Jewish Theological Seminary. United Jewish Communities, an organization that represents 157 Jewish federations across North America, has recorded a severe drop in donors over the past twenty years, even as the total amount raised has continued to grow.

Because of the Madoff scandal, Jewish philanthropy may once again need to go back to being a shared effort, rather than the province of a powerful few. Lagnado doesn't believe this would be a bad thing, extolling the virtues of the pushke—the collection box that used to be found in every Jewish home. Although she doesn't want to see Jewish charities unable to continue their good work, she does find herself "longing for the kind of more humble, more individual *tzedakah,* or personal charity, that took place before the rise of the uber-Jewish foundations and zillionaire philanthropists."

It's a story we're seeing a lot these days: "too big to fail" giving way to "smaller is better."

to do next to support nonprofits with funding cutoffs or reductions; to provide bridge loans; and to establish consulting services, including a "pro bono human resources group" for the smaller organizations.

In a *Boston Globe* interview, network president Mark Charendoff admitted that "there's no question there will be a shakeout. There are organizations we will see, within the next couple of months, close down, and others will merge, and others will be changed forever. . . . Just to be clear, we're not under any impression that we can solve or fix this."

So, charities will find help, look for white knights, merge where it makes sense, and close down where there's no other option. Most foundations haven't yet decided whether they're going to cut everyone back, or make selective cuts while still fulfilling some pledges 100 percent. They may honor current pledges but refrain from making new pledges for a few years, in order to rebuild assets. It won't be unlike what for-profit companies do during hard times. We're just not used to seeing it in the charity world, especially as a result of a community member's misdeeds.

"There They Go Again"

Bernard Madoff cheated a lot of people and a lot of organizations, and the majority of them were Jewish. That fact didn't seem to occur to—or restrain—those given to anti-Semitic feelings and rhetoric. The predictable result: a dramatic increase in anti-Semitic comments in blogs, on the air, and really, everywhere.

The Anti-Defamation League described it as the "brayings of bigots about 'the greed and corruption of the Jews.'" Blogs lit up with ugly comments like the following that appeared from "Adolf" on www.PalmBeachPost.com:

Just another jew money-changer thief. It's been happening for 3,000 years. Trust a Jew and this is what will happen. History has proven it over and over. Jews have only one god— money.

Ugh. Not surprisingly, there were worse examples, but they're not worth repeating. Most carried inflammatory remarks about Jews and money, or suggested that "only Jews could perpetrate such a fraud," or that "the Jews, once again, are stealing money to benefit Israel." According to Abraham H. Foxman, National Director of the Anti-Defamation League, the Madoff event, plus the financial collapse that preceded it, provided a perfect context for the "Jew haters" to take to the Internet, "where they can give voice to their hateful ideas without fear of repercussions."

Like the scandal itself, anti-Semitic sentiment centered itself on popular news sites and blogs in New York and Florida, but other outbreaks occurred on the comment-enabled parts of *Forbes, New York Magazine,* the *New York Post,* and Israel's *Haaretz* and the *Jerusalem Post,* among others.

A Jewish Reckoning

While the Madoff story cut a wide swath through philanthropic circles, affecting the financial and organizational resources that help to advance Jewish causes, it also had a profound impact on the Jewish psyche. It left many questioning what it truly meant to them—the fact that Madoff is Jewish—and what it meant that he was able to attack so many inside and outside the culture and faith, seemingly without compunction.

In a much milder echo of the Holocaust, it brought up the "how could it happen" question, leading some Jews to reevaluate their values, beliefs, and indeed, their very culture. The nuance is, of course, that the Holocaust was driven by forces quite external to Jewish faith and culture, while Jews saw Madoff as "one of us." Aside from being a public relations disaster of epic proportions for the Jewish community, the question remains: What steps should be taken next, as faithful and practicing Jews? What will the future hold for the Jewish community?

Much has been said, written, and done since the Madoff revelation. The following examples provide a flavor of Jewish sentiment.

"Where Did This Man Come From?"

The YIVO Institute for Jewish Research traces its origins to the Yiddish Scientific Institute, founded in 1925 in Lithuania. Today, the YIVO Institute is headquartered in New York, and describes itself as "dedicated to the history and culture of Ashkenazi Jewry and to its influence in the Americas. It is the world's preeminent resource center for East European Jewish Studies; Yiddish language, literature, and folklore; the Holocaust; and the American Jewish immigrant experience."

On January 15, 2009, the YIVO Institute held a panel discussion entitled "Madoff: A Jewish Reckoning." As the Institute put it: "The sheer magnitude of Bernard Madoff's crimes and his apparent preference for fleecing Jews and Jewish institutions have left many of his co-religionists wondering, 'Where did this man come from?' "

The five-person panel included a collection of scholars, businessmen, and philanthropists from the community: Mort Zuckerman; Simon Schama, a Columbia University professor and expert on the relationship between Jews and capitalism; Michael Walzer, a political philosopher specializing in the "practical application of Jewish ethics in a modern economy"; and two hedge-fund managers also involved in Jewish philanthropy.

According to an account of the event in the *New York Times*, "seventeen-degree weather, airport-style security and a mandatory coat-check queue longer than the Rockettes chorus line did not deter an overflow crowd. . . ."

Most interesting were Zuckerman's comments. He started off by objecting to the basic premise of the event—that "somehow Jews should have to account for a sociopath." He cited the fact that Kenneth Lay of Enron wasn't held to account as a "prominent Protestant energy fraudster," and that impeached Illinois governor Rod Blagojevich isn't referred to as a "prominent Serbian-American politician." Zuckerman added: "I don't accept this as a Jewish thing. . . .We should not have to account for this man."

Although some disagreed with this notion, most did acknowledge there would be some backlash against the Jewish community—it's just a question of how much and for how long. Another question is whether the central issue was the backlash, or preventing Jews from feeling a deeper sense of shame and insecurity. Walzer, the philosopher, said the shame "arose from a Jewish sense of responsibility for one another and a commitment to speak out against wrongdoing." He then advised the group to "pay attention to those feelings and let them grow."

Lessons Learned—Yeshiva

At New York's Yeshiva University, the syllabus for a graduate seminar in social philosophy was changed. Normally oriented to such typical topics as repentance and atonement, the subject matter was expanded to include Madoff. The debate, according to a *New York Times* story, centered on "whether Mr. Madoff's actions were sins, and whether it mattered that he was Jewish."

Students in the class shared their thoughts with *Times* reporter Javier Hernandez. Some said that "Mr. Madoff's religious affiliation was unimportant." Others felt that "his Judaism might tarnish their own," and that "outside eyes would not be able to see past the faith." Just like the YIVO panel—same debate, different place.

More widely, the Yeshiva student body fears "resentment" and a "revival of the ugly, old stereotypes; and after the fall of a favorite son, uncertainty about how Jewish institutions like theirs should choose role models," according to Hernandez's account.

Like many religiously affiliated schools, Yeshiva "aims to inculcate ethics and interpersonal morale in its students along with academics." The Madoff scandal "turned into a consummate teaching moment." Indeed, faculty member Rabbi Benjamin Blech stated that he was using the event as "an opportunity to convey to students that ritual alone is not the sole determinant of our Judaism, that it must be combined with humanity, with ethical behavior, with proper values, and most important of all, with regard to our relationship with other human beings."

And university president Richard Joel added: "We should use these times to reflect on our blessings but also reflect on our responsibilities . . . the times are appropriate for us to reflect on our core values, to practice and refine them, and to share them with the world."

Rabbi Blech also offered that Jewish students had been steering away from community service jobs like teaching and into more lucrative professions—translation, Wall Street. "In elevating to a level of demi-worship [of] people with big bucks, we have been destroying the values of a future generation . . . we need a total rethinking of who the heroes are, who the role models are, what we should be honoring."

A third-year law student echoed that thought: "One of our religious imperatives is to be morally upstanding, to be the exemplar of what it is to be a moral citizen, and this is a very

HOT SAUCE HUMOR

Jews, as much as any culture in history, are known for their ability to not only keep their sense of humor, but also to create it, even in the face of adversity. After this chapter's grim account of damage done to the Jewish community, perhaps a small dose of this sort of humor is in order.

So here, again from the *Jewish Daily Forward*'s Bintel Blog, is a culinary response to Bernie Madoff.

Toward the end of January 2009, Nathan Burstein posted the following announcement of a special new Madoff-related product. Burstein noted that although Madoff has been "bad for the Jews and catastrophic for American capitalism . . . perhaps [he] might make a good condiment."

Apparently, the world's most hated swindler has inspired a hot sauce, called Bernie in Hell. The five-ounce bottle of Habanero-style hot sauce can be ordered online for $10 per bottle. The label features a picture of Madoff—complete with horns and flames.

Alex Gardega, an artist in New York City, was moved to create the product after watching a television story about a seventy-five-year-old man who lost his entire retirement savings in Madoff's alleged Ponzi scheme. Visitors to Gardega's website (texasketchup .net) can write in to share their own stories of how the Madoff scandal has affected them—or they can buy a couple bottles of hot sauce.

Burstein notes that the label on the hot sauce bottle "challenge[s] consumers with a question Madoff himself might currently be pondering: 'You can take the money, but can you take the heat?!'"

If you buy five bottles, you'll get a sixth one for free—a better percentage return than what Madoff was promising before his arrest.

It's worth a try on your next cheese blintz.

public case of a failure of that religious ideal." Another instructor wanted the students to "look at and talk about and contextualize this," urging the students to "see themselves as future agents of change." The instructor added: "[W]e have to train them to reflect the morals of society in the most positive ways."

Rabbi Blech summed it up: "Just because you eat kosher and observe the Sabbath does not make you good . . . if you cheat and steal, you cannot claim you are a good Jew."

And so Yeshiva, one of the financial epicenters of the blast with its $110 million loss from Madoff and J. Ezra Merkin, tries to lead the way forward in moral and religious thinking for the Jewish community. Chapter 9 takes a wider look at the issue of trust and how the Madoff scandal destroyed it—and how the Madoff mind could have produced such an event in the first place.

CHAPTER 9

The Psychology of Trust

I can calculate the motions of heavenly bodies, but not the madness of people.

—Sir Isaac Newton

Why do people trust others with anything? It's a great question. People trust other people with their hearts. With their kids. With a couple thousand bucks for a used car. And, as we've now uncovered with great astonishment, with millions of dollars earmarked for their retirement or their favorite charitable cause.

Why did people trust Bernard Madoff to the degree they did? And what was going through Madoff's mind—how could he, and why did he, violate that trust? With the help of several experts on the subject of trust and criminal psychology, this chapter will attempt to shed some light on those questions.

Selling the Dream: How Did Victims Come to Trust Madoff?

Perhaps the best place to start unraveling the mystery is to try to understand why people might have been so accepting of Madoff's offering. Madoff seems to have brought people into his sphere of influence with the greatest of ease, and sold them on his prowess, no questions asked. How did he do that? He certainly operated in a world where slick salesmen would have generally failed.

So how did he do it? One way to look at it is through an examination of the standard sales cycle Madoff (or any professional money manager) might have employed to convince clients to buy his product.

Riding the Sales Cycle

The decision of whether to give someone something of value in exchange for something else has been studied intensely in the last half century by business academics and coaches. The process of hearing the facts and making the choice, or choices, is popularly known as the *sales cycle*. The presenter goes through the cycle, and then the audience makes the choice.

So now we come to Bernard Madoff. How did he get so many of the best, brightest, and wealthiest individuals around the world to bite on his scheme? The answer is more psychological than technical.

Ken Clark, a Little Rock, Arkansas, psychotherapist and certified financial planner, explains the so-called five-step selling cycle as it has been taught by everyone from Brian Tracy to Zig Ziglar. As will be shown, the Madoff approach relied heavily on the first two parts of the cycle, designed to establish trust in the salesperson. The belief in the product—in this case, Madoff's investment fund—hardly comes into question. And unlike most sales, particularly for big-ticket items, there were few objections and little remorse. How a typical car salesman would like to be in that position!

The Approach

The first two steps of the classic five-step cycle start out by establishing trust. The all-important first impression, known as "The Approach," is both an art and a science in selling circles. The Approach is how a salesperson gets in front of potential clients in the first place, and it can take many forms. In the case of a high-wealth investment manager, the first contact is more likely to come from an introduction from an influential friend, not a cold call or an invitation to free informational dinners. The goal is the same, however, whether you are selling ShamWows or stocks: to introduce yourself in a compelling way. Madoff's manner and exclusive word-of-mouth marketing was subtle, but oh so effective.

The Qualification

The second step is "The Qualification." It's where the potential client determines if the salesperson is a good fit. Does he have a verifiable track record? What are his values? Does he know what he is talking about? Ultimately, this is where the potential investor decides if he can trust this person.

Trusted referral endorsements can be a significant factor at this point. When nine people have invested and recommended a person, you, as the tenth, feel secure that you don't have to do as much due diligence as if you were considering investing with an unknown quantity. This kind of groupthink has been blamed for everything from pet rocks to the Holocaust.

More to the point, as a prominent Wall Street stock trader for decades, chairman of the NASDAQ Stock Market, frequent consultant for the SEC and other agencies, and a well-established member of the Jewish philanthropic community to boot—why *wouldn't* a potential investor trust Madoff?

The Positioning

Next comes a closer examination of the product or service. This is known as Positioning. How does the widget work? Does it fulfill my needs? Is it the best solution for me? Is the price fair? This step was almost nonexistent in a Madoff transaction. If anyone asked too many questions about his methods, that person was denied the opportunity to participate. A few inquisitive types, who could not get a clear picture of the Madoff "strategy" from what he disclosed, did not invest, but these were the exception, rather than the rule.

Overcoming the Objections
In a typical sales cycle, the next step is "Overcoming Objections." The tuned-in salesperson, by this time, has determined the customer's priorities and will be explaining the benefits and downplaying the negatives of what seems to be the best fit based on the first three steps. Again, this step was all but absent with Madoff; potential investors were plainly in awe of the man, and anyone who objected would have simply been turned away.

The Commitment
The final step in the classic selling relationship is asking for "Commitment." This is where the actual exchange of money and product occurs. Bernie jumped right to this step, bypassing the normal qualification process. He was able to do this because clients had already sold themselves on the idea of investing with Madoff, or they had been convinced by their friends. *They* approached *him,* begging to be let in; he would simply agree to do them a favor by taking their check.

Ego and the Fear of Being Left Out
By positioning his fund as an exclusive product, Madoff created a sense of scarcity. The call to action was a warning that the prospective millionaire may never see this particular opportunity again. Ken Clark compared the sense of urgency around investing in Madoff Securities to the frenzy of the tech bubble

in the late 1990s. "What drives people is fear, not greed; greed is simply a stepchild of fear," Clark said. "People were afraid of being left out of the club if they took too long to decide or asked too many questions."

Ego is also a great motivator. Madoff's victims were led to believe that they were special. Because they were insiders, they were privy to an exclusive opportunity. Who could resist joining any group that included media moguls like Steven Spielberg and consistent placeholders on *Forbes*'s wealthiest Americans list, like Mort Zuckerman? Heck, a Madoff investor would be one degree of separation away from actor Kevin Bacon and his lovely wife, Kyra Sedgwick—and we all know that the *Footloose* star is connected to everyone somehow.

Ignoring the Voice of Reason

Stephen Greenspan, author of *Annals of Gullibility: Why We Get Duped and How to Avoid It,* and a Madoff victim himself, pointed to four basic causes for getting caught in everything from an inheritance scam involving a Nigerian prince to the "irrational exuberance" of a tulip or technology bubble: situation, cognition, personality, and emotion.

- *Situation:* This refers to the social micro-context in which a decision is made—peer pressure, in other words. Peer pressure combines well with the magnetic pull of a market and the glorious notion of something new (again, tulips or tech stock). In this case, the prominence of Madoff, the social circles of Jewish wealth, the cutting-edge romance of hedge-fund investing, and the pull of the well-respected feeder funds and banks, all came together to make the scheme appear to be legitimate.

- *Cognition:* This refers to the lack of knowledge in key areas and the inability to make decisions about financial investing products, which leads investors to believe what the "experts" tell them.
- *Personality:* A person's personality or gullibility quotient refers to how likely that person is to naturally trust others. When that internal desire to say "yes" is paired with impulsiveness, then the odds of being gulled increase exponentially.
- *Emotions:* Many emotions come into play in any financial decision. Money is deeply connected to our sense of self-worth, right and wrong, family roles, and justice. An opportunity that links the promise of financial reward with acceptance into an exclusive club and the approval of a man thought to be smarter than God can no doubt make people act irrationally.

The Gates of Trust

Ira Wolfe, president of Pennsylvania-based Success Performance Solutions and author of *Understanding Business Values and Motivators,* explained Bernie's ability to undermine the judgment of sophisticated people who should have known better: He knew how to open the gates of trust. According to Wolfe, people use a "graduated gate" system to sort the trustworthy from the unworthy. Each "gate" represents a test which narrows the pool of applicants and acts as a sort of virus protection for our lives.

The first "gate" is pretty simple: Does the person in question *speak the same language?* It follows the old adage that we follow people we like and who are like us. That can mean believing in the same God or going to the same temple or church. A majority of Bernie's victims were people who led the same lifestyle or aspired to do so; they had the same lifestyle model. This is the idea behind the term affinity in *affinity fraud.*

A talented and truly charismatic individual can adjust his or her communication style to match the personality of whomever he or she is trying to persuade. That can mean being more businesslike with someone who likes to cut to the chase, or avoiding too much shop talk with a more gregarious person. It can mean talking sports with someone who likes sports, and so forth. Charisma doesn't have to be high-profile or in-your-face mannerisms like an Arnold Schwarzenegger. It can be quite subtle; a soft-spoken and mild-mannered person like Madoff can be considered charismatic as long as people identify with him.

Bernard Madoff clearly had a quiet confidence that made people feel at ease. With Ruth at his side, he built a reputation that was more alluring for being so understated. Recall New York hedge-fund adviser Charles Gradante's quote from chapter 4: "He wasn't the kind of guy that walked into the room and filled the room with his presence. If you had to pick one of the nicest guys on Wall Street—and there aren't too many— he would've been one of them. He was not a ruthless, tycoon type." Victim Joyce Greenberg recalled, "The man was very low-key. He was not a salesman."

A crafty person can fake their way through the first gate, so the next two gates become important to establishing and verifying trust. The second gateway to trust is *common knowledge, values, and expertise.* By serving on philanthropic boards, being a member of the right clubs, and serving high-profile clients, Madoff gave the appearance of having values that were similarly aligned with those of his clients.

The third and last gate is *performance*—whether the source being considered can deliver. This not only maintains trust, once established, but it also leads to referrals. The record of consistent market-beating returns—on paper, at least—gave the illusion that Bernie Madoff was trustworthy, and led lots of people who should have known better to open the door without asking questions.

Playing to the Physical Side

Most people think of financial decision making as a highly cerebral and deliberate activity with a dash of emotion added in. But there's evidence that very real physical and hormonal reactions to certain stimuli affect our investing practices, and, more generally, how much we trust people.

Dr. Paul J. Zak, founding director of the Center for Neuroeconomics Studies at Claremont Graduate University and author of *Moral Markets: The Critical Role of Values in the Economy* (Princeton University Press, 2008), posited that too many people rely on their ancient, instinctive brain to make financial decisions. He calls this the "lazy Republican" side of decision making because it is conservative and doesn't consume unnecessary energy to make decisions.

This instinctive part of the brain is motivated by neurotransmitters activated by the chemical dopamine. It is the same system that makes us smile when we smell a sizzling steak, see a cute guy or girl, or take methamphetamines. Madoff probably didn't know this, but the brain also releases oxytocin when we shake a hand or see a familiar face. These responses are primitive but highly automatic and strong.

Madoff seemed to hijack these systems through personal relationships and regular contact. Something as simple as going by the name "Bernie" instead of "Bernard" triggered primitive bonding mechanisms that led to blind faith, according to Dr. Zak. By taking advantage of friends and neighbors Bernie saw regularly, he got people to turn their analytical brains off and follow the hormonal trail of their instinctive brains, which in turn doped them into thinking he was trustworthy.

"These people were not yahoos," Zak concluded. "Madoff manipulated smart people using the methods of survival that have served people well for thousands of years."

Once Trust, Always Trust

Once trust has been established, it can cause people to rule out evidence to the contrary. One painfully obvious reason is that you would have to admit you were wrong! That reluctance to admit fault may be why some people overlooked red flags like consistent returns quarter after quarter, regardless of the market.

Christopher Bauer, author of *Better Ethics NOW: How To Avoid the Ethics Disaster You Never Saw Coming* (Aab-Hill Business Books, 2007), explained that most people are motivated by instinct and experience to avoid pain and increase comfort. When an activity goes on for a long time and the reward is consistent, that action becomes habitual. People become addicted to the reinforcement of positive financial statements. Likewise, in down markets, the same people refuse to open those statements!

This consistent return "habit" made it possible for what they once called a "confidence man" to pull off a scam incredible for its simplicity. If the allegations are true, Madoff was not much more sophisticated than a nickel-and-dime street swindler. He was not writing complex software or taking on new identities. He was simply moving money from his right pocket to his left and into someone else's hands while filling the pocket again with someone else's money, all the while using people's most basic emotional responses to shift their attention from his sleight of hand.

When Trust Collides with Reality

Like all addictions, the abrupt end to the steady supply of above-market returns left many experiencing painful withdrawal. Psychotherapist/CFP Ken Clark compared the process of dealing with the news that you had lost your life savings to Elisabeth Kübler-Ross's Five Stages of Grief, outlined in her 1969 book, *On Death and Dying*. Making a long story short, people deal with loss by going through five stages: denial, anger, bargaining, depression, and acceptance.

Clark argued that once people could no longer deny they had been cheated in an enormous and personal way, many placed themselves firmly in the anger camp, which was tempered only by embarrassment. They lashed out at the SEC for not uncovering the scheme sooner. They berated their fund manager, if they had one. And they berated themselves for not asking questions before it was too late.

Clark and Kübler-Ross are quick to point out that people don't go through the steps in any particular order, or stay in each one for any set length of time. They can repeat certain steps and skip others altogether. For many, the anger and bargaining steps overlapped, as days after the announcement of Madoff's arrest, a cottage lawsuit industry sprang up. Securities attorneys started special Madoff practice groups to sue Madoff, his company, his family, investment brokers, hedge funds, and former investors who divested before the plot was uncovered.

Sadly, in a tragedy of this magnitude, depression can set in quickly. Within a week of the scandal breaking, as described in earlier chapters, French financier René-Thierry Magon de la Villehuchet slit his wrists. The seventy-four-year-old had lost $1.4 billion of his own money, plus millions he had invested for friends and family. His suicide is probably consistent with the idea that, for some, good money management is a measure of their ability to make good decisions; if they make poor ones, it's a personal indictment on their character. Said another way, some may not be able to separate out their self-worth from their wealth. The reality of poverty can be hard to live with in some circles.

The final step, acceptance, comes with great difficulty and a lot of time when talking about such large sums of money. Fortunately, many victims didn't have all their net worth tied up in the Madoff scheme; they still have plenty left to maintain a comfortable lifestyle. But for others, it will take a considerable length of time to adjust, and many will stay at the anger phase for a while, fighting for what they can get in court. And others, victims of charities or the causes they support, will lose their jobs and eventually move on. Some support networks have been created to keep victims informed of legal developments and to offer help and consolation, but for the most part, Madoff victims have not been from a group of people who have spent much time with support groups.

A Question of Values

Harriet Rossetto, founder of Beit T'Shuvah, a Culver City rehabilitation center whose Hebrew name means "house of return and repentance," was circumspect about the loss of $3.6 million in endowments to the Ponzi scheme. "Maybe there is a big message here about redefining values," Rossetto was reported to have said. "Maybe Bernie Madoff is the messenger."

Clark noted that organizations, including the numerous nonprofits that lost considerable sums in the scheme, often take longer to get through the denial phase because so many people and meetings are involved in determining what happened. However, nonprofits also seem to find it easier to get to the acceptance phase, possibly because executives are not as personally invested as individuals. Also, blame can be passed around the group more easily. The bottom line is that unless they had to close, executives still believe in their group's mission and are focused on finding a way to continue to deliver value without the resources they thought they had.

The Criminal Mind

So much for how Madoff built trust with his victims and how those victims are dealing with the breaking of that trust. We know *how;* the obvious next question is *Why?* Why did he do it?

Madoff turned out to be a man who could stab his closest friends, burn his most strongly affiliated charities and service organizations, and even dupe and embarrass his own wife, yet somehow go on sleeping at night and carrying on his ordinary routine each day, surrounded by the trappings of wealth in his multiple mansions. He also appeared to have no pangs of guilt or conscience as he socialized with the very people he was cheating.

It's a hard nut to crack, so a number of experts were consulted to get a peek inside his mind. Several theories came forth, ranging from the more-trendy diagnoses of obsessive-compulsive disorder and narcissism to the more garden-variety failings of maliciousness and greed.

Here, to conclude this chapter, are some of the theories.

Was It Just about Hate?

Right off the bat, one psychiatrist put forth a fairly simply explanation. He identified Madoff as a sociopath with deep feelings
of self-hatred as a Jew, and a need to seek revenge against those
whom he despises and envies. Have we not heard this story
once before about a certain dictator of the Third Reich? It's a
bone-chilling possibility, particularly since Madoff didn't pos-
sess any of the outward signs of meanness or hatred so rampant
in the other man. His charitable contributions in the Jewish
community also tend not to support this theory.

. . . Or Was It about Self-Love?

Shmuel "Sam" Vaknin, an Israeli-born psychologist and financial analyst and author of *Malignant Self Love: Narcissism Revis-
ited* (Narcissus Publications, 2001), concluded that Madoff is
likely a psychopathic narcissist. Vaknin defined this personality disorder as a lifelong pattern of infatuation and obsession
with one's self, to the exclusion of all others. This unhealthy
extreme of narcissism—also known as megalomania—results
in the egoistic and ruthless pursuit of one's gratification, domi-
nance, and ambition.

Such narcissistic character traits, according to Vaknin,
include the exaggeration of accomplishments, talents, and
skills to the point of lying about them. The true narcissist
demands automatic and full compliance with his suggestions,
and priority treatment. Stories have been emerging about Madoff's obsession with perfection and cleanliness in his office: It's
been reported that he once derided an employee for spilling
some juice on the carpet, and then went to a closet to get a
replacement carpet square in front of the rest of the staff. Is
this evidence of his high expectations and requirement for
"full compliance?"

Vaknin's self-centric version of Madoff is also devoid of empathy. He is unable or unwilling to identify with, acknowledge, or accept the feelings or needs of others. In the narcissist's world, only the end result matters, regardless of the means used to achieve that end. They act on their malicious choice, even if it inflicts misery and pain on others, because it is expedient to do so. Lacking empathy, the narcissist is rarely remorseful. Because he feels entitled to do so, exploiting others is second nature.

The narcissist abuses others absentmindedly, even offhandedly. He objectifies people and treats them as expendable commodities to be discarded once his needs have been met. It is the mechanical, thoughtless, heartless face of narcissistic abuse—devoid of human passions and of familiar emotions—that renders it so alien, so frightful, and so repellent. Remember Madoff's cold lines—"There is no explanation" and "It is all a big lie"—delivered when he was arrested? His inability to acknowledge the impact of his crime on his victims is chilling but typical of this personality type.

With the psychopathic narcissist, ego can overcome ethics by causing seemingly sane people to obsess over the trappings of success in order to prove a point. For these intensely competitive people, many of whom work in the financial world and travel in the same circles as Madoff, too much is never enough.

SORRY, BUT FOR THE WRONG THINGS?

In fact, as a side note, Madoff hasn't apologized to anyone, formally or informally—except to the other residents in his Upper East Side building, expressing his regret for the inconvenience of continuous monitoring and press coverage.

The drive to accomplish, have, and do more than anyone else can be caused by the person's embarrassment over their race, or a perceived lack of proper lineage or education—all of which could have played a role in Bernie's case, as observed in chapter 2.

Taking this a bit further, a self-conscious man who felt embarrassed about his past could end up creating an omnipotent, invulnerable "False Self" as a defense mechanism to deflect the hurt felt by the "True Self." The narcissist often believes this fictional creation more than reality and refuses to admit the truth even to his closest family and friends. In the end, the constant vigilance required to maintain such an untenable facade can lead to desperate actions.

But is an obsessive ego enough to make someone steal millions from a charity? Perhaps—if that person with the delusional ego reasoned that he was smarter, savvier, and more ethical than everyone else. This "Robin Hood Syndrome" could have led Madoff to believe that his contributions to good causes were reason enough to rip off the wealthy. He was simply taking from the rich to give to justice, equality, human dignity, and tolerance causes. But how could this explain his take from Steven Spielberg's Wunderkinder Foundation, or any of the other well-intentioned investors who joined the scheme early on?

Unfortunately, this theory doesn't hold up either, given that he bilked so many millions in endowments from causes he himself purported to support.

Plain and Simple: A Mind Disorder?

Let's return for a moment to neuroeconomics expert Dr. Paul Zak and his theory about oxytocin and other hormones linking various stimuli to pleasurable responses. Zak suggests that the problem with Madoff may be physical. According to Zak, some people who suffer from a deep pathology linked to a trauma in early life or some other dysfunction may have a problem with oxytocin levels, called Oxytocin Deficit Disorder (ODD, as it is known in the business). This pathology, commonly found in sociopaths, would put the sufferer in constant survival mode, wiping out his ability to feel empathy. That inability to comprehend the damage he was inflicting on his friends and neighbors could explain the lack of guilt Madoff displayed after his scheme was uncovered. One wonders what this trauma or other dysfunction might have been, as there's certainly nothing in the official record.

Did It Simply Spin Out of Control?

Author Chris Bauer proposed that Madoff may not have been malicious at all. He may have simply gotten in over his head and found that he didn't know how to get out. Like many investors today, he may have simply turned his fortunes over to hope—hoping that a better day, a big market rally or some such, would arrive, while tending the fires with the Ponzi scheme in the meantime.

But as day after day passed without the arrival of that gravy train, it became increasingly challenging for Madoff to find new ways to stay alive. Life for him may have become a hamster wheel, speeding up and needing ever more money to keep it going. In Bauer's view, when the panic of falling off this spinning wheel becomes all-encompassing, it can become difficult to differentiate between right and wrong. The most important thing is just to keep that wheel spinning; you can worry about the consequences later.

A lot of what Madoff did has this feel—the pulling in of more and more money from more places, the final plea to

Carl Shapiro for $250 million, the stress and strain observed in these last days, the utter secrecy. When asked whether he feels that Madoff simply spun out of control in this manner, Bauer gives a terse reply: "We may never know."

The Thrill of the Chase?

CFP psychotherapist Ken Clark agrees that committing a crime can change the way the mind operates going forward. Once he's crossed that line, the criminal gets a sense of abandon, and part of that is feeling excitement over getting away with something, saying to himself, "Let's see if I can ride this out and enjoy it."

Like a compulsive gambler, and, consistent to a degree with the "spinning out of control" theory, Madoff may have felt a need to have just one or two more big hits to get even again. At some point, he might have numbed himself to the risk, not allowing himself to think of what could happen if that elusive payoff never came. In essence, he started to believe his own lie—that he knew something other people didn't know (perhaps his "proprietary" trading system?)—and that he was able to do what others could not: make money in a down economy without investing anything.

Someone in this situation lives in fear of being discovered. All of his actions are built around developing a counter case to offset what may come out someday, although we haven't yet seen that counter case. Behind that calm demeanor could have been a single-minded focus on covering his tracks.

Will the Real Madoff Please Stand Up?

Another theory is that the sweet, comforting smile that lured so many to their financial deaths was genuine. However, if so, it lived in the same body as a conniving thief. Some have suggested that a multiple personality disorder caused him to do things a normal person would never even conceive of, let alone consider and carry out.

Multiple Personality Disorder (MPD)—or Dissociative Identity Disorder as it is now known, can mean that a person perceives the world using as many as 100 distinct, disaggregated self states, and each one may not know what the other "state" did when it was up to bat. The disorder became popular after the broadcast of the 1976 television film, *Sybil.* Some 40,000 people were subsequently diagnosed with the disorder between 1985 and 1995. Although it sounds bad, it can get you off the hook from time to time. The MPD diagnosis in the trial of the "Zoo Man," who admitted to killing four women when in an alternate personality state, resulted in a hung jury.

Dr. Keith Ablow, a celebrity psychiatrist and high-profile expert witness, suggested that dementia or bipolar disorder may have caused Madoff to act erratically. Dementia, which is normally associated with a decline in memory due to aging, has been known to sporadically disorient younger people who suffer from diseases as diverse as Huntington's, vitamin B deficiency, or syphilis. It can also be a side effect of bipolar disorder, which has played a role in the lives of a number of repeat offenders. Technically, bipolar disorder (or manic depression) often takes the form of severe mood swings. It can also impair judgment.

This last theory doesn't seem to hold up given Madoff's placid demeanor—at least in public.

Going after a Bigger Fish: The SEC?

Was Bernard Madoff simply a greedy manipulator out to get rich and have his way with his clients—or is it more complex than that? There's an emerging school of thought that Bernard Madoff really had it in for the SEC, perhaps the biggest fish in the pond of victims.

As reported by the *New York Times,* several crime experts, including former FBI agent Gregg O. McCrary, suggest that Madoff had a psychopathic personality, and, like many criminals, thought he was "above the law," and in particular, could not be caught. Madoff's long-standing relationships with regulators and his subsequent immunity to their repeated investigations would have been a "heady, intoxicating" experience that may have fueled a "sense of entitlement and grandiosity."

McCrary added that "[I]t's not too far-fetched to compare Mr. Madoff to serial killers . . . they have control over the life or death of people . . . they're playing God." Sort of a financial God, really, asserting complete control by taking their money. This sense of godliness may have been extended through his control of the SEC. Perhaps Madoff was getting the SEC back for years of sticky compliance and annoying investigations. Maybe it was just for fun, or to achieve a sense of power and entitlement.

We may never find out.

How Crazy Is Insane?

If one doesn't accept that Madoff was a coolheaded and cunning criminal, perhaps his ability to cheat so many people—particularly well-intentioned charitable organizations—could be viewed as pure insanity. Fortunately, such a label would not translate to an insanity plea for any future court proceedings. Some have suggested that Madoff may reach back to the insanity defense established in ancient Greece and supported by King Edward II's proclamation that a person must have a mental capacity "greater than a Wild Beast" in order to stand trial. However, in the United States, justice requires that the insanity defense pertain to the state of the accused *at the time the crime was committed*. An attorney would have to prove that Madoff could not appreciate the nature of his actions during the decades in which he pulled off his crime.

While in the days following his arrest Madoff was exceptionally quiet, wore a creepy grin during his perp walks, and was prescribed a sedative, this probably doesn't reach the bar of "unfit to stand trial." And claiming a mental disorder would not be enough. He would also have to show that he was unable to make a rational decision. Psychotherapist Ken Clark finds it difficult to believe that a jury would buy any insanity defense that covered behavior exhibited over a period of decades.

And even if Madoff is determined to be found "not guilty by reason of insanity," that is not a get-out-of-jail-free ticket. He would then be committed to a psychiatric facility until it is determined that he is no longer a threat to himself or others. The investors who lost millions may have some suggestions for when that might be.

Regardless of the causes that led so many well-intentioned investors into this mess, and regardless of what happens to Bernard Madoff, there remains one important question: What will happen next? What will the Madoff legacy do to modify, enhance, or amend the investing world; its regulations and their enforcement; our approach; and the approach of professionals to investing itself?

That is the subject of the final chapter.

CHAPTER 10

The Madoff Legacy

I have never heard of an entity that could make money in all kinds of markets consistently, year in and year out. Yet we continue to believe that there will be one. It is, like much else in finance, a myth that will not die.

—*Ben Stein*

So what does the Madoff scandal mean? Financial scandals aren't all that uncommon, and most have a handful of victims and interesting news stories, but little else.

But some have a much larger impact than that. In recent years, the Enron and WorldCom scandals went far beyond victims and news stories to usher in a whole new era of financial regulation and caution. We got the Sarbanes-Oxley Act in 2002. That dramatically stepped up financial reporting accountability with a significant corporate price tag for compliance. We got more transparency, disclosure, and even-handed treatment from Wall Street analysts and firms. And those scandals drilled into individual investors' heads the fact that, no matter how good an investment idea looked, understanding the investment and not putting too many eggs in one basket were important.

Those two corporate scandals are behind us. But as the Madoff debacle unfolds, we have yet another securities fraud perpetrated on an unsuspecting public with dire and most newsworthy consequences. So once again we should expect to see some regulatory loopholes tightened, some Wall Street and financial industry reform, and some greater "due diligence" on the part of the investing public.

And this is all happening in a greater context of a public enormously weary of scandal, lying, cheating, greed—you name it. From the greed-driven, mortgage-driven financial crisis and the somewhat suspect Troubled Asset Relief Program bailout to Blagojevich, Eliot Spitzer, the U.S. automakers, the peanut butter in your sandwich—whom can you trust these days? How far should you trust them, and what should the government and others do to bake more trust into the system?

The natural questions are: *What* regulation? *How much* regulation? *What* Wall Street reform? *What* investor due diligence? Beyond the massive losses and the guilt and punishment eventually rung up for Madoff, Ezra Merkin, Frank DiPascali, and others, the answers to these questions will ultimately be the legacy of Bernard Madoff.

The Regulatory Legacy

Despite the best intentions and the millions upon millions spent to fund the FBI, CIA, and other agencies, and despite known clues to the plot, September 11, 2001, happened anyway. And despite the best intentions and the millions spent to fund the SEC, FINRA, and other agencies, along with known clues to the plot, Bernard Madoff happened anyway.

There's a pattern here. Assuming the SEC had the "best intentions"—and some are questioning the influence Madoff may have had over that agency—the SEC simply blew it. They didn't see the Madoff scandal even with its broad-daylight, almost elephant-in-the-room nature, revealed most vividly by the Harry Markopolos exposé.

Like the terrorist attacks and most other government failures of the sort, Congress is wasting no time taking a closer look.
Shortly after the Madoff arrest, U.S. Rep. Paul Kanjorski, chair of
the House Capital Markets Subcommittee, promised a congressional inquiry in early 2009. According to Kanjorski, "A rewrite
of U.S. regulations to prevent a relapse of the Madoff fiasco will
be high on the agenda of the new U.S. Congress."

And with that, the investigation gained steam.

The Debate: More Laws, Better Laws, More Enforcement?

It's an age-old debate: Are the laws sufficient to ensure justice?
Or are there cracks you can stick your fist through? Is it the
laws themselves, or their enforcement, or simply the fact that
the laws are out of date? The Madoff scandal just gave that old
debate a lot of new fuel.

Ronald Cass, former dean of the Boston University School
of Law, said the Madoff scandal "illustrates the limits of the law,
not the need for more of it." Were the laws themselves inad-
equate? The investment company and trading laws enforced
by the SEC are pretty complete and concise on issues of disclosure, producing accurate and complete financial statements,
and generally not misleading the public. But how far do they
extend into the largely unregulated hedge-fund world?

Securities attorney and SEC executive committee member Marc Morgenstern believes "early detection and effective
enforcement" would offer a better solution than "dramatic
new legislation." He suggests that fraud is more likely to be prevented by operational changes, like expanding enforcement
and creating better coordination between and within regulatory agencies, rather than by creating new laws.

Morgenstern also points to the eleven "branch" offices of
the SEC as a problem, as we saw to a degree with the handling

of Markopolos in Boston and New York. He thinks it should all be centralized. Morgenstern cautions against overreaction and political posturing. He uses Sarbanes-Oxley as an example of a law that was "passed in an emotional cauldron, while well-intentioned . . . [having] significant adverse consequences." He warns that the consequences tend to be borne by smaller, well-meaning enterprises, and "ultimately by investors."

Called onto the Senate Carpet

Like 9/11 and other national disasters, Congress got moving quickly, first with a House Financial Services Subcommittee inquiry on January 5, 2009, followed by a hearing in front of the Senate Banking Committee on January 27. In both hearings, the mood was tense and scolding; congressional leaders want answers. And both hearings took aim more at enforcement than the laws themselves. The SEC pointed to resource and process problems that hinder enforcement and allow frauds like Madoff to slip through the cracks.

Upon questioning, as reported by CBS News, SEC officials described their agency as "dedicated to preventing fraud, but overwhelmed by the sheer volume of investigations, with just 425 examiners tracking hundreds of thousands of tips every year." SEC director of enforcement Linda Thomsen added: "We simply do not have the resources to investigate them all."

Senate Banking Committee chairman Sen. Christopher Dodd (D–CT) has asked regulators for regular reports to the Committee on their progress to improve fraud detection. Thomsen said that the agency is committed to improving fraud detection, but "needs to improve its internal processes for pursuing cases." She also asked Congress for more enforcement resources.

Others were more graphic, including Sen. Charles Schumer (D–NY): "Madoff's fraud was so immense and obvious, and took place over such a long period of time, it is simply inexplicable how the SEC missed it. It's as if there was a giant elephant standing next to the SEC in a rather small room for 25 years, and the SEC never noticed the elephant or even the smell of peanuts on its breath."

Schumer does support expanding enforcement resources, funding 100 new enforcement staff members. He also suggested centralizing these resources—but in Wall Street, not in Washington.

However, not everyone agrees it's an issue of resources, process, or location; problems may run deeper than that. Said former SEC chief accountant Lynn Turner in a Bloomberg report: "The SEC is in worse shape today than the French army was after its defeat at Waterloo." But he cautions against replacing the SEC with another agency, which "would be to the detriment of investors." Congress did take away a feeling that problems were "deeper and more systemic" than previously thought, and still isn't calling for more regulation—just more effective regulators.

Where this will lead remains to be seen. What is clear is that new director Mary Schapiro has her work cut out for her.

The Wall Street Legacy

Apart from the obvious question of regulation and regulatory bodies being answered by Congress and the federal government, one also wonders what scars Bernard Madoff will leave on Wall Street—that is, the network of firms who make their living managing other people's money.

To say that Wall Street had a bad year in 2008 is, to be sure, a horrific understatement. Markets tanked, people lost money—but that's only where it starts. Big blue-chip firms like Bear Stearns, Lehman Brothers, and Merrill Lynch bit the dust, or nearly did so. Tens of thousands lost their jobs. A few scandals, as outlined in chapter 1, seeped into the media and public mind. Then, along comes the Madoff bombshell. One of the largest industries in America slipped into an abyss of opacity and mistrust.

Those who weren't hurt so much by the financial collapse and bad news itself were still caught in the maelstrom of bad publicity. If Wall Street needed to polish its image before Madoff, it needed a complete detailing and Simoniz job after Madoff.

For this chapter, Wall Street divides into two parts: funds and fund managers; and retail client money managers, brokers, and financial planners. Funds and fund managers divide further into unregulated funds—hedge funds—and their regulated counterparts—mutual funds and other regulated investment companies.

Hedge-Fund Futures

The $1.7 trillion hedge-fund industry, already besieged with poor returns (losses) and a handful of scandals, was already on the ropes, as described in chapter 5. Because of the "Wild Wild West" nature of hedge-fund investing, and the effects both on investors and markets (witness the 2008 oil price spike), many are calling for greater regulation of hedge funds. But it's tricky: With too much regulation, they would cease to be hedge funds.

There are two likely outcomes: First, even some light regulation would probably call for more transparency and disclosure, and a greater requirement for registration, both for funds and their advisers, may come with that. And beyond such mandates from Congress and the regulators, it's likely that natural forces will cause hedge funds to clean up their acts. Their investors will demand it, as the Madoff lesson clearly points to the hazards of secretive, "black box," "secret sauce" investment practices and how they're marketed to the public. In addition, realizing that the outsized hedge-fund returns *do* come with risk, thousands of investors worldwide are reevaluating and redeploying their investments, and hundreds of hedge funds will close as a result.

As 2009 unfolds, the congressional mandate on hedge funds is still a work in progress. In late January 2009, SEC commissioner Luis Aguilar asked Congress "to close the glaring loopholes in securities regulation" and give the agency authority to regulate hedge funds. Aguilar also recognizes difficulties with the split between the SEC and the Commodity Futures Trading Commission, another regulatory body covering favored hedge-fund investments. So he advocates combining the agencies. In the end, like many, Aguilar believes greater regulation would not only cut down on fraud but also reduce market turmoil. Finally, Mary Schapiro, the new SEC chair, has come out in favor of mandatory registration for hedge funds.

Another area likely to get some review is the "funds-of-funds" business—the fund companies like Fairfield Greenwich and Tremont that famously took investor money and simply passed it on to Madoff, collecting exorbitant fees along the way. No specific proposals have emerged as of late January, but greater requirements to disclose what they're doing with the money, and to do "due diligence" on the downstream funds, would be reasonable.

Whatever happens, investors will need better ways to separate the good guys from the bad, and to make informed decisions about their investments. Just exactly what form that takes—what combination of regulatory change and internal hedge-fund-industry change actually happens—remains to be seen.

A British Model?

The United States is far from the only place where the Madoff bomb exploded, and far from the only place where there's a public outcry for the investment industry to clean up its act. It turns out that hedge-fund concerns—and the regulatory reform needed to deal with them—got a head start in the UK. The Hedge Fund Standards Board (HFSB) was formed in January 2008, and is just implementing standards that might find a way into the U.S., too. As the UK *Telegraph* reports, HFSB's standards "stipulate that hedge funds should have separate processes for fund administration, valuation, custody and brokerage that are completely independent of the fund manager, something that Mr. Madoff's operation did not do." In light of the affair, HFSB is considering whether the standards should be tougher.

Interestingly, most in Britain seem to be in favor of the enhanced regulation. A poll indicated that "more than half of leading fund managers . . . said their industry should face more regulation." Some 71 percent were "resigned to governments extending regulation, and 60 percent thought more hedge-fund scandals "would emerge in the coming year."

Regulated Funds

Other than the pall cast over the investment business in general, it doesn't seem likely that the Madoff scandal will affect traditional regulated funds—that is, mutual funds and their counterparts—very much. In fact, there could be an uptick in business as "smart" dollars flee funds and look for more dependable investments.

The one area that continues to get scrutiny—more from investors than from regulatory agencies—is the fees charged by these firms for managing investments. Just how much is it worth to manage a portfolio for someone? In light of recent investment performance, some of the exorbitant fees exposed by the Madoff scandal, and reduced customer commitment to the markets in general, the comfortable ¾ to 1½ percent charged by most funds may decrease.

Retail Wall Street: A Public Relations Nightmare?

The public hasn't been happy with retail Wall Street for years, having endured the dot.bomb crash, fueled and pumped by Henry Blodget and scores of other Wall Street analysts. The public has also endured sales schemes and minor investing scandals, high fees, bad investments, commercials that make investing look like child's play, and now the destruction of many a nest egg by the latest "unforeseen" market downturn.

Now, we have Madoff.

And so the question becomes one of trust. Can you trust your financial adviser, who may be part of this mess? Who, if less than thorough, could have just dumped your money into Madoff's fund? Like most other professions, the vast majority of participants are honest and diligent—it just takes a few bad apples to poison the entire barrel.

But the Madoff apple is so poisonous that, as recounted in chapter 7, 86 percent of financial advisers polled suggest that they would like their industry trade groups to "project a more positive image of advisers." As reported by *InvestmentNews,* "[I]t is important for all financial services industry associations"—like the Financial Planning Association (FPA), the National Association of Personal Financial Advisors (NAPFA), FINRA, and others—"to partner in creating a national ad campaign to help educate consumers and gain [back] their confidence."

So far in 2009, such campaigns haven't come forth; in fact, the FPA sees it as "more of a public relations problem for the SEC" than for financial planners. FPA executive director Marvin Tuttle expressed a rather confident view: "The Madoff scandal raises awareness of the differences between true financial

---

DID THEY SMELL A RAT?

Due diligence, did they know something, or was it just plain luck? That remains to be seen, too, as reports arrive showing that big Wall Street firms pulled money out of Madoff accounts before the scandal broke. Merrill Lynch, J.P. Morgan Chase, and Morgan Stanley all reportedly steered clients away, and Morgan withdrew some $250 million in mid-2008, "after a mid-year review of its hedge fund risks."

That said, three top executives at Merrill Lynch did not do their own due diligence, and it cost them an undisclosed sum as they lost part of their investments through another hedge-fund family known as Spring Mountain Capital LP. Spring Mountain, run by another former Merrill guy, had some Madoff investments, and is planning to close down in the wake of the scandal and client redemptions.

But not all the news is bad. Two firms—J.P. Morgan Chase and The Bank of New York Mellon—sent $535 million to the trustee liquidating the Madoff firm, as they found assets to be returned to defrauded investors per stipulation of the Securities Investor Protection Act (SIPA). As more firms "come clean" this way, there may yet be some recovery in store for Madoff victims.

---

planners and those who use the term without proper credentials, intent or ethics."

That may be true, and it may be that more individual investors may see the need for professional financial help, and decide to bring their assets to be managed in a "flight to safety" movement. The final impact on the retail financial industry remains to be seen.

The Legacy for Individual Investors

Finally, we get to what you, as an individual investor, as custodian and steward of your own nest egg, as "CFO" of your finances, should learn and do in the wake of Madoff. The big thing, of course, is to avoid such a calamity yourself. Despite the scandal and the public-image problem it created, Wall Street is still a solid place to put your money. But the scandal certainly reinforced the notion that there *are* risks—and you have to know what you're doing.

The Madoff scandal should not convince anyone that investing is a bad idea. It simply sends a clear signal to do it wisely. And "do it wisely" means two things: First, be careful what you invest in; and second, be careful who you invest it with.

Choosing and Managing Your Financial Adviser

Financial advisers come in many colors and stripes and do everything from giving you advice to managing your money 100 percent, giving only month-end and year-end statements showing you what you have and whether or not you gained or lost money in the most recent period.

As a client, you have choices as to what kind of adviser to use. And if they manage money for you, you have a duty and a responsibility to know where it is, and what they're doing with it. The Madoff debacle serves as a clear reminder of what can happen when people, for whatever reason, choose to throw their money management responsibility "over the wall" to someone else.

The two best and most obvious pieces of advice are: (1) know what your adviser is doing; and (2) make sure you're getting the value you pay for. These two, of course, are related.

Following are three logical "checks" to use to protect yourself, based on advice published by NAPFA shortly after the scandal broke:

1. *Know where your money is.* Whether the adviser manages 100 percent on your behalf, or whether you make the decisions, know where your money is held. Bernard Madoff made the decisions, did the administration, and held the money all in one mysterious seventeenth-floor operation that investigators are still trying to sort out. Your money should be administered and held by a third-party administrator or "custodian," with trades cleared through that firm, and that firm's identity should show on your financial statements, with contact information and account numbers. If that's not obviously the case, it makes sense to ask what's going on. Transparency is important.

2. *Read monthly or quarterly financial statements.* The custodian firm, typically a retail broker, bank, or trust company, must provide at least quarterly financial statements; most will provide them monthly. Those reports should come directly from the custodian firm—not the adviser.

3. *Stay in contact with your adviser.* You should have at least some personal contact with your adviser, with at least an annual in-person visit. Regular phone calls or e-mails will help. Watch for vague or evasive or techno-speak answers;

if you don't understand what they're saying, get them to clarify. Remember—you're the client, and you're still in charge. If the adviser seems to be taking charge of your investments without clarity and without your consent, it may be time to find another adviser. Says Diahann W. Lassus, CFP and national chair of NAPFA: "It's your money, so you need to stay involved."

4. *Remember "fiduciary responsibility."* Qualified advisers take an oath that they will put client needs first (over their own need to generate sales commissions, for instance). If you see any signs that they aren't acting in your best interests, it's time to reevaluate. Remember that many "advisers," especially stockbrokers, put their primary fiduciary obligation with their employers, not their clients. Ask about NAPFA or FPA membership, and ask if they've taken a fiduciary oath.

5. *Understand their track record.* It's important to know what an adviser has done for other clients, and how they've done it. They won't give names, but they should be able to in some way show concrete examples of how they've managed money for other clients. If they use anything other than traditional stocks, bonds, and mutual funds traded on major exchanges, they should be able to tell you about those off-market investments in clear detail.

Lessons for the Individual Investor

Guys like Madoff are smart, savvy, and experienced at bucking the system. So, finally, how can you, as an individual investor, avoid a Madoff event? You're busy, and you simply can't check out everything. So here are a few final words of wisdom to avoid becoming part of such a titanic financial news story:

1. *Do the smell test.* If an investment just doesn't seem right, or isn't understandable, or is too good to be true, take the time to check under the hood. As we saw with Madoff, blindness can happen in plain sight—unknown auditors or administrators, unrealistically high returns, unrealistically consistent returns. If your friend tells you he shoots an 82, an 83, or an 84 every time he plays golf, would you believe that, without seeing it? If it seems too good to be true, it probably is.

2. *Know that high returns mean high risk.* Nobody can give you above-market returns—for long—without taking some commensurate risks. If there really was a high-return, low-risk investment available to you, a member of the general public, then others would know about it too, and they'd be flocking to it and driving up the price. Lead is lead, and gold is gold, and not even the smoothest marketing pitch can turn one into the other.

3. *Know your middlemen.* The financial services industry is complicated, and there are a lot of players looking to take a few crumbs—a percent or two, a dollar or two—here and there from your investments. Take responsibility for finding out what they do, how much they charge for it, and whether the value-add is worth the charge. Shop carefully—like you would for a new car, a new house, or any other big-ticket item. This is your financial life.

4. *Diversify.* The Madoff scheme looked so attractive that an amazing number of smart individuals simply tossed everything over the wall to him. We all know what happened. Even if an asset seems irresistibly attractive, it shouldn't comprise more than 10 or 20 percent of your investable wealth—even if there is diversification within the asset, i.e.,

a fund. There is just too much at stake, and as we've discovered, disaster can come from unexpected directions.

As we move on from the Madoff nightmare, it helps, just as in any disaster event, to understand what happened, to learn the lessons, and move on. Investors should keep an eye on the revelations in the Madoff case and what comes forward in the form of new rules, new enforcement, and other changes in the investing climate. Some individuals will be able to pick up the pieces and move on; others will hide under the bed at the sound of thunder for fear of another tornado—at least for a while. We can only hope that in the end—fingers crossed—the Madoff scandal ultimately leads to a better financial and investing world for all of us.

Epilogue

There is no doubt that the story of Bernard L. Madoff—and the legacy—will continue to evolve for years to come. And no doubt, even more surprises will come to the surface.

As the investigation proceeds, Madoff's victims and his methods will continue to make headlines. The legal challenges will go on for years. They will go beyond the resolution of the federal criminal and bankruptcy cases and into hundreds of cases against intermediaries and others who, through deed or neglect, steered clients toward financial oblivion. A revamping of regulation and regulatory enforcement will almost surely result. Less clear, but also on the table, is Wall Street's voluntary response to the matter. But it's reasonable to expect some real climate change—not just a change in the weather—in Washington and on Wall Street.

As this treatment of the Madoff matter comes to an end, three new headline developments serve as a fitting close.

"It Took Me About Five Minutes to Figure Out He Was a Fraud"

On February 4, 2009, Harry Markopolos finally got his chance. He got the visibility so long deserved in the form of a hearing of the House Financial Services subcommittee led by Paul E. Kanjorski (D-Pa).

And not surprisingly, he made the best of his chance. He took off his gloves with the SEC, and warned of more to come, in a well-prepared testimony of some sixty pages.

Well, actually, he put on his gloves, too. Markopolos describes his own fear and trepidation in the matter. He was one guy, assembling "damning evidence" against a powerful guy whom he believed to be a "mobster," with "close ties to organized crime including the Russian mafia and Latin American drug cartels." He feared for his own safety and that of his family. "If he knew my name, I didn't think I was long for this world," he told the subcommittee. To avoid leaving fingerprints, Harry Markopolos wore gloves as he put together his Madoff dossier.

Then, about the SEC, Markopolos said:

- The SEC "roars like a lion and bites like a flea" and "is busy protecting the big financial predators from investors."
- "I gift-wrapped and delivered the largest Ponzi scheme in history to them, and somehow they couldn't be bothered to conduct a thorough and proper investigation because they were too busy on matters of higher priority."
- "It is both a captive regulator and a failed regulator . . . captive to the industry it regulates and afraid" to bring big cases against prominent individuals.

Echoing sentiments expressed by others, Markopolos stated his belief that the SEC is intimidated by the big guys and spends disproportionate amounts of time and money chasing down compliance issues with smaller securities operators. He also questioned the experience and maturity of SEC investigators: "the people who are coming to the SEC are too young" and the agency should look to hire "old foxes." He also suggested, as others have, a central office to handle whistle-blower complaints (instead of the current regional offices) and that the SEC replace its senior staff.

In a somewhat bland response, falling far short of a Madoff mea culpa, the head of the SEC inspections office said the agency has hired many former traders to boost the expertise of its examination staff, that ". . . in the last four or five years, it's a much better situation in terms of the caliber and the experience of the investigation staff."

Markopolos also warned of more problems to surface with feeder funds: "There are twelve more out there lying low in the weeds in Europe that you have not heard of yet."

The prepared testimony can be found in its entirety at: http://online.wsj.com/public/resources/documents/Markopolos Testimony20090203.pdf.

Madoff's List

During the same week in early February that Markopolos testified in front of the House subcommittee, the New York bankruptcy court made the Bernard L. Madoff Securities client list public.

And what a list! Some 162 pages, eighty-four client entries per page. That would be over 13,000 clients! But not all of the entries represent unique clients—some are apparently multiple entries for multiple family accounts, family trusts, and so forth. Oddly, the list, submitted as a PDF file, was sorted in alphabetical order by *first* name, and there was no mention of account numbers or size of the accounts.

According to one analysis, the actual number was 11,374 clients in forty-four states and forty countries, with most concentrated in the New York and Florida area.

There were a few more famous names on the list: Sandy Koufax, World Trade Center developer Larry Silverstein, and about twenty players and personnel from the New York Mets baseball team. It also confirmed most of the names. More striking were the large numbers of ordinary folks nobody had ever heard of.

The list may include a few who had an account or a relationship but didn't invest or lose money. Apparently, or at least so claimed, Madoff's attorney Ira Sorkin is one of them; he claims not to have invested with Madoff and not to know why his name is on the list. The list does not include those who came to Madoff through feeder funds. So we still don't have a clear view of how many people actually lost money, nor how much they lost, and we apparently won't for some time.

The size and scale of this list makes it even more of a mystery as to how Madoff administered this fraud supposedly by himself. We may learn more about that as investigators sift through the 7,000 boxes of records recently found stored in a Queens warehouse.

The more we know, the more we don't know.

The list can be found in many places, including: http://online.wsj.com/public/resources/documents/ madoffclientlist020409.pdf.

Warning: before opening this file, make sure to have a pair of reading glasses handy.

Schapiro Speaks Out

A day after the "official" Madoff victims' list went public, Mary Schapiro, the new SEC chair, went public, too. In her first speech since assuming the title, she announced a crackdown on fraud and promised several enforcement changes, including speedier inquiries and tougher settlements.

Among the changes was the dismantling of an old Christopher Cox program requiring all five commissioners to agree and approve actions, including subpoenas and corporate penalties. She also announced the formation of an advisory group of investors, and says the agency is looking for improved ways to handle tips, like the rather large and loud one that would have implicated Madoff.

Other topics addressed, and long overdue for review: improved audits (no more three-person accounting shops) and separation of investing and custodial (administrative) activities. She also revealed efforts to fill key managerial vacancies—the head of the New York office, the head of the corporation-finance division, and Chief Accountant—as well as strengthen the leadership in the Enforcement division.

"A strong and reinvigorated SEC will be on the beat like never before to catch wrongdoers," Ms. Schapiro said.

What that ultimately means remains to be seen.

FINALLY, MR. MARKOPOLOS'S LETTER

For his right-on prophecy of the Madoff scandal, Harry Markopolos has become a legend of the time. As with other legends of their time—Abraham Lincoln comes to mind—much can be learned by examining the detail and thought process evident in their writings. In that spirit, for those of you who have the time and stomach for detail, the famous letter "The World's Largest Hedge Fund is a Fraud" is an excellent read, and can be found in its full girth at: http://online.wsj.com/documents/madoff_SECdocs_20081217.pdf.

As Lincoln himself said at Gettysburg, "It is rather for us to be here dedicated to the great task remaining before us." In this case, that "task" would be to use lessons learned from the Madoff scandal to bring about a Wall Street and a regulatory foundation more of an "of the people, by the people and for the people" character. Let's all hope the Markopolos letter finally lights the way to make that happen.

Bernard L. Madoff Investment Securities Company Profile

Following is how Bernard Madoff Investment Securities LLC describes its own business, from an archive of its website, www .madoff.com, captured from 2005. Source: archive.org's "Way-back Machine."

Note especially the last section: "The Owner's Name Is on the Door."

A Global Leader in Trading US Equities

Bernard L. Madoff Investment Securities LLC is a leading international market maker. The firm has been providing quality executions for broker-dealers, banks, and financial institutions since its inception in 1960. During this time, Madoff has compiled an uninterrupted record of growth, which has enabled us to continually build our financial resources. With more than $500 million in firm capital, Madoff currently ranks among the top 1% of US Securities firms. Our sophisticated proprietary automation and unparalleled client service delivers an enhanced execution that is virtually unmatched in our industry.

Madoff Securities' clients include scores of leading securities firms, banks and financial institutions from across the United States and around the world. The firm is a leading market-maker in all of the S&P 500 stocks as well as over 350 NASDAQ issues. The firm is known for its fine pricing as well as its ability to execute most orders in seconds.

Madoff Securities' superior service is made possible by a sophisticated dealing staff backed by the securities industry's most advanced technology. It is underpinned by the personal commitment of founder Bernard L. Madoff and his brother Peter B. Madoff, who is the senior managing director. Their dedication to providing quality executions has enabled the firm to become a leader in the US "third market," which trades US listed equities away from the exchange floor. Madoff Securities is a registered US broker/dealer regulated by the Securities and Exchange Commission and the National Association of Securities Dealers.

An Intricate Interweaving of Advanced Technology and Sophisticated Traders

One of the critical ingredients in creating the added value which Madoff Securities offers its clients is the firm's intricate interweaving of advanced technology and experienced traders. The firm's position at the forefront of computerized trading is widely acknowledged in the US financial community.

Madoff Securities' leading edge information processing technology means clients can choose to communicate their buy and sell orders to the firm's trading room by electronically inputting them or by making a telephone call. In either case, once an order is received, Madoff's systems scan prevailing prices in all markets to establish an execution price. Because this process may take only seconds, clients can receive immediate confirmation of their transactions.

Sophisticated computers are integral to every aspect of the firm's activities, from executing trades to clearing and settling them, from monitoring prices to identifying trading opportunities around the world.

Madoff Securities also utilizes its computers to seek out opportunities for hedging its inventory of securities. The firm uses a variety of futures, options, and other instruments to hedge its positions and limit its risks. While these hedging strategies are an important tool in protecting the firm's financial position, ultimately, these highly prudent risk management policies protect the interests of clients as well.

At Madoff Securities, Clearing and Settlement Are Rooted in Advanced Technology

The combination of quality and value that is inherent in every Madoff Securities transaction continues beyond execution. At Madoff, the clearing and settlement process is also rooted in advanced technology, which minimizes errors and maximizes efficient processing and rapid communications.

Madoff Securities is a full clearing firm and a member of all US clearing corporations and depositories. The firm's highly automated clearing and settlement systems interface with the Depository Trust Company, the Options Clearing Corporation, and the National Securities Clearing Corporation, of which Bernard Madoff is a past chairman. The firm's systems also interface fully with the systems of all major global custodians and clearing & Settlement systems.

Madoff Securities' extensive network of relationships with other broker/dealers enables the firm to ensure timely delivery and settlement of all client transactions.

Moreover, Madoff Securities' computerized transaction processing means that the firm can customize client reports and deliver them electronically in whatever format best meets the needs of clients.

Important Information about Procedures for Opening a New Account

To help the government fight the funding of terrorism and money laundering activities, Federal law requires all financial institutions to obtain, verify, and record information that identifies each person who opens an account.

What this means for you: When you open an account, we will ask for your name, address, date of birth and other information that will allow us to identify you. We may also ask to see your driver's license or other identifying documents.

Sophisticated Disaster Recovery Facilities, Reflects the Attention to Every Detail

Madoff Securities has one of the most sophisticated disaster recovery facilities found anywhere in the securities industry. In addition to its offices in Manhattan, Madoff Securities maintains a fully equipped and staffed facility located near LaGuardia Airport. This office duplicates all of the features of the primary Madoff Securities offices. Madoff Securities' disaster recovery facility is not just an alternative trading room, but rather a full-fledged office which is equipped to receive and transact orders and to handle the clearing and settlement process as well.

Under the supervision of a facilities manager, this unique on-line facility is tested continuously to ensure that it is prepared to take over the firm's operations if any kind of disaster were to affect the Manhattan office. Members of the firm's staff are rotated through the facility and regularly perform their work from it. Thus, there is always staff on hand in case disaster strikes at the firm's main office.

The disaster recovery facility is on a different electric power grid than the main office, and it is served by a different telephone central office. The facility also has its own electrical generator.

Since this facility was created in 1992, it has been used as an adjunct to Madoff Securities' main office, and it has not been confronted with a major emergency. But the existence of this facility testifies to the high priority the firm places on being available to meet the needs of its clients under all conditions.

The Owner's Name Is on the Door

In an era of faceless organizations owned by other equally faceless organizations, Bernard L. Madoff Investment Securities LLC harks back to an earlier era in the financial world: The owner's name is on the door. Clients know that Bernard Madoff has a personal interest in maintaining the unblemished record of value, fair-dealing, and high ethical standards that has always been the firm's hallmark.

Bernard L. Madoff founded the investment firm that bears his name in 1960, soon after leaving law school. His brother, Peter B. Madoff, graduated from law school and joined the firm in 1970. While building the firm into a significant force in the securities industry, they have both been deeply involved in leading the dramatic transformation that has been underway in US securities trading.

Bernard L. Madoff has been a major figure in the National Association of Securities Dealers (NASD), the major self-regulatory organization for US broker/dealer firms. The firm was one of the five broker/dealers most closely involved in developing the NASDAQ Stock Market. He has been chairman of the board of directors of the NASDAQ Stock Market as well as a member of the board of governors of the NASD and a member of numerous NASD committees.

One major US financial publication lauded Bernard Madoff for his role in "helping to make NASDAQ a faster, fairer, more efficient and more international system." He has also served as a member of the board of directors of the Securities Industry Association.

Reflecting the growing international involvement of the firm, when Madoff Securities opened a London office in 1983, it would become one of the first US members of the London Stock Exchange. Bernard Madoff was also a founding member of the board of directors of the International Securities Clearing Corporation in London.

Peter B. Madoff has also been deeply involved in the NASD and other financial services regulatory organizations. He has served as vice chairman of the NASD, a member of its board of governors, and chairman of its New York region. He also has been actively involved in the NASDAQ Stock Market as a member of its board of governors and its executive committee and as chairman of its trading committee. He also has been president of the Security Traders Association of New York. He is a member of the board of directors of the Depository Trust and Clearing Corp. He is a member of the board of the Securities Industry Association.

Bernard and Peter Madoff have both played instrumental roles in the development of the fully computerized Cincinnati Stock Exchange. Peter Madoff has been a member of its board of governors and has served on its executive committee. They have helped make the Cincinnati Exchange the fastest growing regional stock exchange in the United States.

These positions of leadership not only indicate the deep interest Madoff Securities has shown in its industry, they also reflect the respect the firm and its management have achieved in the financial community.

Bernard Madoff Investment Securities Order Handling and Execution

Following are excerpts from the trading (broker/dealer) side of Bernard Madoff Investment Securities' website, 2005, a discussion of order handling and execution. This content gives a glimpse of the primary broker/dealer business of BMIS and the transparent description of its activities, a clear contrast to the opacity of its investment management business.

Site: www.madoff.com

Source: "Wayback Machine," www.archive.org.

Madoff's Guide to Order Handling—Nasdaq Securities

Introduction

A Primer for Execution Quality

Bernard L. Madoff Investment Securities LLC has been providing quality executions for broker-dealers, banks, and financial institutions since the firm's inception in 1960. During this time, Madoff has compiled an uninterrupted record of growth, which has enabled us to continually build financial resources. With more than $500 million in firm capital, Madoff currently ranks among the top 1% of U.S. Securities firms. Our sophisticated proprietary automation and unparalleled client service delivers an enhanced execution that is virtually unmatched in our industry.

The hallmarks of our system are price improvement, speed, and enhanced liquidity delivered with a level of client service that sets us apart from our competitors. Madoff utilizes a market based, algorithmic approach to defining price improvement and enhanced liquidity.

Discussions with many of our clients have brought to light several key concerns with the decimal-pricing environment: The difficulty of defining "meaningful" price improvement when stocks trade in pennies, the possibility of significantly reduced liquidity at the quoted national best bid/offer (NBBO), and the prospect of an increased number of "split tickets" or multiple-piece fills even on their smaller sized orders. We have designed our system to address all of these concerns.

To help you fully understand the services we offer, we have developed this guide to illustrate how our execution system works. The cornerstones of a quality execution—Price, Liquidity, Speed, and Limit Order Protection—are highlighted below.

Price

Market Order Price Improvement

Madoff has been a market innovator in providing quality executions for its clients. Our clients can confidently state that their clients' orders will have one of the highest rates of price improvement available in the industry today. In addition, we also offer an on-line audit trail documentation system. This will provide you with additional information to assist you in your obligation under the SEC's Order Handling Rules to ". . . regularly and rigorously examine execution quality likely to be obtained from different markets or market makers trading a security."

Automatic Price Improvement for All Nasdaq Securities

Madoff provides automated price improvement opportunities for all Nasdaq securities in which we make a market. Our systems automatically price improve all eligible market and marketable limit orders by 20% of the NBBO spread. Eligible orders will include immediately executable market and marketable limit orders that are greater than 99 shares and are within the liquidity threshold for that stock where the NBBO is greater then two cents ($0.02). The amount of improvement will be based on the NBBO spread at the time we receive your order and will be rounded to the nearest penny. The improvement will be no less than a penny per share. Orders larger than the liquidity guarantee will not be eligible for automatic price improvement.

Liquidity

Madoff's Enhanced Liquidity

Madoff offers immediate liquidity for eligible orders under normal market conditions at the displayed price available in the marketplace as defined by the national best bid and offer (NBBO) at the time of receipt of your order and enhanced by our price improvement mechanisms. In Nasdaq securities, immediately executable market and marketable limit orders up to 2,000 shares will be automatically executed in their entirety immediately upon receipt regardless of the size at the NBBO. Orders from 2,000 up to 10,000 shares will receive an automated execution that is based on a predetermined combination of Madoff's own capital and use of our smart router to efficiently access multiple points of liquidity. Orders 10,000 shares and greater will be handled manually. In certain less liquid securities, the guarantee for automatic execution may be less than 1,999 shares, at management's discretion. During periods of unusual market conditions, we reserve the right to adjust our execution parameters to appropriate levels. During periods when the NBBO is locked or crossed, our liquidity guarantee is reduced automatically. Madoff's liquidity guarantee is intended for regular and continuous, two-sided, non-momentum based business. Orders that do not meet this description may be subject to lower liquidity guarantees. In addition, our liquidity guarantee is intended to cover individual orders. Multiple orders that are the result of a single investment decision may be treated as a single order to the extent that the aggregate size of these orders exceeds our guaranteed liquidity threshold. Madoff reserves the right to adjust liquidity guarantees on a client by client basis.

Speed

Automation Delivers Faster Executions

By incorporating an algorithmic approach to defining price improvement, Madoff is able to reduce overall execution speeds for market and marketable limit orders. Madoff's clients do not sacrifice speed in their efforts to achieve a quality execution.

Limit Order Exposure

Superior Limit Order Handling

Madoff offers its clients superior limit order protection. The SEC has mandated that all market centers and their participants reflect their clients' interest in their quote. Our automated systems automatically execute or display all held limit orders less than block size (10,000 shares or $200,000) that are priced equal to or better than Madoff's quote or that will add to the size associated with such quote unless an express request is made by our client not to display the order. Our systems also guarantee client limit orders priority over any Madoff proprietary trader interest, in compliance with our Manning obligations. As a result, many of your clients' limit orders will be executed with greater speed by our system than by our competitors. This occurs not only because your order is exposed in the Intermarket Trading System (ITS) and NASDAQ quotes where it can interact with other NMS interest, but also because your order will interact with our other clients' orders if there is a matching interest or activity at the limit price.

SPECIAL SITUATIONS

Under certain circumstances orders will be subjected to automated or manual verification. This may be done through the use of orders sent to other market centers. An example of when this may happen would be locked and crossed markets, actively moving markets, and widely spread markets. In addition, orders may be subjected to clarification of the terms of the order (i.e. limit price, special instructions, etc.). In these instances the price at execution time may be different (favorable or unfavorable) from the price at receipt time. Madoff also employs the following policies for special situations:

SEC ORDER HANDLING RULES

Madoff's systems and its procedures are designed to search out and provide a quality execution for all its clients' orders. Madoff considers a quality execution to include opportunities for price improvement beyond the inside quote (National Best Bid and Offer). Madoff employs its own proprietary automation, the Madoff Integrated Support System (MISS), when seeking a quality execution. MISS considers all quotation information from National Market System (NMS) participants as well as readily accessible quotation information from qualified electronic communication networks (ECNs) that may be disseminated in the NMS.

Madoff's automated systems have been designed and are continually enhanced to automatically provide the highest level of regulatory compliance and execution quality available. While Madoff's automation provides a level of quality and consistency that would not otherwise be available in a manual environment, Madoff's employees remain the cornerstone of our execution service.

Senior management, as well as trading, systems, and operations personnel are all aware of the significance of the SEC's Order Handling Rules. Management meetings are held regularly to ensure that the firm is meeting its regulatory and competitive goals. Quality and consistency are rigorously monitored through Madoff's on-line supervisory systems, which allow management to review each trade for its execution quality on a regular and continuous basis.

Under certain circumstances orders will be subjected to manual verification (i.e. locked and crossed markets), or clarification of the terms of the order (i.e. limit price, special instructions, etc.). In these instances the price at execution time may be different (favorable or unfavorable) from the price at receipt time.

APPENDIX C

Federal Complaint: *U.S. v. Bernard L. Madoff Investment Securities LLC*

This is the criminal complaint served by FBI agent Thomas Cacioppi on December 11, 2008, based on his interview with "two senior Madoff employees."

Source: Findlaw.com

Approved: _____ **08 MAG 2735** COPY
MARC LITT
Assistant United States Attorney

Before: HONORABLE DOUGLAS F. EATON
United States Magistrate Judge
Southern District of New York

- -x

UNITED STATES OF AMERICA	:	**COMPLAINT**
- v. -	:	Violation of 15 U.S.C. §§ 78j(b),
BERNARD L. MADOFF,	:	78ff; 17 C.F.R. § 240.10b-5
Defendant.	:	
	:	COUNTY OF OFFENSE: NEW YORK

- -x

SOUTHERN DISTRICT OF NEW YORK, ss.:

THEODORE CACIOPPI, being duly sworn, deposes and says that he is a Special Agent with the Federal Bureau of Investigation, and charges as follows:

COUNT ONE
(Securities Fraud)

1. From at least in or about December 2008 through the present, in the Southern District of New York and elsewhere, BERNARD L. MADOFF, the defendant, unlawfully, wilfully and knowingly, by the use of the means and instrumentalities of interstate commerce and of the mails, directly and indirectly, in connection with the purchase and sale of securities, would and did use and employ manipulative and deceptive devices and contrivances in violation of Title 17, Code of Federal Regulations, Section 240.10b-5, by (a) employing devices, schemes, and artifices to defraud; (b) making untrue statements of material facts and omitting to state material facts necessary in order to make the statements made, in the light of the circumstances under which they were made, not misleading, and (c) engaging in acts, practices, and courses of business which operated and would operate as a fraud and deceit upon persons, to wit, MADOFF deceived investors by operating a securities business in which he traded and lost investor money, and then paid certain

investors purported returns on investment with the principal received from other, different investors, which resulted in losses of approximately billions of dollars.

(Title 15, United States Code, Sections 78j(b) & 78ff; Title 17, Code of Federal Regulations, Section 240.10b-5; and Title 18, United States Code, Section 2.)

The bases for my knowledge and the foregoing charges are, in part, as follows:

2. I have been a Special Agent with the Federal Bureau of Investigation ("FBI") for approximately six and one-half years, and I have been personally involved in the investigation of this matter. The information contained in this Complaint is based upon my personal knowledge, as well as information obtained from other sources, including: a) statements made or reported by various witnesses with knowledge of relevant facts; and b) my review of publicly available information relating to BERNARD L. MADOFF, the defendant. Because this Complaint is being submitted for the limited purpose of establishing probable cause, it does not include every fact that I have learned during the course of the investigation. Where the contents of documents and the actions, statements and conversations of others are reported herein, they are reported in substance and in part, except where otherwise indicated.

3. I have reviewed the publicly available web site of a securities broker dealer named Bernard L. Madoff Investment Securities LLC, from which I have learned the following: (a) BERNARD L. MADOFF, the defendant, is the founder of Bernard L. Madoff Investment Securities LLC; (b) Bernard L. Madoff Investment Securities LLC is a securities broker dealer with its principal office in New York, New York; (c) Bernard L. Madoff Investment Securities LLC "is a leading international market maker. The firm has been providing quality executions for broker-dealers, banks and financial institutions since its inception in 1960;" (d) "[w]ith more than $700 million in firm capital, Madoff currently ranks among the top 1% of US Securities firms; (e) BERNARD L. MADOFF, the defendant, is a former Chairman of the board of directors of the NASDAQ stock market; and (f) "Clients know that Bernard Madoff has a personal interest in maintaining an unblemished record of value, fair-dealing, and high ethical standards that has always been the firm's hallmark."

4. I have interviewed two senior employees of Bernard L. Madoff Investment Securities LLC ("Senior Employee No. 1", and "Senior Employee No. 2", collectively the "Senior Employees").

The Senior Employees informed me, in substance, of the following:

a. The Senior Employees are employed by Bernard L. Madoff Investment Securities LLC, in a proprietary trading, and market making capacity. According to the Senior Employees, BERNARD L. MADOFF, the defendant, conducts certain investment advisory business for clients that is separate from the firm's proprietary trading and market making activities. According to the Senior Employees, MADOFF ran his investment adviser business from a separate floor in the New York offices of Bernard L. Madoff Investment Securities LLC. According to Senior Employee No. 1, MADOFF kept the financial statements for the firm under lock and key, and stated that MADOFF was "cryptic" about the firm's investment advisory business.

b. In or about the first week of December, BERNARD L. MADOFF, the defendant, told Senior Employee No. 2 that there had been requests from clients for approximately $7 billion in redemptions, that he was struggling to obtain the liquidity necessary to meet those obligations, but that he thought that he would be able to do so. According to the Senior Employees, they had previously understood that the investment advisory business had assets under management on the order of between approximately $8-15 billion. According to a Form ADV filed by MADOFF on behalf of Bernard L. Madoff Investment Securities LLC with the SEC on or about January 7, 2008, MADOFF's investment advisory business served between 11 and 25 clients and had a total of approximately $17.1 billion in assets under management.

      c.   On or about December 9, 2008, MADOFF informed Senior Employee No. 1 that he wanted to pay bonuses to employees of the firm in December, which was earlier than employee bonuses are usually paid. Accordingly to the Senior Employees, bonuses traditionally have been paid in February of each year. On or about December 10, 2008, the Senior Employees visited MADOFF at the offices of Bernard L. Madoff Investment Securities LLC to discuss the situation further, particularly because it MADOFF had appeared to the Senior Employees to have been under great stress in the prior weeks. At that time, MADOFF informed the Senior Employees that he had recently made profits through business operations, and that now was a good time to distribute it. When the Senior Employees challenged his explanation, MADOFF said that he did not want to talk to them at the office, and arranged a meeting at MADOFF's apartment in Manhattan. According to Senior Employee No. 2, MADOFF stated, in substance, that he "wasn't sure he would be able to hold it together" if they continued to discuss the issue at the office.

      d.   At MADOFF's Manhattan apartment, MADOFF informed the Senior Employees, in substance, that his investment advisory business was a fraud. MADOFF stated that he was "finished," that he had "absolutely nothing," that "it's all just one big lie," and that it was "basically, a giant Ponzi scheme." The Senior Employees understood MADOFF to be saying, in substance, that he had for years been paying returns to certain investors out of the principal received from other, different, investors. MADOFF stated that the business was insolvent, and that it had been for years. MADOFF also stated that he estimated the losses from this fraud to be at least approximately $50 billion. One of the Senior Employees has a personal account at Bernard L. Madoff Investment Securities LLC in which several million had been invested under the management of MADOFF.

      e.   At MADOFF's Manhattan apartment, MADOFF further informed the Senior Employees that, in approximately one week, he planned to surrender to authorities, but before he did that, he had approximately $200-300 million left, and he planned to use that money to make payments to certain selected employees, family, and friends.

      f.   At MADOFF's Manhattan apartment, MADOFF further informed the Senior Employees that he had also recently informed a third senior employee ("Senior Employee No. 3"), of the facts that MADOFF had just told the Senior Employees.

     5.   On December 11, 2008, I spoke to BERNARD L. MADOFF, the defendant. After identifying myself, MADOFF invited me, and the FBI agent who accompanied me, into his apartment. He acknowledged knowing why we were there. After I stated, "we're here to find out if there's an innocent explanation." MADOFF stated, "There is no innocent explanation." MADOFF stated, in substance, that he had personally traded and lost money for institutional clients, and that it was all his fault. MADOFF further stated, in substance, that he "paid investors with money that wasn't there." MADOFF also said that he was "broke" and "insolvent" and that he had decided that "it could not go on," and that he expected to go to jail. MADOFF also stated that he had recently admitted what he had done to Senior Employee Nos. 1, 2, and 3.

     WHEREFORE, deponent prays that BERNARD L. MADOFF, the defendant, be imprisoned, or bailed, as the case may be.

DEC 1 1 2008

THEODORE CACIOPPI
Special Agent
Federal Bureau of Investigation

Sworn to before me this
_____ day of December, 2008

HONORABLE DOUGLAS F. EATON
UNITED STATES MAGISTRATE JUDGE
SOUTHERN DISTRICT OF NEW YORK

Bernard Madoff's Victims List

Composite list compiled from the *Wall Street Journal* and Hedge
FundBlogger.com, originally sourced from various news stories.

BERNARD MADOFF'S VICTIMS LIST			
Region	Madoff Investor	Investor type	Potential Exposure
	Fairfield Sentry (Fairfield Greenwich Group)	FOF feeder fund	$7.5 billion
	Tremont Group Holdings	FOF feeder fund	$3.3 billion
E/LA	Banco Santander	Bank	$2.87 billion
	Kingate Management	FOF feeder fund	$2.8 billion
E	Bank of Medici of Austria	Bank	$2.1 billion
	Ascot Partners (Madoff feeder fund)	Hedge fund	$1.8 billion
E	Access International Advisors	Hedge fund	$1.5 billion
E	Fortis Bank Nederland	Bank	$1.35 billion
E	HSBC	Bank	$1 billion
	J. P. Jeanneret Associates	Asset manager	$946 million
	Benbassat & Cie	Bank	$935 million
E	Union Bancaire Privee	Bank	$790 million
E	Natixis	Bank	$554.4 million
	Sterling Equities (Sterling Stamos Capital Mgt.)	Asset manager	$500 million
E	Royal Bank of Scotland	Bank	$492.76 million
E	BNP Paribas	Bank	$431.17 million
	Fix Asset Management	Hedge fund	$400 million
	Carl and Ruth Shapiro	Individuals	$400 million
E	BBVA	Bank	$369.5 million
	Man Group PLC (RMF)	Hedge Fund	$360 million
E	EIM Group	Asset Manager	$330 million
E	Reichmuth & Co. (Reichmuth Matterhorn)	Bank	$327 million
APJ	Nomura	Bank	$304 million
	Normal Holdings	Asset manager	$302 million
	Maxam Capital Management (Madoff feeder fund)	FOF feeder fund	$280 million
	Pioneer Alternative Investments	Hedge fund	$280 million

BERNARD MADOFF'S VICTIMS LIST (continued)

Region	Madoff Investor	Investor type	Potential Exposure
	Ira Rennert	Individual	$200 million
E	Bank Austria	Bank	$192.1 million
	Jerome Fisher (Nine West founder)	Individual	$150 million
	Carl and Ruth Shapiro Family Foundation	Charity	$145 million
APJ	Aozora Bank	Bank	$137 million
E	AXA	Insurer	less than $135 million
E	Credit Industriel et Commercial	Bank	$125.4 million
	Yeshiva University	University Endowment	$110 million
	Dexia	Bank	$106.9 million
E	UniCredit SpA	Bank	$92.38 million
	Hadassah	Charity	$90 million
E	Unione di Banche Italiane	Bank	$84.9 million
E	Swiss Life Holding	Insurer	$78.9 million
	MorseLife (elder care facility)	Charity	$73 million
E	Nordea	Bank	$59.1 million
E	M&B Capital Partners	Asset Manager	$52.8 million
E	Hyposwiss	Bank	$50 million
APJ	Korea Life Insurance Co.	Insurer	$50 million
E	Banque Benedict Hentsch	Bank	$48.8 million
	Royal Dutch Shell	Pension	$45 million
APJ	Great Eastern Holdings	Bank	$44.26 million
	Fairfield, CT town pension fund	Pension Fund	$42 million
C	Royal Bank of Canada	Bank	$40.4 million
	Wolosoff Foundation	Charity	$38 million
E	Oddo et Cie	Asset manager	$36.957 million
	Bramdean Asset Management	Asset manager	$31 million
	Mortimer B. Zuckerman Charitable Remainder Trust (*New York Daily News* owner's charity)	Charity	$30 million
	Family of Sarah Chew	Family office	$30 million
	Arthur I. and Sydelle F. Meyer Charitable Foundation	Charity	$29.2 million
APJ	Sumitomo Life Insurance Co.	Insurer	$22 million
E	Banco Espirito Santo	Bank	$21.4 million
	Madoff Family Foundation	Charity	$19 million
	Jewish Community Foundation of Los Angeles	Charity	$18 million
	Phyllis Molchatsky	Individual	$17 million

BERNARD MADOFF'S VICTIMS LIST (continued)

Region	Madoff Investor	Investor type	Potential Exposure
	Foundation for Humanity (Elie Wiesel's charity)	Charity	$15.2 million
	KSM Capital Advisors	Investment firm	$15 million
	Harel Insurance Investments and Financial Services	Insurer	$14.2 million
	Alicia Koplowitz	Individual	$13.7 million
E	Baloise	Insurer	$13 million
	Lautenberg Family Foundation	Charity	$12.8 million
E	Credit Agricole SA	Bank	$12.32 million
E	Societe General	Bank	$12.32 million
E	Groupama	Insurer	$12.32 million
	Kas Bank	Bank	$12.3 million
I	Phoenix Holdings	Insurer	$12.6 million
	Massachusetts Pension Reserves Investment Management	Pension	$12 million
E	Caisse d'Epargne	Bank	$11.1 million
	Mitsubishi UFJ Financial Group	Financial institution	$11 million
	Richard Spring (Boca Raton recruiter)	Individual	$11 million
	Hampshire County Council	Pension	$10.7 million
	RAB Capital	Hedge fund	$10 million
	Richard Roth	Individual	$10 million
	United Jewish Endowment Fund	Charity	less than $10 million
E	Banco Popolare	Bank	$9.86 million
APJ	Korea Teachers Pension	Pension	$9.1 million
APJ	Mitsui Sumitomo Insurance Co.	Insurer	$8.8 million
	Robert I. Lappin Charitable Foundation	Charity	$8 million
	Michael Roth	Individual	$7.5 million
	Chais Family Foundation	Charity	$7 million
	Jewish Federation of Greater Los Angeles	Charity	$6.4 million
I	Technion-Israel Institute of Technology	University	$6.4 million
	Vincent Tchenguiz	Individual	$6.3 million
	Julian J. Levitt Foundation	Charity	$6 million
	Irwin Kellner (named plaintiff on first lawsuit against Madoff)	Individual	$6 million
	Ramaz School	School	$6 million
	North Shore—Long Island Jewish Health System	Pension fund	$5.7 million
	Stony Brook University Foundation	University endowment	$5.4 million
E	Neue Privat Bank	Bank	$5 million

BERNARD MADOFF'S VICTIMS LIST (continued)

Region	Madoff Investor	Investor type	Potential Exposure
	Burt Ross	Individual	$5 million
	David Berger	Individual	$5 million
	International Olympic Committee	Non-profit	$4.8 million
	Dorset County Pension Fund	Pension	$3.5 million
	Congregation Kehilath Jeshurun (New York)	Synagogue	$3.5 million
E	Caja Madrid	Bank	$3.1 million
I	Clal Insurance	Insurer	$3.1 million
	Roger Peskin	Individual	$3 million
E	Swiss Reinsurance Co.	Insurer	$3 million
	Merseyside Pension Fund	Pension	$3 million
	Maimonides School (Boston)	School	$3 million
	New York Law School	School	$3 million
	Bard College, New York	University	$3 million
	Global Specialised Opportunities 1	Hedge fund	$2.8 million
E	Banca March	Bank	$2.7 million
	The Diocese of St. Thomas (Catholic church, Virgin Islands)	Charity	$2 million
	American Friends of Yad Sarah	Charity	$1.5 million
I	Yad Sarah	Charity	$1.5 million
	Caisse des dépôts et consignations	Government-owned bank	$1.38 million
	Robert and Sarah Chew	Individuals	$1.2 million
	SAR Academy (New York)	School	$1.2 million
APJ	Aioi Insurance	Insurer	$1.1 million
	Maiji Yasuda Life Insurance Co.	Insurer	$1.1 million
	Harold Roitenberg	Individual	$1 million
	Ira Roth	Individual	$1 million
	Arnold and Joan Sinkin	Individuals	$1 million
	Steven Abbott	Individual	less than $1 million
	Allegretto Fund	Hedge fund	$790,000
E	Mediobanca	Bank	$671,000
E	GeniumAdvisors	Asset manager	$281,400
APJ	Taiyo Life Insurance Co.	Insurer	$221,000
	Optimal Investment Services (Grupo Santander)	Alternatives firm	n/a
E	Genovator, Benbassat & Cie	Asset manager	n/a
APJ	Allianz Global Investors	Bank	n/a
	Banesto	Bank	n/a

BERNARD MADOFF'S VICTIMS LIST (continued)

Region	Madoff Investor	Investor type	Potential Exposure
	Erste Bank	Bank	n/a
	Gutmann	Bank	n/a
	KBC	Bank	n/a
	LLBW	Bank	n/a
	Mirabaud & Cie	Bank	n/a
E	Notz, Stucki & Cie	Bank	n/a
E	UBS	Bank	n/a
	Chair Family Foundation	Charity	n/a
	Fair Food Foundation	Charity	n/a
	JEHT Foundation	Charity	n/a
	The Moriah Fund	Charity	n/a
	Palm Beach Country Club	Country Club	n/a
	Engelbardt family	Family office	n/a
	Loeb Family	Family office	n/a
	Thyssen family	Family office	n/a
	SNL Reaal Groep	Financial services firm	n/a
	AWD	Financial services provider	n/a
	Austin Capital Managemet	Fund of hedge funds	n/a
	Gabriel Partners (Merkin)	Fund of hedge funds	n/a
	INTAC Global Preservation Hedge Portfolio (via Rye Investment Management)	Fund of hedge funds	n/a
	Last Atlantis Capital Management	Fund of hedge funds	n/a
	Barbara Flood	Hedge fund	n/a
	Thema (Madoff feeder fund)	Hedge fund	n/a
	Ed Blumenfeld (Long Island real estate developer)	Individual	n/a
	Eric Roth (screenwriter)	Individual	n/a
	Frank Lautenberg (NJ Senator, family foundation)	Individual	n/a
	Fred Wilpon (owner of NY Mets)	Individual	n/a
	Henry Kaufman (former chief economist at Salomon Brothers)	Individual	n/a
	J Gurvin Foundation	Individual	n/a
	Jeff Tucker (Stone Bridge horse farm owner, Fairfield Greenwich Group founding partner)	Individual	n/a
	Jeffrey Katzenberg (DreamWorks)	Individual	n/a

BERNARD MADOFF'S VICTIMS LIST (continued)

Region	Madoff Investor	Investor type	Potential Exposure
	John Robbins	Individual	n/a
	Joyce Z. Greenberg	Individual	n/a
	Larry King	Individual	n/a
	Larry Leif	Individual	n/a
	Lawrence Velvel (dean, Massachusetts Law School)	Individual	n/a
	Leonard Feinstein (Bed Bath & Beyond co-founder)	Individual	n/a
	Leonard Litwin	Individual	n/a
	Marc Rich (fugitive financier, pardoned by President Clinton)	Individual	n/a
	Norman Braman (former Philadelphia Eagles owner)	Individual	n/a
	Stephen Fine	Individual	n/a
	Steven Spielberg (Wunderkinder foundation)	Individual	n/a
	Zsa Zsa Gabor	Individual	n/a
	Avram and Carol Goldberg (Stop & Shop founders)	Individuals	n/a
	Family of former New York Governor Eliot Spitzer	Individuals	n/a
	Kenneth and Jeanne Levy-Church (donors to Fair Food and JEHT foundations)	Individuals	n/a
	Kevin Bacon and Kyra Sedgwick (actors)	Individuals	n/a
	Members of the Hillcrest Country Club (St. Paul, MN)	Individuals	n/a
	Members of the Oak Ridge Country Club (Hopkins, MN)	Individuals	n/a
	Knowsley MBC	Pension	n/a
	Liverpool City Council	Pension	n/a
	Sefton MBC	Pension	n/a
	St. Helens MBC	Pension	n/a
	United Association of Plumbers & Steamfitters Local 267	Pension fund	n/a
	West Palm Beach Pension Fund	Pension fund	n/a

Region is region of primary influence. Key: E=Europe, LA=Latin America, APJ=Asia Pacific/Japan, I=Israel, C=Canada

n/a = not available or not disclosed

Source: *Wall Street Journal,* HedgeFundBlogger, various published reports

Bernard Madoff Chronology

Following is a list of highlights from the Madoff story. By necessity it isn't complete and some exact dates still aren't known for sure.

BERNARD MADOFF CHRONOLOGY		
Year	Precise date (if important)	Event
1920		Charles Ponzi begins his scheme with international postal reply coupons. He is arrested in August and convicted in November of that year.
1938	4/29	Bernard Madoff is born in Queens, New York.
1949		Charles Ponzi dies in Brazil.
1956		Bernard Madoff graduates from Far Rockaway High School, Far Rockaway, New York.
1956		Madoff enrolls at the University of Alabama, attends one year.
1957		Madoff returns to Queens, enrolls in Hofstra College, Hempstead, New York.
1958		Ruth Alpern graduates from Far Rockaway High School.
1960		Bernard Madoff graduates from Hofstra with a bachelor's degree in political science.
1960		Madoff attends Brooklyn Law School for one year.
1960		Madoff starts Bernard L. Madoff Investment Securities (BMIS) with $5,000 earned as a lifeguard and sprinkler installer.
1961		Ruth Alpern graduates from Queens College with a degree in psychology.
1961		Bernard Madoff and Ruth Alpern get married.
1961		Bernard Madoff starts managing and investing money for others, probably Carl Shapiro (exact year unknown).
1964		First son Mark Madoff born, Queens, New York.

BERNARD MADOFF CHRONOLOGY (continued)

Year	Precise date (if important)	Event
1965		Brother Peter Madoff graduates from Queens College and starts with BMIS.
1966		Second son Andrew Madoff born, Queens, New York.
1967		Niece Shana Madoff born, Queens, New York.
1975		Madoff invests $250,000 in computerizing Cincinnati Stock Exchange, becomes first all-electronic exchange (year approximate).
1975	5/1	"May Day": date the securities industry was deregulated allowing price competition and more deal making in brokerage industry.
1981		Madoff family buys beachfront home in East Hamptons, 216 Old Montauk Highway.
1984		Madoff family moves from Roslyn, New York, on Long Island to duplex in Upper East Side, Manhattan.
1986		Son Mark graduates from University of Michigan, starts with BMIS.
1988		Son Andrew graduates from Wharton School of Business, U. of Pennsylvania, starts with BMIS.
1989		Madoff handles more than 5 percent of total NYSE stock trading volume. *Financial World* ranked him as "one of the highest paid on Wall Street. His trading operations are reported to be automated for all but the largest orders."
1989		Walter Noel and Jeffrey Tucker merge operations into what would become Fairfield Greenwich Securities.
1990		Madoff becomes non-executive chairman of the NASDAQ Stock Market.
1992		SEC investigates investment firm Avellino & Bienes based on a tip, requires refund to investors of $440 million in unregistered securities to 3,200 investors that were invested with Madoff; Madoff refunds most of money in a weekend.
1992		Describes "convertible arbitrage" investment strategy to the *Wall Street Journal*.
1992		Ruth Madoff graduates from New York University with a Master of Science in Nutrition.
1994		Madoff buys Palm Beach mansion, 410 N. Lake Way, for $3.8 million, puts it in Ruth's name.
1995		Shana Madoff graduates from Fordham University law school, joins BMIS as compliance attorney.

BERNARD MADOFF CHRONOLOGY (continued)

Year	Precise date (if important)	Event
1996		Ruth Madoff gets published as co-editor of *Great Chefs of America Cook Kosher: Over 175 Recipes from America's Greatest Restaurants.*
1996		Bernard Madoff joins board of trustees of Yeshiva University, New York.
1998		Madoff posts a 9.8 golf handicap, with not one of over 20 scores exceeding 89.
1999		Madoff is recognized as a leading market maker in after-hours and off-exchange trading, BMIS is ranked in the top 1 percent of all U.S. securities firms.
1999		Harry Markopolos starts his analysis of Madoff's outsized performance.
1999		SEC investigates violations of the limit order protection rule; Madoff outlines new procedures for BMIS and moves on.
2000		Madoff becomes chairman of the board of the Sy Syms School of Business at Yeshiva University.
2001		*Barron's* article calls Madoff's returns into question, suspects front-running and other deceptive trading practices.
2002		Madoff is elected treasurer of Yeshiva University; J. Ezra Merkin joins the board and becomes chairman of the investment committee.
2003		Shana Madoff meets Eric Swanson, an assistant director of compliance for the SEC, at an industry conference.
2003		Ruth Madoff commissions family scrapbook for Bernie's sixty-fifth birthday; she then changes her mind.
2004		SEC investigates BMIS for front-running; "no evidence found."
2005		SEC filings show Bernie, Mark, Andrew, and at least one other BMIS employee holding board positions and key advisory posts at NASD and the NASDAQ Stock Market.
2005		Harry Markopolos writes his letter "The World's Largest Hedge Fund is a Fraud."
2006		Madoff is asked by SEC to comply with registration rules and registers as an investment adviser, but the SEC concludes that there is "no evidence of fraud."
2007		Shana Madoff marries Eric Swanson.

BERNARD MADOFF CHRONOLOGY (continued)

Year	Precise date (if important)	Event
2007		FINRA uncovers irregularities, including the absence of reported trades in the investment fund, during a biannual exam, but doesn't do anything; later claimed to be outside its jurisdiction.
2008	1/7	Files annual report with SEC, reporting "eleven to twenty-five clients with $17.1 billion under management."
2008	12/1	Bernard Madoff tells his sons of $7 billion in redemptions, says "he's having trouble finding enough money."
2008	12/1	Madoff gets $250 million loan/investment from Carl Shapiro.
2008	12/3	Madoff gets last funds from client, $10 million from oil dealer Martin Rosenman.
2008	12/9	Madoff discloses to sons that he wants to pay bonuses early, later reveals entire story after being confronted by the sons.
2008	12/10	"Senior employees," presumably Mark and Andrew, contact FBI, talk to Special Agent Theodore Cacioppi. FBI and SEC draw up a complaint.
2008	12/11	After agreeing to do so with Madoff, Theodore Cacioppi serves the complaint at 8:30 a.m. Madoff greets him in a robe and slippers.
2008	12/11	Madoff appears in court that afternoon, charged with both a criminal and civil complaint.
2008	12/12	Bail hearing sets bail at $10 million and orders house arrest.
2008	12/12	Civil case becomes a bankruptcy case; trustee is appointed.
2008	12/12	Robert I. Lappin Foundation announces closure of programs.
2008	12/16	Christopher Cox, outgoing SEC chair, says he is "gravely concerned about the multiple failures of his agency."
2008	12/19	Jeffry and Barbara Picower announce the closure of their foundation.
2008	12/23	Investor and feeder-fund manager René-Thierry Magon de la Villehuchet commits suicide in his New York office.
2008	12/24	Bernard Madoff mails $1 million in jewelry in five packages to family and friends.
2008	12/31	Madoff submits client list per court order.
2009	1/5	House Financial Services Committee holds a hearing. Rep. Spencer Bachus (R–Ala.) declares "What we may have in the Madoff case is not necessarily a lack of enforcement and oversight tools, but a failure to use them."

BERNARD MADOFF CHRONOLOGY (continued)

Year	Precise date (if important)	Event
2009	1/5	Because of the jewelry mailing, prosecutors request bail be revoked.
2009	1/12	Bail hearing is held, bail is maintained with new conditions to protect assets.
2009	1/15	YIVO Institute holds panel: "Madoff: A Jewish Reckoning."
2009	1/27	Senate Banking Committee holds a hearing. A very testy Sen. Charles Schumer (D–NY) grills the SEC: "Madoff's fraud was so immense and obvious, and took place over such a long period of time, it is simply inexplicable how the SEC missed it. It's as if there was a giant elephant standing next to the SEC in a rather small room for 25 years, and the SEC never noticed the elephant or even the smell of peanuts on its breath."

Index

National Association of Securities
Dealers (NASD), 54. *See also*
FINRA
New York
charities, 161–67
real estate investments,
163–64
New York City Center, 56
New York Law School, 79, 153
New York Mets, 163, 229
New York Public Library, 177
New York Public Theater, 162
New York Stock Exchange,
48–49
Noel, Walter and Monica, 80–81
nonprofit organizations. See
charities and foundations
North Shore–Long Island Jewish
Health System, 163
NYSE Hybrid Market, 49

O
Objections, overcoming, 194
OEX options, 100–101,
134–35, 137
On Death and Dying (Kübler-
Ross), 200
options contracts, 100, 135–37
OTC (over the counter)
trading, 48
OTCQX, 41–42
oxytocin, 205–6

P
Palm Beach, 34, 76, 142
victims, 156–61
Palm Beach Country Club, 35,
74–76, 142, 157
Palm Beach County school
district, 177

Palm Healthcare Foundation, 82
Palmer, Daren, 11
payment for order flow, 46–47,
50, 103
Pearlman, Lou, 6–7
peer pressure, 195
penetration strategy, 72–73
penny margins, 44
pension funds, 63, 150–51
performance, 197–98
personality, 196
philanthropy. *See* charities and
foundations
Picard, Irving, xi, 126
Picower Foundation, 77, 150,
166, 177–78
Piedrahita, Andrés, 81, 84, 114
pink sheets, 40–42
pinksheets.com, 41
Pioneer Alternative
Investments, 145
Ponzi, Charles (Carlo), 1, 13–14
Ponzi scheme, 1–2, 97, 98, 112,
113, 139
Positioning, 193–94
positive reinforcement, 199
postal-reply coupons, 13–14
premium, 135–36, 137
Prep for Prep, 162
PricewaterhouseCoopers, 116
product, 65–67
pushkes, 183
put options, 101, 135
pyramid scheme, 1–2

Q
Qualification, The, 193
Queens College, 26, 162–63,
177–78

Securities Act, 88, 90
Securities and Exchange
    Commission. *See* SEC
    (Securities and Exchange
    Commission)
Securities Exchange Act, 88, 90
securities fraud, 111
Securities Industry Association, 55
Securities Investor Protection
    Corporation (SIPC), 125–
    26, 131–33, 220
securities trading, 37, 42–44
Sedgwick, Kyra, 155
self-hatred, 203
self-love, 203–5
Senate Banking Committee,
    214–15
Sentry Fund, 81
Serwer, Andrew, 173
Shapiro, Carl, 38, 58, 83, 119,
    147, 148, 149, 207
Sigma Alpha Mu, 24
Silverstein, Larry, 229
Simon, Scott, 165
single-stock put options, 102
situation, 195
Skakun, Michael, 27–29
Slatkin, Reed, 4–5
slatkinfraud.com, 6
smell test, 224
sociopath, 203
software, 52–54
Sorkin, Ira, 230
Sorkin, Lee, 94, 133
Spielberg, Steven, 77, 154
Spitzer, Eliot, 105
split strike conversion, 115, 137
spread, 39, 40, 43–44, 46
Spring, Richard, 147
Spring Mountain Capital, 220

Stanton, Louis L., xi, 124, 126
statements, financial, 222
Stellar US Absolute Return, 85
Sterling Stamos investment fund,
    155, 163
Stern, Richard, 50–51, 53–54
strike price, 135
Stuyvesant Fuel Service, 117
Success Performance Solutions,
    196
suicide, 9, 83, 201
Swanson, Eric, 32, 87
swindlers, famous, 1–15
Swiss Life Holding, 153
Sy Syms School of Business, 56, 77

T

Tanner, Robert, 70
Tchenguiz, Vincent, 147
Technion-Israel Institute of
    Technology, 152
Technology Advisory Council, 55
third market, 49–52
Thomsen, Linda, 214
3(c)(1) funds, 61
3(c)(7) funds, 61
Toub, Philip Jamchid, 82, 85
Tremont Capital Management,
    79, 144, 145, 217
Trimark Securities, Inc., 50
trust, xiii–xiv, 71, 72, 219
    psychology of, 191–210
Trust Associates, Inc., 71
truth in securities law, 90
Tucker, Jeffrey, 81
Tufts University, 153
Turner, Lynn, 215
Tuttle, Marvin, 220–21
2 and 20 compensation rule,
    61–62

About the Author

Peter Sander is a personal finance author, researcher, and consultant. His eighteen books include *The 250 Personal Finance Questions Everyone Should Ask* and *The Complete Idiot's Guide to Day Trading Like a Pro*. He has developed more than 200 personal finance columns for MarketWatch and TheStreet.com, and has appeared on *NBC Today*, *CNNfn*, and *Fox News*. He lives in Granite Bay, California.